Exemplary Science
in Grades 9–12

Standards-Based Success Stories

Exemplary Science in Grades 9–12

Standards-Based Success Stories

Robert E. Yager, Editor

NATIONAL SCIENCE TEACHERS ASSOCIATION

Arlington, Virginia

KH

NATIONAL SCIENCE TEACHERS ASSOCIATION

Claire Reinburg, Director
Judy Cusick, Senior Editor
J. Andrew Cocke, Associate Editor
Betty Smith, Associate Editor
Robin Allan, Book Acquisitions Coordinator

ART AND DESIGN, David Serota, Director
PRINTING AND PRODUCTION, Catherine Lorrain-Hale, Director
   Nguyet Tran, Assistant Production Manager
   Jack Parker, Electronic Prepress Technician

NATIONAL SCIENCE TEACHERS ASSOCIATION
Gerald F. Wheeler, Executive Director
David Beacom, Publisher

Library of Congress Cataloging-in-Publication Data
Exemplary science in grades 9–12: standards-based success stories / [edited] by Robert Yager.
   p. cm.
   ISBN 0-87355-257-1
   1. Science—Study and teaching (Secondary)—Case studies. 2. Science—Study and teaching (Secondary)—
Standards. I. Yager, Robert Eugene, 1930-
   Q181.E85 2005
   507'.1'2—dc22
                        2004030526

NSTA is committed to publishing quality materials that promote the best in inquiry-based science education. However, conditions of actual use may vary and the safety procedures and practices described in this book are intended to serve only as a guide. Additional precautionary measures may be required. NSTA and the author(s) do not warrant or represent that the procedure and practices in this book meet any safety code or standard or federal, state, or local regulations. NSTA and the author(s) disclaim any liability for personal injury or damage to property arising out of or relating to the use of this book including any recommendations, instructions, or materials contained therein.

10/19/06

Contents

Implementing the Changes in High School Programs Envisioned in the National Science Education Standards:

Where Are We Nine Years Later?

Robert E. Yager
Science Education Center University of Iowa

How This Book Came About

Nine years have elapsed since the 1996 publication of the National Science Education Standards (NSES) (NRC 1996). The critical issues in science education now are these: How far have we progressed in putting the vision of the NSES into practice? What remains to be done? What new visions are worthy of new trials?

The four monographs in the NSTA Exemplary Science Monograph series seek to answer these questions. The monographs are *Exemplary Science: Best Practices in Professional Development* (currently available); *Exemplary Science in Grades 9–12* (the book you are reading); *Exemplary Science in Grades 5–8;* and *Exemplary Science in Grades K–4* (the latter two books are in development.)

The series was conceived in 2001 by an advisory board of science educators, many of whom had participated in the development of the National Science Education Standards. The advisory board members (who are all active and involved NSTA members; see p. xiii for their names) decided to seek exemplars of the NSES' *More Emphasis* conditions as a way to evaluate progress toward the visions of the NSES. The *More Emphasis* conditions provide summaries of the NSES recommendations in science teaching, professional development, assessment, science content, and science education programs and systems. (See Appendix 1 for the six *Less Emphasis/More Emphasis* lists.) The board sent information about the projected series to the NSTA leadership team and to all the NSTA affiliates, chapters, and associated groups. A call for papers on exemplary programs also appeared in all NSTA publications. In addition, more than a thousand letters inviting nominations were sent to leaders identified in the *2001–2002 NSTA Handbook*, and personal letters were sent to leaders of all science education organizations.

After preliminary responses were received, the advisory board identified teachers and programs that it felt should be encouraged to prepare formal drafts for further review and evaluation. The goal was to identify 15 of the best situations—in each of the four areas: professional development and grades 9–12, 5–8, and K–4—where facets of the teaching, professional development, assessment, and content standards were being met in an exemplary manner.

The most important aspect of the selection process was the evidence the authors of each article could provide regarding the effect of their programs on student learning. This aspect proved the most elusive. Most of us "know" when something is going well, but we are not well equipped to provide real evidence for this "knowing." Many exciting program descriptions were not among the final titles—simply because little or no evidence other than personal testimony was available in the materials forwarded. The 15 high school models that make up this monograph were chosen by the advisory board as the best examples of programs that fulfill the *More Emphasis* conditions; each has had a clear, positive impact on student science learning.

The History of the National Science Education Standards

Before discussing the contents of this book at greater length, I would like to offer a brief history of how the National Science Education Standards came to be.

Most educators credit the National Council of Teachers of Mathematics (NCTM) with initiating the many efforts to produce national standards for programs in U.S. schools. In 1986 (10 years before the publication of the National Science Education Standards), the board of directors of NCTM established a Commission on Standards for School Mathematics with the aim of improving the quality of school mathematics. An initial draft of these standards was developed during the summer of 1987, revised during the summer of 1988 after much discussion among NCTM members, and finally published as the *Curriculum and Evaluation Standards for School Mathematics* in 1989.

The NCTM standards did much for mathematics education by providing a consensus for what mathematics should be. The National Science Foundation (NSF) and other funding groups had not been involved in developing the math standards, but these groups quickly funded research and training to move schools and teachers in the direction of those standards. Having such a "national" statement regarding needed reforms resulted in funding from private and government foundations to produce school standards in other disciplines, including science.

NSF encouraged the science education community to develop standards modeled after the NCTM document (1989). Interestingly, both the American Association for the Advancement of Science (AAAS) and the National Science Teachers Association (NSTA) expressed interest in preparing science standards. Both organizations indicated that they each had made a significant start on such national standards—AAAS with its Project 2061 and NSTA with its Scope, Sequence, and Coordination project. Both of these national projects had support from NSF, private foundations, and industries. The compromise on this "competition" between AAAS and NSTA leaders led to the recommendation that the National Research Council (NRC) of the National Academy of Sciences be funded to develop the National Science Education Standards. With NSF funding provided in 1992, both NSTA and AAAS helped to select the science leaders who would prepare the NSES. Several early drafts were circulated among hundreds of people with invitations to comment, suggest, debate, and assist with a consensus document. A full-time director of consensus provided leadership and assistance as final drafts were assembled. Eventually, it took $7 million and four years of debate to produce the 262-page NSES publication in 1996.

There was never any intention that the Standards would indicate minimum competencies that would be required of all. Instead, the focus was on visions of how teaching, assessment, and content should be changed. Early on, programs and systems were added as follow-ups to teaching, assessment, and content.

The NSES goals were meant to frame the teaching, staff development, assessment, content, program, and system efforts as visions for change and reform. These goals represent a step beyond those central to Harms' earlier Project Synthesis. The four goals (justifications) for K–12 science listed in the NSES encompass preparing students who:
1. experience the richness and excitement of knowing about and understanding the natural world;
2. use appropriate scientific processes and principles in making personal decisions;
3. engage intelligently in public discourse and debate about matters of scientific and technological concern; and
4. increase their economic productivity through the use of the knowledge, understanding, and skills of the scientifically literate person in their careers (NRC 1996, p. 13).

Basically, the goals do not suggest any content or any glamorized process skills that must be transmitted or experienced for their own sake. Paul Brandwein has called for teachers and schools to ensure that each high school graduate have one full experience with science (1983). He suggested that this would create a revolution in science education—something we still badly need. Some NSES enthusiasts suggest that one such experience each year would be a better goal during the K–12 years—a 13 year continuum of science in school—and perhaps one each 9-week grading period would be an even better goal!

The NSES volume begins with standards for improved teaching. That chapter is followed by chapters on professional development, assessment, science content, and science education program and systems. Content was placed in the document after the other three for fear that placing it first would invite a focus only on what should be taught—almost relegating teaching, staff development, and assessment to "add-on" roles. The major debates, however, centered on what should appear in the content chapter.

NSES and Science Content

A major direction in the NSES with respect to content was the identification of eight facets of content. These facets change the focus from a traditional discipline focus with a list of major concepts under each discipline, to a much broader listing that is more indicative of the goals (justifications) for science in high schools. These eight facets of content elaborated in NSES are

1. Unifying Concepts and Processes;
2. Science as Inquiry;
3. Physical Science;
4. Life Science;
5. Earth and Space Science;
6. Science and Technology;
7. Science in Personal and Social Perspectives; and
8. History and Nature of Science.

Just as the first NSES goal is considered the most important one, the first facet of content (Unifying Concepts and Processes) is similarly considered the most important. It was envisioned as being so basic that it was first thought to be included as the preamble for each content section of NSES. However, many felt that too many would simply move to a new listing of basic discipline-bound concepts and ignore the preamble. Although life, physical, and Earth/space science still appear, some lists combine them into a listing of basic science concepts as a single content focus—thereby suggesting a more integrated approach to the major concepts comprising modern science. Major debates occurred in identifying these eight content constructs and the specific content included in each of the "discipline-bound" content areas.

Important current reforms must focus on the four less familiar content facets, namely: (a) science for meeting personal and societal challenges (referring to goals 2 and 3); (b) technology—which now enjoys a whole set of standards produced by International Technology Education Association (ITEA 2000); (c) the history and philosophy of science; and (d) science as inquiry.

The *More Emphasis* conditions for inquiry represent what the current reforms are all about and indicate why the use of social issues is considered essential. The *More Emphasis* conditions for inquiry are meant to reverse the failures in 1981 in finding examples of teaching science by inquiry in U.S. schools. After the Project Synthesis report, Paul DeHart Hurd (1978) reported:

> *"The development of inquiry skills as a major goal of instruction in science appears to have had only a minimal effect on secondary school teaching. The rhetoric about enquiry and process teaching greatly exceeds both the research on the subject and the classroom practice. The validity of the enquiry goal itself could profit from more scholarly interchange and confrontation even if it is simply to recognize that science is not totally confined to logical processes and data-gathering." (p. 62)*

Issues related to student lives, their schools, and their communities can provide the contexts that invariably require the concepts and skills that appear in science programs in typical schools.

However, instead of starting with a high school curriculum and proceeding through it, the student is more central and becomes the magnet for the need for what is generally taught. To many students it seems that the typical science content has been dictated by teachers or textbook authors who merely assume its relevance for all learners. Generally, everything is taught "because it will be useful—trust me!" But, for most students such use is never found. Instead science content is seen only as something useful to those who wish to pursue college/university study, especially in medicine, health sciences, and engineering—and also important for performing well on college entrance examinations. It can be argued that our major problem with high school science remains: science is viewed as merely a stepping stone to further study of science at the next level, whether grade by grade in schools or for the college track in high school and for college entrance. It is not seen as something important and useful for *all*.

The NSES broaden the focus to something other than a consideration of the concepts that characterizes biology, chemistry, physics, and to a much lesser extent, the Earth/space sciences. It also includes technology (the human-made world) as well as a focus on the objects and events in the natural universe. Moreover, it includes society, which is easy for life science enthusiasts since it represents a level of focus in biology (i.e., ecology). It is also related to the social studies (such as sociology, economics, government, geography, and psychology).

However, it is insufficient to assume a universal understanding of science itself. To most persons, science is what is studied in school. What is studied usually ends up as topics or chapters organized around precise concepts that are traditional features of textbooks, and often coincide to courses in college departments where science teachers have had direct experience as students during their preparation.

Science needs to be understood and seen as appropriate for all—as a human endeavor that all people can understand, experience, and use. The NSES goals exemplify a holistic view of science. Carl Sagan emphasized a vital point when he observed that every human starts as a scientist (NRC 1998). However, as the child grows and attends school, he/she is discouraged from practicing real science and is taught skills in science classes that are alien to science itself. Science consists of four essential features—all of which should be a part of school and every child's experience:

1. Asking questions about the objects and events observed in the natural world;
2. Proposing answers (possible explanations) to these personally constructed questions;
3. Designing tests or preparing logical reasons to establish validity for the proposed answers; and
4. Communicating the question, proposed explanations, and the evidence assembled to support the explanation to others (especially others, who have pondered and investigated similar objects and events in nature).

Science is a human endeavor that is characterized by curiosity and wonderment, by attempts to explain, by the desire to determine the accuracy of each explanation advanced, and by responsibility for sharing and communicating the process to others (in science at the research level, this means to others constituting the science establishment). If science were advanced with this four point sequence, goal one of NSES would be met. Yet it rarely occurs and remains a major issue in science education, especially in high school and college programs. The question arises: how would real science *ever* be offered in a textbook, a teacher's lecture, or a state framework? For complete science is what current reforms are all about—and science for all!

Conclusion

The fifteen high school exemplars all show great progress for implementing the Standards and the stated goals for science in grades 9–12. Each author team was asked to reflect on the *More Emphasis* conditions that were recommended for teaching, assessment, and content (and to some degree those concerned with the continuing education of teachers). To what extent these conditions were met by the exemplars is discussed in the final chapter.

This monograph indicates where we are with respect to meeting the visions for reforms in science for high schools. It is important to know how our efforts during the four-year development of the NSES have impacted science classrooms. We feel that an exhaustive search has occurred during the past three years and are impressed with what the search has revealed. We hope others reading about these exciting programs will find new ideas to try and that they will want to share more stories of their successes, especially in terms of similar experiences with their own students. We trust that this volume is an accurate record of what can be done to meet the Standards while also pinpointing some continuing challenges and needs. The exemplary programs described in this monograph give inspiration while also providing evidence that the new directions are feasible and worth the energy and effort needed for others to implement changes.

We also hope that the exemplars included will bring new meaning and life to the *More Emphasis* conditions. In many respects, the *Less Emphasis* conditions are not bad, but they do not usually result in as much learning or in ways the four goals for science teaching can be exemplified.

Hopefully the fifteen examples in this monograph will serve as generators for new questions and new ideas for developing even more impressive programs so that the decade following the publication of the NSES results in even more exciting advances by 2006.

References

Hurd, P. DeH. 1978. The golden age of biological education 1960–1975. In: W.V. Mayer (Ed.), *BSCS biology teacher's handbook* (3rd edition). (pp. 28–96). New York: John Wiley & Sons.

International Technology Education Association. 2000. *Standards for technological literacy.* Reston, VA: Author.

National Council for Teachers of Mathematics. 1989. *Curriculum and evaluation standards for school mathematics.* Reston, VA: Author.

National Research Council (NRC). 1996. *National science education standards.* Washington, DC: National Academy Press.

National Research Council (NRC). 1998. *Every child a scientist: Achieving scientific literacy for all.* Washington, DC: National Academy Press.

Acknowledgments

Members of the National Advisory Board for the Exemplary Science Series

Hans O. Andersen
Past President of NSTA
Professor, Science Education
Indiana University-Bloomington
Bloomington, IN

Charles R. Barman
Professor
Science and Environmental Education
Indiana University School of Education
Bloomington, IN

Bonnie Brunkhorst
Past President of NSTA
Professor
California State University-San Bernardino
San Bernardino, CA

Rodger Bybee
Executive Director
Biological Sciences Curriculum Study
Colorado Springs, CO

Audrey Champagne
Professor
State University of New York
Albany, NY

Fred Johnson
Past President of NSTA
Consultant
McKenzie Group
Memphis, TN

Roger Johnson
Professor
University of Minnesota
Minneapolis, MN

Mozell Lang
Science Consultant
Pontiac Northern High School
Pontiac, MI

LeRoy R. Lee
Past President of NSTA
Executive Director
Wisconsin Science Network
DeForest, WI

Shelley A. Lee
Past President of NSTA
Science Education Consultant
Wisconsin Dept. of Public Instruction
Madison, WI

Gerry Madrazo
Past President of NSTA
Clinical Professor—Science Education
University of North Carolina
Chapel Hill, NC

Dick Merrill
Past President of NSTA
University of California, Berkeley
Berkeley, CA

Nick Micozzi
K–12 Science Coordinator
Plymouth Public Schools
Plymouth, MA

Edward P. Ortleb
Past President of NSTA
Science Consultant/Author
St. Louis, MO

Jack Rhoton
President of NSELA
Professor of Science Education
East Tennessee State University
Johnson, TN

Gerald Skoog
Past President of NSTA
Professor and Dean
Texas Tech University
Lubbock, TX

Emma Walton
Past President of NSTA
Science Consultant
Anchorage, AK

Sandra West
Associate Professor
Science Education
Southwest Texas University
Canyon Lake, TX

Karen Worth
Senior Scientist
Education Development Center
Newton, MA

Assistant Editors at the University of Iowa

Suzanne Butz
Kris Dolgos
Brian J. Flanagan
Nancy C. Rather Mayfield

About the Editor

Robert E. Yager—an active contributor to the development of the National Science Education Standards—has devoted his life to teaching, writing, and advocating on behalf of science education worldwide. Having started his career as a high school science teacher, he has been a professor of science education at the University of Iowa since 1956. He has also served as president of seven national organizations, including NSTA, and been involved in teacher education in Japan, Korea, Taiwan, and Europe. Among his many publications are several NSTA books, including *Focus on Excellence* and *What Research Says to the Science Teacher*. Yager earned a bachelor's degree in biology from the University of Northern Iowa and master's and doctoral degrees in plant physiology from the University of Iowa.

It's the "Little Things" That Can Change the Way You Teach

David L. Brock
Roland Park Country School

Setting

My school is an urban college preparatory school for girls, located in Baltimore, Maryland. An independent school, we teach grades K–12, and in our high school division we currently have 284 young women in grades 9–12, with a 35% minority enrollment, 21% of them receiving financial assistance. Our typical class size in the sciences is between 18 and 20 girls, and classes meet for three 70-minute periods each week in an alternating "A-day/B-day" block schedule. In the 2000–01 school year, we completed construction of a new science wing in accordance with the national recommendations for size and pupil number in combined lab-lecture rooms (Biehle, Motz, and West 1999). Among other renovations to the building at that time, we became a laptop computer school with a wireless network for all students grades 7–12 (with a separate dedicated computer lab for K–6). While our science program is a required academic component of all K–12 grades (including biology, chemistry, *and* physics in the high school), the specific program I will be discussing here—"The Little Things That Run the World"—is only part of the ninth-grade honors biology course.

Changing the Classroom's Quality

This program emphasizes the "student-as-player/teacher-as-coach" approach to the classroom (NRC 1996). A student-centered curriculum, it provides a model for the teaching standard on how to guide students through an extended, focused scientific inquiry, where students bear the primary responsibility for their learning. Because the project requires regular drafts of students' pre-lab research, experimental protocols, data charts, graphs, and mathematical analyses, it also provides a model for the assessment standards with respect to examining ongoing student work with a view to helping them gain a steadily richer understanding of both their topics and their investigative skills (NRC 1996).

During "Little Things," each team of students chooses, performs, and manages its own experimental investigation into a focused topic in the ecology of soil microbes (e.g., "What impact did a recent drought have on protozoa levels?"). Thus, the project provides a model that emphasizes *all* of the National Science Education Standards' (NSES) preferred content standards for the life sciences (NRC 1996). But even more important is the fact that, as a result of participating in field study projects like this one, students walk away from the experience with a richer understanding of humanity's place in the web of environmental relationships as well as the knowledge of their own power to understand the intricacies of the natural world. Since this kind of wisdom is ultimately what any of us who teach science are all about in the first place, projects like "Little Things" can help all of us come closer to the "spirit" that lies at the heart of the all good science education.

Who We Are

My students and I have been running "The Little Things That Run the World" project since the 1999–2000 school year. Originally part of our school's involvement in the NSF's Baltimore Long-Term Ecological Research Study (BES), it has evolved over the past four years through my involvement with the Paul F. Brandwein Institute (Brock 2002), and has generated considerable funding interest during its four years, including grants from the Toshiba America Foundation, the Captain Planet Foundation, and the ReliaStar/Northern Life *Education's Unsung Heroes* program. It continues to serve as the culminating end-of-year exam for my ninth grade honors biology students, and several of its alums have gone on to participate in the school's science research seminar, and publish related work. "Little Things" has even led to the creation of a three-week summer research internship—the Environmental Science Summer Research Experience for Young Women—that just completed its third successful year. In the spring of 2003, the program was honored with the Gustav Ohaus Award from the National Science Teachers Association (NSTA).

The Program

The "Little Things" project is a unique curriculum unit on the soil ecology of microbes that has five major goals:

- to provide students with the opportunity to engage in real scientific research where none of the answers are known ahead of time and in so doing present them consequently with the chance to develop their own hypotheses, to design and perform their own experimental protocols, and to analyze and evaluate their own results, submitting them for peer review and to various community stakeholders;
- to give students the chance to learn how to work with, identify, and estimate

populations of diverse, unknown microbes using standard microbial research techniques and technologies;

- to develop in students an understanding of the biochemistry of soil microbes and their immediate micro-environment (pH, temperature, humidity, etc.);
- to generate in students a comprehension of the role microbes play in the overall health of the soil and its ecosystem and how they influence and interact with the multicellular organisms of that system (e.g., invertebrates, plants, etc.);
- and, finally, to cultivate in students an appreciation of how human uses of the soil (e.g., as playing fields, gardens, etc.) impact the viability of soil microbes and, hence, of the greater soil ecosystem itself.

During the five weeks of the project, students work in independent research teams of three to four members, on research topics of their own choosing, and with the provision that it must have something to do with how our school's use of the campus grounds might be impacting soil ecology. Each team starts by finding information on the role(s) of various microbe populations in the soil using internet and library resources (Figure 1) until they have learned enough about what microbes are doing in the soil to begin narrowing their focus to a specific interest (e.g., the role of protozoa in the soil food chain). From this focus, students then start to develop a specific experimental question related to the fields, grassy areas, and woodlands on our school's campus (e.g., "What impact does the chalk used to mark the lines on the lacrosse field have on the density of bacteria living in that soil?"). Finally, they use the knowledge from their research to generate a specific hypothesis and begin to design their experiments.

Figure 1: Performing Background Research

Throughout the year, the students have already had to generate almost every one of their controlled experiments from scratch, determining the specific steps they will take, what their controls will be, and so on. Hence, experimental design itself is something with which they are quite familiar. However, to accomplish this task during their project, they first have to learn some basic, standard methods for studying soil microbes, methods with which most of them are initially unfamiliar (Hall 1996). Therefore, while they are working on their background research at the start of the project, they are also learning how to use augers to take soil samples, how to perform serial dilutions and soil saturations to extract microbes for analysis, and how to operate soil analysis test kits (see Figures 2 and 3). Also, once the students begin working on the design phase of their experimental protocols, they have access to a professional soil microbiologist (through the project's original participation in BES), who comes in for one day during the early part of "Little Things" to consult with each research team on their individual investigation (see Figure 4). Thus, in spite of the practical challenges that come from studying soil microecology, the students in this project are able to achieve the necessary mastery of some rather sophisticated research strategies and procedures in a relatively short period (about two weeks).

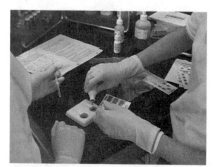

Figure 2: Learning Lab Activities

Figure 3: Learning Lab Activities

Figure 4: Consulting with Scientists

Furthermore, they are doing all of this research and design in an educational climate of continuous assessment and feedback. Throughout the preliminary stages of their investigations, the student teams must submit a minimum of four regular, written updates about the progress of their inquiry for formal evaluation. Each time, the students learn additional questions they need to answer about their topic and about ways to improve their experiments, and with each submission and each new trial of an experiment, they receive the necessary pragmatic encouragement and support they need in order to discover how best to achieve their individual team goals. Students may submit these updates for formal feedback *more* often than is required, but regardless of how often they do so, they must demonstrate an increase in the level of intellectual rigor with each update submitted; in this way, they come to understand that learning (about science, or, for that matter, anything else) is always about stretching one's understanding.

The consequence of all of this ongoing appraisal, research, and experimentation is that, if you were a fly on the wall during "Little Things," what you would see is active young women simultaneously exploring the internet, plating serial dilutions, testing for inorganic nutrients, peering through microscopes, quantifying microbe densities, and a whole host of additional possible activities (see Figure 5). You would see their teacher roaming the room, coaching and prompting, using informal discussions to evaluate and guide, but the real teaching and learning—and, most importantly, the *responsibility* for it—would reside with the students. They themselves attain the objectives described above, and what they accomplish each year can be truly amazing. Recent projects have included everything from an examination of the impact of different soil aeration methods on protozoa (see Figure 6) to a study of which method of restoring disturbed areas following the construction of the science wing (e.g., sodding versus seeding) returned microbe levels to healthy levels the fastest (see Figure 7). Each spring brings new challenges and new ideas, and what their young minds come up with in a given year is eagerly anticipated.

One other thing students learn by the end of this project, though, is that real research is never done in a vacuum. It is always submitted to peer review, critique, and to verification and substantiation. Consequently, the students who participate in "Little Things" must present their findings in the form of a formal research paper (including graphs and analysis of their data)—the best of which the class decides to post to the project's website for others to read and evaluate—and each team must present their findings to their peers, other teachers, and the administration during a class colloquia at the program's end (see Figure 8). The best are also posted to the project's website, and everything is updated each June to reflect the work of a given year.

Figure 5: Counting Microbes

Alignment With *More Emphasis*

Clearly, as challenged in the content standards of the NSES, engaging in a project like this one allows one to emphasize understanding a "few fundamental science concepts" about ecology (e.g., the impact of the microbial food chain on the health of the soil) versus knowing random definitions (like "food chain"), and it allows students to learn those concepts within the framework of an inquiry that has ramifications for decisions our community makes (e.g., Should we fertilize?). Furthermore, as explicitly challenged in the 9–12 Content Standard A, it involves implementing an inquiry that allows students to learn about the process itself as they pursue and analyze an actual scientific investigation over an extended period of time, learning multiple process skills within a specific context. The program also requires students to manage ideas and information in order to generate a complex argument that explains what the students discovered, and to apply this argument in communicating to their peers and others the consequences of what they found.

Figure 6: Setting Up Research Plots

Figure 7: Studying the Effects of Soil Restoration on Bacteria

Figure 8: The Final Presentation

To see how "Little Things" can accomplish these things, let us look briefly at some excerpts from a final report a student team submitted this past year. They began their project by examining the role of nitrogen in ecological systems, and during the course of their background research, they found that:

- *… All life requires nitrogen compounds in order to live because nitrogen is an element that everything living must have to make proteins and DNA (Johnson 1998). Nothing can live without DNA or proteins. DNA copies itself into RNA, which makes proteins. Proteins cause chemical reactions that cause the chemicals of the cell (lipids, carbohydrates, water, proteins, and nucleic acids) to react between each other. These chemical reactions are how the cell performs its four tasks: reproduction, manufacture of chemicals, respiration, and synthesis.*

- *Air, which is 79% nitrogen gas, is the major reservoir and most abundant source of nitrogen (Nitrogen Cycle 2001). However, most organisms, including plants, cannot obtain nitrogen from the air. And as stated before, everything needs nitrogen to live. Plants must secure their nitrogen in "fixed" form, such as nitrate ions, ammonia, or urea (Nitrogen Cycle 2001). Plants convert nitrogen into a form that they can use through a process called Nitrogen Fixation (Nitrogen Cycle 2001). This is where bacteria come into play…*

- *… Fertilizer has the number one effect on plants, soil, and microbes. The nutrients and chemicals that fertilizer consists of alter the soil composition and thereby affect everything that relies on, or works for soil … by using fertilizer the nitrogen cycle is modified because of the input of nitrogen quantity (from the fertilizer), hence, having an effect on the bacteria by giving them more "food" to perform their job in the nitrogen cycle…*

- *… The purpose of our experiment is to determine whether adding additional fertilizer to a plot of soil will increase or decrease the density of bacteria in that plot and also have an effect on the soil composition, especially the nitrogen cycle. We will see if different concentrations of fertilizer have a different effect on the total number of bacteria along with the nitrate level in the soil … also, by performing our experiment we hope to see what particular impact humans carelessly have on the microbe environment they rely on so much. People have little or no knowledge about microbes and how much they are needed in and for the human life, and by adding fertilizer to their grass they could really be hurting something very significant. We hope to draw many conclusions from our experiment.*

From the text, it is plain to see that by focusing on a single core concept in ecology, the students were better able not only to learn about the nitrogen cycle itself but to place this knowledge within both the larger body of biology (i.e., the "value" of nitrogen in the fundamental biochemistry of living things) and an important social context (i.e., the school's decision to fertilize our grounds). A key idea in life science stopped being merely an abstraction for them and became part of an understanding they could apply in a way that had valid meaning for them *and* simultaneously demonstrate a richer understanding of important and significant scientific knowledge. Or, to put it another way, not only did this specific project enable students to achieve and demonstrate mastery of NSES 9–12 Content Standards, it allowed them to do so in ways that changed their paradigms about the world as well as their knowledge of it.

What is more, when students in a situation such as this one are able to perceive and then develop an experimental investigation that requires them to apply new found understanding such as described, they become exactly the kinds of critical thinkers who can generate the kind of data seen in Figure 9 and the sort of following final argument called for in the 9–12 Content Standards:

- *… Through the various trials of our experiment, our group confirmed our hypothesis was incorrect. We stated that the No Aeration plot would have the most protozoa, the Hollow Tine [method of aeration] plot would have the least amount and the Forking plot [method of aeration] would be somewhere in the middle. The No Aeration plot did have the highest amount of protozoa; however, the Forking and Hollow Tine plots were so close in data that we cannot say definitely whether or not one was higher than the other...*

- *… Looking at the data and the similar patterns in both plots, our group concluded that there was not substantial enough difference in the amounts of protozoa to confidently say that the difference was significant, and not just the result of some counting problem or other source of error... Looking back at conditions on that particular day, we noticed that it rained an extensive amount, enough to make a big difference in our data and the levels of protozoa. This goes to show that different weather conditions are also a factor in determining whether or not aeration is a good idea. For instance, on Day 3 and Day 7, when the weather was clear, no aeration was obviously the best method in obtaining high levels of protozoa. However, on Day 5, when it was raining, aerating the soil actually proved helpful in maintaining protozoa levels. Between the two aeration methods, Forking is better when the weather is clear and sunny because there is less surface desiccation and therefore less water is evaporated out of the soil. On rainy days, Hollow Tine aeration is best because bigger holes in the soil lead to more water infiltration. Water is important to protozoa levels because they "swim" through the soil and therefore more water would make it easier to move and catch prey.*

It is complex arguments such as this one that are precisely what the NSES demands that we emphasize more in our classroom, and analysis like that in Figure 9 can only come from the implementation of a real investigation, using authentic research methods. Combine this evidence with the example from the nitrogen cycle research, and you can see why programs like the "Little Things" project can generate just the sort of learning we all want to be about in our classrooms.

However, projects like mine are about more than the NSES *content* standards, they are also about *teaching* and *assessing*. Hence, the other major challenges one can tackle using a program like "Little Things" are the teaching standards and assessment standards. First, this project enables teachers both to guide students through a continual appraisal of their progress during an extended scientific inquiry and to adapt this guidance to meet the needs, interests, strengths, and experiences of each team of students. In addition, it encourages informal discussion while they work on improving their experiments, helping them learn how to evaluate their own work through this process. So, for example, in a group whose research question was on the impact of mulch on pH and bacteria levels, the original list of potential variables to control consisted of: *how much soil is taken in sample, what samples are tested for, what kind of mulch sampled*; whereas after four weeks of discussion and feedback, the final list of potential variables the team of students finally understood needed to be controlled for consisted of: *time soil samples taken, amount of soil samples taken, number of times experiment is replicated, how much soil is taken in sample, what samples are tested for, where normal levels are taken, what kind of mulch sampled, flower bed in which mulch is taken from, date soil samples taken, where in plotted area soil sample is taken from, the*

Figure 9: Sample Student Graph

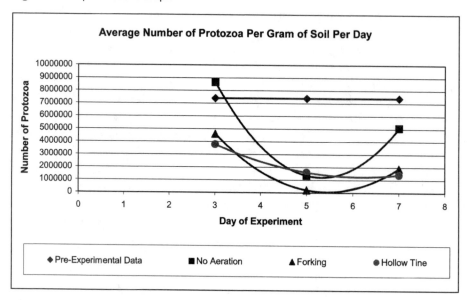

amount of soil from each sample used for the pH testing, amount of demineralized water used in pH testing, amount of soil flocculating reagent used in pH testing, amount of solution transferred to spot plate, which depression used on spot plate, amount of duplex indicator used in pH testing, whether you use the duplex indicator or another indicator first, amount of soil in culture tube, amount of sterile water in each culture tube, amount of water you remove from each culture tube to the next, amount of soil dilution placed in to nutrient agar plate, the level of soil dilution tested, type of agar used.

Second, such projects allow students to own the responsibility for completing the project and gain from it what they choose to invest in it (Teaching Standard B.1). Compare the concluding argument presented earlier with the excerpt that follows; the range of what is possible with "Little Things" becomes abundantly evident:

...From the data shown, we are able to conclude that our hypothesis was correct. PH affects protozoa population greatly. The graph which displays the correlation between pH and protozoa shows that as the pH values increase, it appears that the number of protozoa increases as well. The decrease in the protozoa population in Plot 2 is expected because Plot 2 was the experimental plot where we changed the pH deliberately by adding sulfuric acid. This was also the soil that had a lower pH. From the graph of pH vs. Protozoa, population we can see that the optimal range for protozoa levels is between 7.0 and 8.0. Since we did not collect data from the other end of the pH range, we cannot determine whether the optimal range is only between pH values of 7.0 and 8.0 or if there is another lower range as well.

Third and finally, a significant component of the project is a final presentation to peers and administrations. Therefore, it provides a chance for formal discussion of student findings as they present them to the larger school community. Given that another major component is the four required drafts, "Little Things" also plainly assesses whether students are achieving a rich, scientifically accurate understanding of a body of critical knowledge and whether they can reason effectively about its larger implications through the ongoing give-and-take that accompanies the regular submissions of student preliminary reports.

Conclusion

In the course of four years, more than 150 young women have successfully completed the "Little Things That Run the World" program, which promotes student understanding of the scientific research process and enhances the way students envision and understand their world, cultivating in them a sense of ecological stewardship. As project director, it is my sincere hope that by discovering for themselves "the little things that run the world," my students will learn firsthand how their cognitive skills uniquely endow them to wisely manage their fragile legacy and to walk away equipped to transform their lives, their communities, their society, and ultimately their world.

Please come visit us at our website at *http://faculty.rpcs.org/brocka*; just click on the "Little Things" link.

References

Biehle, J., L. Motz, and S. West. 1999. *NSTA guide to school science facilities*. Arlington, VA: NSTA Press.

Bramble, J. E. 1995 *Field methods in ecological investigation for secondary science teachers*. St. Louis: Missouri Botanical Garden.

Brock, D. 2002. "Risk Taker." *Ecology in action: Biodiversity field studies, vol. 2. of the Paul F. Brandwein summer leadership institute*. 31.

Cothron, J. H., R. N. Giese, and R. J. Rezba. 2000. *Students and research: Practical strategies for science classrooms and competitions, 3rd ed.* Dubuque: Kendall/Hunt Publishing Company.

Hall, G. S., ed. 1996. *Methods for the examination of organismal diversity in soils and sediments*. Paris: CAB INTERNATIONAL.

National Research Council (NRC). 1996. *National science education standards*. Washington, DC: National Academy Press.

Samuels, M. L. 1989. *Statistics for the life science*. Englewood Cliffs: Prentice Hall.

Technology and Cooperative Learning:

The IIT Model for Teaching Authentic Chemistry Curriculum

Therese Forsythe
Northeast Kings Educational Centre

Gregory MacKinnon
Acadia University

Setting

Computer technology is emerging as a viable tool for classroom instruction. This chapter reflects upon a case study of a high school chemistry classroom where the computer is being used in a unique way to deliver and direct curriculum on acids and bases. The authors have developed a learning model in which computer technology is both *integrated* with the curriculum and *interactive* for the student. This Integrated Interactive Technology (IIT) model has been piloted and studied with very promising results. The classroom research has been helpful in defining how to best incorporate computer technology in a meaningful and productive fashion while defining a new role for the teacher. This chemistry classroom is not only innovative in its use of technology; more importantly, it adopts a truly constructivist framework for learning. In doing so it responds to many of the challenges posed by the National Science Education Standards. The chapter will carefully articulate how the IIT model has measurably met these challenges while providing insight into how science learning can be enhanced through computer technologies.

The school where the IIT project took place is a rural high school comprised of students ranging from grades 7 through 12. The school is one of ten high schools in a school board that covers a geographical area of approximately 2569.4 square miles in the midwestern region of the province of Nova Scotia. The school board is responsible for the education of more than 16,000 students.

This rural school, located in a farming community, houses approximately 600 students, 300 of whom are in grades 10–12. Most students in the school come from low- to middle-socioeconomic backgrounds. The school can be defined as technology poor with only two computer labs having no more than 60 computers total for all of the students. With such a lack of facilities, the sole access of students to computer technology is through computer science courses or casual computer use during break periods when students typically use word processing and PowerPoint software.

The students enrolled in grade 12 chemistry were all involved in the project of implementing our interactive software as part of an acid/base unit, which is a core component of the curriculum. In total, 30 students participated in the study. To initiate a computer integration exercise requires uninterrupted access to computers for extended periods. In this school this was not possible. Through community collaboration with Acadia University, an arrangement was made to donate six computers to the high school, thus empowering the teacher to pursue the action research project described in this chapter.

Relevance of the NSES to the Canadian Context

The National Science Education Standards (NSES 1996) are recognized in Canada as seminal and visionary. Canadian science education curriculum reform has been most heavily influenced by the NSES initiative. A brief discussion of the curriculum documents guiding our reform will help the reader to see the obvious influences and overlaps between our regional efforts and the NSES.

The Council of Provincial Ministers of Education in 1995 adopted the Pan-Canadian Protocol for Collaboration on School Curriculum. Under this protocol a document was developed entitled *Common Framework of Science Learning Outcomes K–12.* The intent was to propose a nationwide template for science education. The framework highlights foundations and research-informed progressive education with science literacy as a key focus. This focus was reiterated later in a regional document known as the *Foundation for the Atlantic Canada Science Curriculum* (ACSC 1997). Three processes of scientific literacy are delineated in the ACSC document, namely: (1) scientific inquiry; (2) problem solving; and (3) decision making. Within this framework, and building on the strengths of the Pan-Canadian Protocol, science literacy was linked to general essential graduation outcomes and specifically to science through four strands: (1) Science, Technology, Society, and the Environment (STSE) curriculum; (2) skill development; (3) knowledge; and (4) attitudes. From these were developed key-stage curriculum outcomes and specific curriculum outcomes. At each step of curriculum reform, the NSES has provided a wealth of direction through its comprehensive treatment of science education. In short, this reliance on the pivotal NSES document has guaranteed significant overlap with Canadian curriculum initiatives.

More Emphasis/NSES

The Interactive Integrated Technology model developed for this project was based heavily on a cooperative learning model that involved interactions between: (a) grouped students; (b) groups of students; (c) teacher and individuals; (d) teacher and groups; and finally between (e) teacher and the entire class. This extensive interaction allowed for unique opportunities for students to learn individually, from peers and from teacher-led activities. With respect to the IIT model, interactivity was also promoted through the use of the computer. The teacher (T. Forsythe) and researcher (G. MacKinnon) carefully designed the software to regularly prompt students to investigate the subject of acids and bases, and to subsequently input different types of information into the computer as they proceeded through the unit of study. This information might be anything from numerical data for calculations, to responses to multiple-choice questions, to testing of content knowledge, to providing feedback from laboratories or classroom activities. The computer acted as an interactive curriculum and class work organizer. More specifically, the computer was used to: (a) introduce curriculum through multimedia i.e. pictures, sound and video; (b) provide historical context to relevant theories; (c) prompt students to perform various laboratories and activities; (d) provide feedback through regular assessment items; and (e) remind students to compile their understandings to address a unit challenge problem. In the context of the developed IIT model, "integrated" meant developing software that directed students through the content in their specific curriculum (MacKinnon, Deveau, and Forsythe 2000). In this instance there were provincial curriculum documents that dictated precisely what curriculum students would be responsible for on a standardized regional examination. Students in groups of three visited their group work station and proceeded through the unit at their own pace, accessing the teacher for explanations, clarifications, laboratory supplies, and assessment materials.

Real-world problems were embedded throughout the unit curriculum. The impact of acids and bases on our lives was evident in examples ranging from soft drinks to issues of pollution and other environmental concerns. The unit challenge was a multifaceted problem in lake pollution, which could only be addressed by students when they had achieved a working knowledge of the entire curriculum unit. Students were regularly prompted by computer and teacher to revisit the unit challenge as they constructed component understandings around acid-base theory. The acidification of lakes is a relevant issue in our region and as such has a measure of authenticity and motivational interest for the chemistry students. In their final assessment of the unit, students were expected to present, in a professional way, a solution to the problem posed in the unit challenge. In this way students acted as a team to solve a problem situated in a meaningful context and presented the solution as if they were apprentice chemists.

Active debate was fostered by the examination of historical context with regard to acid-base theory. Rather than provide meaningless vignettes of important scientists and their theories, students were asked to consider why the scientists arrived at the conclusions they did about acids and bases, considering the facilities, state of knowledge, and conceptual understanding at that time. Understanding the "way" scientists came to conclusions and the context in which it took place is a useful exercise in modeling the true nature of science inquiry.

Based on the NSES (teaching standards), teachers are looking for opportunities to engage students in discussions and debate that allows for negotiation of meaning in a social constructivist framework rather than representing science as a "fait accompli" exercise. This in turn shifts some of the responsibility for learning to the student and opens up the curriculum for a consideration of extended interest areas around the history of science. This adapting of curriculum fosters a community of learners that includes teacher and students alike. The content standards push for more personal and social perspectives on science. The process of considering historical development of theories is aligned with this standard.

Teacher/Student/Classroom

This particular classroom can be described as a teaching laboratory. Eight octagonal tables were distributed throughout the teaching area, with laboratory benches bordering the room. The computer stations were placed on the laboratory benches where student teams performed their assigned technology-related tasks. The chemistry teacher acted as a facilitator, guiding student teams through the curriculum, providing any necessary clarification through informal discussion. The teacher (T. Forsythe) has a Bachelor of Science in chemistry and a Masters of Education in Curriciulum Studies (Science). She has been involved in the development of provincial curriculum documents and has experience teaching chemistry. Researcher G. MacKinnon conducted qualitative research including field studies, interviews, focus groups and audio-visual recordings (MacKinnon 2000). With the researcher a second observer, constant assessment of student understanding provided information as to when the project needed any revisions or when students would benefit from whole class discussions. The students in both chemistry classes were highly self-motivated and exhibited a strong work ethic. The range of student academic abilities varied, as is found in most classes; however, the students were eager to learn, and even more excited to be involved in an interactive technology project. Throughout the six-week unit, students spent little time off task and were frequently found working on assignments and labs during their own free time.

The excitement generated by the study in the classroom was certainly motivational but it also had educational value. Students were exposed to the idea that science can be learned in many different ways that represent some overlap of content and process. That a teacher could study the impact of a new approach was a novel idea to students. The NSES point to students being actively involved in inquiry. In this case study, students were not only learning science in very active and interactive ways but they were also involved in the process of reflecting on the very way we teach science. Their participation in focus groups and member check sessions promoted a community of researchers/learners that the NSES supports. In a unique way, the action research on their classroom added a layer of inherent "buy-in" with respect to them actively impacting their own science learning.

Program Description/NSES Links

The project under study involved the design of multimedia software using Macromedia's Authorware. This software employs many features that allow students ample opportunity to interact with information as they are learning. For example, students can choose appropriate answers or compile and record their own responses.

Enabling students to actively engage in the learning process was the primary goal in the development of the software program. The program was prepared around a group of foundational constructivist ideas noted in the literature (Dick 1991; Duffy and Jonassen 1991; Greening 1998; Merrill 1991; Osborne 1996; Perkins 1991; Willis and Wright 2000). The model used for software development involved a recursive reflective process (R2D2) where students, teachers, and a science education professor had opportunities to impact the development through feedback and iterative discussions and trials (Willis 1995).

There are a number of design features inherent to the implementation of this student-centered learning environment. All of these design features (See Table 1) allowed students to learn science through investigation and inquiry in a collaborative and authentic learning environment.

Table 1. Design Features of the Software

Guideline	Response as manifested in the IIT model
1	A unit challenge acid-base problem serves as an umbrella task.
2	The teacher assists the learner by applying closure to topics.
3	The unit challenge, as well as problems embedded in the unit, is based on real data from authentic chemistry settings.
4	The unit challenge is a multicomponent/multidimensional task which can only be successfully completed by careful consideration of the entire unit of study.
5	Through use of a hypertext environment, students have the flexibility to address topics both sequentially and in a nonlinear fashion. The pace and order of study is only confined by preset curricular deadlines.
6	Because the role of teacher has been shifted away from presenter of knowledge, there is greater opportunity to challenge/assist individual students at their level of conceptual understanding.

The classroom was fitted with six computers. Due to the limited resources, teams of three were constructed to maximize the students' access to the computer stations. These teams worked cooperatively for the duration of the project. While the value of cooperative learning settings has long been recognized (Kagan 1992), more recent research (Johnson and Johnson 1996) has linked innumerable benefits to cooperative learning and the use of technology.

The computer was used in conjunction with other assignments, activities, and laboratory exercises. Students used the computer to gather information and practice a variety of problem-solving exercises. From here, they worked in teams to investigate the information they learned from the computer. This investigation could take many forms, from debate over viable solutions to parts of the unit challenge problem, to the analysis and defense of conclusions obtained from the numerous laboratory experiments.

Students can enter the unit learning cycle at a variety of nodes, and thus two or three computers in a classroom can be quite sufficient to direct the learning of several groups of students. It is also important to note the nonlinear nature of the interactive software. Students were able to enter or leave the computer station whenever they chose to do so. The result is that all student teams were constantly at different points in the curriculum on any given day. Also, with the freedom to come and go on the computer station, and with the wealth of other related activities, minimal computer resources were required. Figure 1 shows the model used to incorporate the IIT model into the classroom setting. The students were first given the umbrella task of solving an environmental problem concerning the acid level found in a local lake. From here, they were able to enter the software to view a timeline, a hypertext page that allowed students to enter the choice of topics wherever they chose to do so.

Depending on the choice from the timeline page, students would be given a series of instructional background information as well as a chance to apply this newfound knowledge. Students at the computer (see Figure 1) were introduced to: (1) new theoretical topics; (2) lab techniques through video clips and pictures; (3) sample calculations; (4) assessment, in the form of mastery learning exercises; and (5) historical context for the topics. Away from the computer, (see Figure 1) students engaged in: (1) laboratory investigations; (2) practicing lab techniques; (3) practice problems; (4) paper and pencil assessment; (5) library research; and (6) assignments, investigations, and activities. As students progressed through theory and practice, both at and away from the computer, they periodically revisited the problem and constructed new understandings about how to solve the problem. This was accomplished by computer prompts that sent students away to consider the application of learned theory and to update their "unit challenge" notes.

A crucial component of this instructional system taps into the established benefits of problem-based learning. Savery and Duffy (1995) contend that, "The more the problem-solving learning situation represents the real world, the more likely the student will transfer skills to other problem solving situations…. Anchoring can do this learning in meaningful contexts which simulate apprenticeship learning." Building on situated cognition (Carr, Jonassen, Litzinger, and Marra 1998) encourages the creation of fruitful generative learning environments (Cognition and Technology Group at Vanderbilt 1991; Grabowski 1996) where reasoning and sustained exploration are the foci.

Figure 1. A Model for Integrating Computers into Curriculum

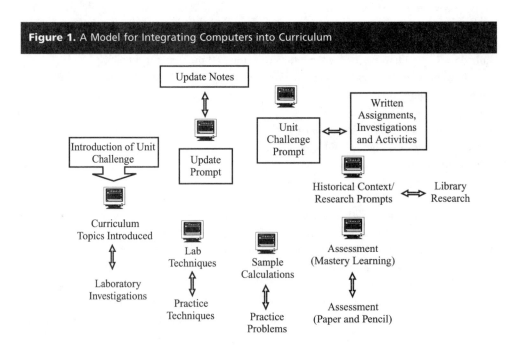

The teacher assumed the role of facilitator as little formal or traditional instruction was given during the six-week unit. As students worked in teams, the teacher would travel from team to team listening, asking and answering questions, and generally providing assistance and clarification as needed. With the assistance of the researcher, students were given ample opportunity to verbalize their learning through informal discussions that allowed the both of us to assess what the students understood up to that point in the acid-base unit.

The Hypertext Environment

The entry interface screen is shown in Figure 2. From this hypertext screen, students could access any individual component of the unit's content. The timeline feature used to outline the topics serves to provide context for students as they study the history of acid-base chemistry.

Research has shown that a well-organized interface and adequate preliminary instruction allows students to become very comfortable with the software. This promotes a "transparent technology" in terms of their learning (Adrianson and Hjelmquist 1993). The technique of using advanced organizers has been linked to better retention and comprehension of instructional content (Ausubel 1960; Mayer 1979). Hypertext menu systems have the additional advantages of promoting open-ended environments for learning (Hannifin, Hall, Land, and Hill 1994), as well as promoting self-regulating learning behaviors in students (Shin 1998).

Changing Emphases: Teaching Standards

The IIT model is an interactive student-centered approach to incorporating technology in learning. Through a team approach, students have the opportunity to direct their own learning through multiple interaction styles with a knowledge base and an instructor. The curriculum is authentic and relevant to students. Students are empowered to assume advisory roles as apprentice chemists solving a real problem. In addressing the unit challenge they are involved in metacognitive processes and extensive synthesis of concepts and process skills in an effort to solve a practical problem. As group members they share responsibility in their cooperative effort to complete the unit. Their approach to solving the unit challenge through a cycle of learning concepts, invoking techniques and finally applying their new understandings, becomes an authentic exercise in inquiry. Students learn to access all of the available resources (content knowledge, experimentation, interaction with peers and teacher) in their effort to direct their own style of inquiry. The promotion of inquiry-based learning is an important thrust of the NSES. Their teacher serves to guide learning through an elaborate scaffolding process based on students "need to know." The teacher becomes director of the classroom experience rather than purveyor of knowledge.

Changing Emphases: Professional Development Standards

For the teacher, the IIT project has functioned as an action research opportunity that has culminated in an extensive case study. This "inquiry into teaching and learning" is an emphasis espoused by the NSES. The entire unit is based on the premise of constructivist learning. Students and teacher addressed the content in an inquiry mode both at the macro level (unit challenge) and the micro level (component theory). The use of an authentic problem that relies on the

Figure 2. Timeline User Interface

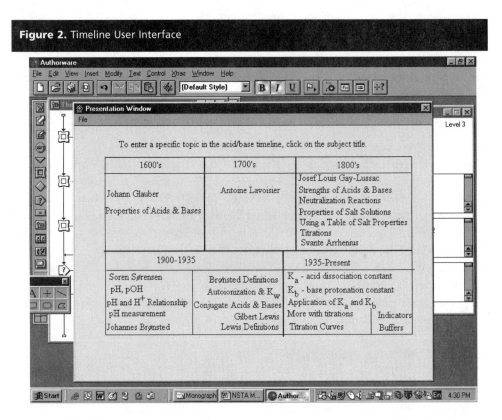

acquisition of component conceptual understandings ensured that students would see the connection between theory and practice. This glimpse of practice allowed students to appreciate what a career in science research might look like. Meanwhile this unique process of scaffolding students knowledge-building relies heavily on the teacher's foundational interest in pedagogy and scientific inquiry. The teacher has generated an environment of inquiry that accesses many learning models and styles and has had opportunities to discuss the progress of the project and elicit feedback and critique from the students. This fosters a collegial spirit, a cooperative effort between student and teacher and an integration of science and science learning. The teacher is perceived as a director of knowledge building with expertise in both content knowledge of chemistry as well as experiential knowledge of the classroom environment and what constitutes substantive learning.

This project allowed the teacher a unique opportunity to employ technology in her teaching and to share and discuss the results with a dedicated collaborator/researcher. The feedback and iterative modifications of classroom instruction follows an action research model that provides ideal opportunities for professional development. The experience of the researcher as a science educator and an observer in the teacher's classroom provided valuable feedback to drive change. The teacher experienced a sense of liberation in that she organized the learning environment but was rarely solely responsible for delivering knowledge through a teacher-lecturer transmission model. Instead, students largely benefited from one-on-one or small group discussions where the nuances of conceptual misunderstandings were much easier to perceive and to clarify. The student's perception of the teacher as a collaborative researcher is very positive. In interviews, students repeatedly expressed gratitude that their teacher was so interested in their education. The IIT project was innovative in this rural school and thus the teacher provided pedagogical leadership through demonstrating risk-taking with a technology experiment. The teacher has had opportunities to share the results of the project with other teachers both informally and through regional conference presentations. The provincial department of education is interested in the leadership that this project and teacher might provide. Based on this project's results, other teachers have been encouraged to apply this model to their own curricular settings. The work has been recognized by the provincial department of education as innovative, forward-looking, and an effective use of technology. The interaction of a researcher (university-based) and a practitioner (school-based) sends an important message to other teachers about the value of collaboration. Teachers can act as "change agents" in their classrooms, their schools, and their professional communities.

Changing Emphases: Assessment Standards

The assessment in this project was designed to sample: (a) content/conceptual understanding; (b) capability to synthesize information; (c) practical application of knowledge; (d) acquisition of process skills; and (e) productive models of inquiry. This was achieved through a blend of practical activities, focused laboratories, tests, computer-assisted feedback activities, peer assessment, written progress reports, a unit challenge response and a regional examination. The regional examination had numerous STS components that relied on students recognizing authentic problems and the means to solve them. The IIT project gave students practice through the acid-base unit to formulate problem-solving approaches. These students performed above average on the examination and, though not conclusive, it appears that the IIT model gave students valuable practice.

The NSES promote an emphasis on assessing what is most highly valued. While individual components of the assessment scheme were given values, the weighting of the assessment favored the ability of students to assimilate, accommodate, and synthesize new knowledge in the context of their daily inquiry. Students were exposed to multiple models of evaluation and provided feedback to the teacher (focus groups and individuals) on the accessibility and suitability of the assessment items throughout the acid-base unit. Students' ultimate success at internalizing concepts of acids and bases was reflected by a style of assessment that valued their process of inquiry-based learning.

Changing Emphases: Content and Inquiry

The nature of the unit was such that students needed to learn concepts not solely because of their inherent significance, but more importantly that the synthesis of related concepts would allow them to solve an authentic problem. The unit challenge ensured that students integrated the learning, demonstrating an overlap of concepts, social issues, and computation in the context of inquiry. Activities and laboratories were all directly related and relevant to building new understandings around the acid-base concepts en route to solving the unit challenge. Embedded within these activities were process skills (prediction, hypothesis, graphing) and practical techniques. Because the ultimate aim was to apply the knowledge through an inquiry-based approach, the teacher worked very hard to encourage students to regularly revisit the unit challenge and assimilate and accommodate their understandings. The classroom had an investigative atmosphere with appropriate scaffolding from the teacher. The teacher periodically assembled the entire group to help congeal the main ideas. Because many of the students worked in a linear sequential pattern through the curriculum and the teacher imposed loosely-defined deadlines, it was possible to have fruitful closure sessions.

Evaluation of Impact

Assessing what students learn from a particular teaching innovation is crucial to the acceptance of that innovation in other classrooms. The research found that students have increased confidence in their knowledge, improved peer interactions, and built on their abilities to complete problem-solving exercises that combine a multitude of scientific principles, within the learning environment. The bottom line however, is that these same students must be able to perform on a standardized test to truly see how this innovative classroom approach compares to other, more traditional, classroom teaching techniques. For the students in this research project, a standardized provincial assessment was administered at the end of the school year. The results demonstrated that these students performed better on the acid-base unit sections of the exam than students had in previous years. On average, students scored 94.1% on these sections of the exam. Previous years found an average of 73.6–74.2 %. In the other units in the course, the average grades were 74.1% and 76.3% respectively. Moreover, students completed all of the examination questions that involved multiple levels of complexity, with few errors. For this reason, we considered the multimedia project to register some success.

The NSES provides teachers with guidelines for assessment standards, shown in Table 2. This table also shows what our research project did to fulfill these guidelines. Both qualitative and quantitative data were collected in the IIT setting and from these sources it was possible to triangulate the findings of the study.

Summary

With the increasing exigency for teachers to implement technology in the classroom and the prescribed outcomes-based curricula subject teachers are required to teach, there is a growing dilemma as to how to effectively use technology. This dilemma provided the impetus for the development of our software and subsequent research project. The impacts for this research in classrooms were seen in the improved student ability to: (1) efficiently carry out a multitude of tasks; (2) apply higher order thinking skills; (3) confidently investigate curriculum rather than rely on the teacher; (4) improve organizational skills; (5) communicate scientific explanations through peer interactions; and (6) improve internalization due to the student acting as teacher in the group process.

Educational research often has as its primary goal and responsibility the growth of understanding about the nature of learning and the promotion of such in the classroom. Teaching, as a profession, predisposes its practitioners to a world of continual reflection and inquiry. What is embedded in this action research approach is the close collaboration with all of the stakeholders

Table 2. NSES Assessment Standards

NSES Guidelines	More Emphasis	Fulfillment of guidelines in research project
1	Assessing what is most highly valued	External provincial assessment
2	Assessing rich well-structured knowledge	Concept mapping, video recordings, and field notes show the increased ability to assimilate information
3	Assessing scientific understanding and reasoning	Completion of activities, assignments, and experiments
4	Assessing to learn what students do understand	Interviews and/or surveys completed in weeks 1, 2, 3, 4, and 7
5	Assessing achievement and opportunity to learn	Collection of daily progress reports and peer debriefing with professional
6	Students engaging in ongoing assessment of their work and that of others	Continual peer collaboration and cross-group discussions of tasks
7	Teachers involved in the development of external assessments	Teacher on team to develop provincial chemistry 12 examination

of the research project. Throughout this project, the interaction with other members of the professional community, such as Dr. MacKinnon, was essential to its success. The very premise of collegial collaboration builds in motivation for the teacher to engage in research that stretches the boundaries of the classroom.

References

Allchin, D. 2000. How not to teach historical cases in science. *Journal of College Science Teaching* 30 (1): 33–37.

Adrianson, L. and E. Hjelmquist. 1993. Communication and memory of texts in face-to-face and computer-mediated communication. *Computers in Human Relations* 9:121–135.

ACSC. 1997. Foundation for the Atlantic Canada Science Curriculum. Available online at *http://apef-fepa.org/pdf/science.pdf*

Ausubel, D. P. 1960. The use of advance organizers in learning and retention of meaningful information. *Journal of Educational Psychology* 51: 26.

Berger, C. F., C. R. Lu, S. J. Belzer, and B. E. Voss. 1994. Research on the uses of technology in science education. In *Handbook of Research on Science Teaching and Learning*, ed. D. Gabel, 466–490. New York: MacMillan.

Carr, A. A., D. H. Jonassen, M. E. Litzinger, and R. M. Marra. 1998. Good ideas to foment educational revolution: The role of systemic change in advancing situated learning, constructivism and feminist pedagogy. *Educational Technology* 5–15.

Cognition and Technology Group at Vanderbilt. 1991. Technology and the design of generative learning environments. *Educational Technology* 31 (5): 34–40.

Dick, W. 1991. An instructional designer's view of constructivism. *Educational Technology* 31 (5): 41–44.

Duffy, T. M. and D. H. Jonassen. 1991. Constructivism: New implications for instructional technology? *Educational Technology* 31(5): 7–12.

Friedlander, L. 1989. Moving images into the classroom: Multimedia in higher education. *Laserdisk Professional* 2 (4): 33–38.

Grabowski, B. L. 1996. Generative learning: Past, present and future. In *Handbook of Research for Educational Communications and Technology,* ed. D. H. Jonassen, 897–918. New York: MacMillan Library.

Greening, T. 1998. Building the constructivist toolbox: An exploration of cognitive technologies. *Educational Technology* 38 (2): 23–35.

Hannafin, M. J., C. Hall, S. Land, and J. Hill. 1994. Learning in open-ended environments: Assumptions, methods, and implications. *Educational Technology* 34 (10): 48–55.

Johnson, D. W. and R. T. Johnson. 1996. Cooperation and the use of technology. In *Handbook of Research for Educational Communications and Technology,* ed. D. H. Jonassen, 1017–1044. New York: MacMillan Library.

Kagan, S. 1992. *Cooperative learning*. San Juan Capistrano, CA: Kagan Cooperative Learning.

Kearsley, G. 1988. Authoring considerations for hypertext. *Educational Technology* 28 (11): 21–24.

MacKinnon, G. R. 2000. The nature of learning in an integrated interactive technology setting: A case study of a high school chemistry classroom. MEd Thesis, University of New Brunswick.

MacKinnon, G. R., K. Deveau, and T. Forsythe. 2000. Integrated interactive science software: A new role for teachers. *Journal of Instructional Science and Technology* 3 (2): 2–10.

MacKinnon, G. R., C. P. McFadden, and T. Forsythe. 2002. The tension between hypertext environments and science learning, *Electronic Journal of Science Education* 6 (3).

Marchionini, G. 1989. Information-seeking strategies of novices using a full text electronic encyclopedia. *Journal of American Society for Information Science* 40: 54–66.

Marsh, E. J. and D. D. Kumar. 1992. Hypermedia: A conceptual framework for science education and review of recent findings. *Journal of Educational Multimedia and Hypermedia* 1: 25–37.

Mayer, R. E. 1979. Can advanced organizers influence meaningful learning? *Review of Educational Research* 49: 371–383.

Means, B. 1994. Introduction: Using technology to advance educational goals. In *Technology and Educational Reform: The Reality Behind the Promise*, ed. B. Means, San Francisco, CA: Jossey Bass.

Merrill, M. D. 1991. Constructivism and instructional design. *Educational Technology* 31 (5): 45–53.

National Research Council (NRC). 1996. *National science education standards*. Washington, DC: National Academy Press.

Osborne, J. F. 1996. Beyond constructivism. *Science Education* 80 (1): 53–82.

Perkins, D. N. 1991. Technology meets constructivism: Do they make a marriage? *Educational Technology* 31 (5): 18–23.

Reidl, J. 1995. *The integrated technology classroom*. Boston, MA: Allyn and Bacon.

Rose, E. 1999. Deconstructing interactivity in educational computing. *Educational Technology* 39 (1): 43–49.

Roselli, T. 1991. Control of user disorientation in hypertext systems. *Educational Technology* 31 (12): 42–46.

Savery, J. R. and T. M. Duffy. 1995. Problem-based learning: An instructional model and its constructivist framework. *Educational Technology* 35 (5): 31–37.

Willis, J. 1995. A recursive, reflective, instructional design model based on constructivist-interpretivist theory. *Educational Technology* 35 (6): 5–23.

Willis, J. and K. E. Wright. 2000. A general set of procedures for constructivist instructional design: The new R2D2 model. *Educational Technology* 40 (2): 5–20.

Inquiring Minds Want to Know All About Detergent Enzymes

Carolyn A. Hayes
Center Grove High School

Setting

Center Grove High School serves 2,100 students in grades 9–12. The high school joins two middle schools and six elementary schools to comprise the Center Grove Community School Corporation in Greenwood, Indiana. Current enrollment in the school district is 6,900 students. This is the result of a 2–3% growth each year in the last 11 years. The school district is located 20 miles south of Indianapolis, Indiana, in White River Township of Johnson County. The people in this township make up 30.5% of the total county population. In Johnson County, 85.7% of the residents have a high school diploma and 23.1% have four or more years of college.

The residents of White River Township have been described as clearly younger, better educated, more fully employed, making more money, and living in more expensive homes. The majority of the residents are employed in the management and professional area and in sales and office positions. The median household income is $69,000 with the average family size being 3.14 persons per family.

Review of *More Emphasis* Conditions

Several *More Emphasis* conditions are incorporated in the design of the enzyme unit. Those from the content and inquiry standards include:

- Implementing inquiry as instructional strategies, abilities, and ideas to be learned;

- Activities that investigate and analyze science questions;
- Using evidence and strategies for developing or revising an explanation;
- Groups of students often analyzing and synthesizing data after defending conclusions;
- Applying the results of experiments to scientific arguments and explanations; and
- Management of ideas and information.

Those from the teaching standards include:
- Guiding students in active and extended scientific inquiry;
- Providing opportunities for scientific discussion and debate among students; and
- Continually assessing student understanding.

The enzyme unit provides experiences that actively engage students in learning about their world. Using activities that require my students to discuss, debate, and evaluate what they know and what they need to know, including hypotheses, experimental designs and experimental results, they not only learn science concepts but also acquire skills to solve problems, both personal and social. This unit provides opportunities for students to demonstrate their new knowledge and skills.

Classroom Setting

My public classroom teaching experience spans 29 years. My educational background includes a B.S. and M.S. in secondary science education; in December 2004 I received an Ed.D. in curriculum and instruction. My success in implementing inquiry-based instruction has been recognized through the receipt of the Presidential Award for Excellence in Science Teaching and the Radio Shack National Teacher Award. The enzyme unit I designed is used in my Honors Biology 1 class, which includes 9th and 10th graders. In addition to honors biology, I also currently teach genetics at Center Grove. The student body at Center Grove includes 2100 students in grades 9–12. This population is approximately 96% White, 2% Asian, 1% Hispanic/Latino and 1% African American and multi-racial. Less than 1% of the student body includes students who do not consider English as their first language. Eighty-three percent of students enrolled in honors biology class have also enrolled in at least one or two other honors level courses.

The Story of Enzymes

This unit is designed to engage students in both guided and open inquiry by including scenarios, materials, and a question sequence. The planned question sequence provides the teacher tools to learn what students already know and to lead them to new levels of understanding.

The design of the unit follows the learning cycle. Students are first engaged using an introductory activity. Then they investigate science concepts and ultimately apply their experiences for assessment. From the teacher's perspective, improvisation is included in the design. Planning questions that I will present, which may be generated by my students, prepares me to alter my instruction based on what my students do. This ensures that each of the students learns.

Engagement: Day 1—Lesson Scenario

You have been hired by the Center Grove Day Care Center because of your expertise in laundry detergents and knowledge of Jello. The day care has been barraged with questions from parents on how to get the Jello stains out of their children's clothing. It seems that this day care center loves to serve Jello to the boys and girls. The day care center wants to make the parents happy and needs your help and advice as to what to recommend to the parents.

After presenting the scenario, students start a journal to record their progression through the lessons. Working individually, each student divides a page in the journal into two columns. On one side, everything already known about the situation is written (i.e., detergents and Jello gelatin desserts). On the other side, everything the student would like to find out about the situation is written down. Each student is asked to state the problem that needs to be solved. These written statements come from questions prompted by the teacher. The questions include:

1. What do you know about the situation? (i.e., detergents, Jello, …). Write your responses in your journal.
2. What would you like to find out about the situation?
3. What is the problem statement?

Next, the students discuss their answers within their lab groups. Each group selects a spokesperson, who reports to the rest of the class. I record their responses on the board for: *What You Know, What You Would Like to Find Out,* and *Problem Statement*. After a classroom discussion of the responses, which results in a unified problem statement, I interject the following question: "If given the following materials (…), how would you go about designing an experiment to find an answer to the problem statement?" Each lab group discusses the question and comes up with a detailed plan, and then shares that plan with the class. Students evaluate the different plans for omissions, vagueness, or errors. Following class discussion, each group writes a hypothesis, revises the design, prepares data tables, and receives teacher approval to begin the experiment. Then, the students conduct the experiment.

Engagement: Day 2—Data Analysis

Students collect their data, analyze the data, and share results with the rest of the class. I prompt the students with the following questions to aid them in their analysis.

1. What do the results suggest to you?
2. Do you have enough information to explain the results and give a sufficient answer to the day care center?
3. Which products increased the size of the well diameters or affected the areas the most?
4. What ingredient in the gelatin dessert do you think was changed? What caused the change?
5. What ingredient in the detergent is probably responsible for the breakdown of the protein, gelatin?
6. Are there any similarities among the different detergents?
7. Where would you look for possible answers?
8. Do you have any other questions you might ask about your results?

9. Are you satisfied with your results?

To help interpret results, students look to other sources, such as the product labels, the internet, the textbook, and the teacher, to find more information. Students construct concept maps to explain what is happening to the Jello and why. (See Figure 1.) The concept map should illustrate that an enzyme is the cause of the digestion of the Jello and how the enzyme works. Assessment during this phase includes *formative* assessment where the teacher interacts with the groups as they are discussing the problem statement, collecting data, analyzing data, and constructing their concept maps. Students write a letter to the daycare center in response to the initial question as an authentic assessment.

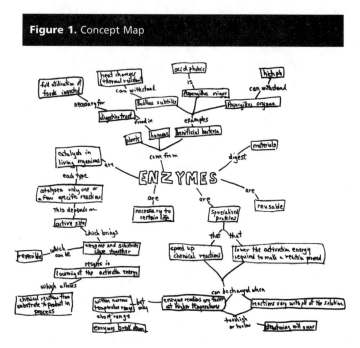

Figure 1. Concept Map

Investigation: Lesson Scenario—Part B

The Center Grove Day Care Center is happy with your results, but has a new dilemma to solve. Children are also going home with grease stains from the French fries, along with the fries smashed into their clothing. To say the least, the parents are not happy about these stains. Will the detergent you have selected also work on these stains?

Students return to their lab groups and look at their original lists of *What I Know,* and *What I Want to Know* and see if any of these items can address the new question. I also reiterate similar questions that were posed to students from the first scenario. Students look at their concept maps to see if they can provide any possible solutions. After class discussion and the finalizing of the problem statement, I share with the class that there are materials available for their experiments. Each group comes up with a detailed plan using the material provided. These plans are shared and evaluated. Following class discussion, each group writes a hypothesis, revises the design, prepares data tables, and receives teacher approval to begin the experiment. Then, students conduct the experiment.

Investigation: Day 2

Students collect their data, analyze the data, and share their results with the rest of the class. Questions posed to students include the following:

1. Were the results the same as the previous experiment? If not, how are they different?
2. What do the results suggest?
3. How were the three substrates affected by the various detergents?
4. What does the evidence tell you about the enzymes in the detergents?
5. Do you have enough information to explain the results and give a sufficient answer to the day care center?
6. Do you have any other questions you might ask about your results?
7. Are you satisfied with your results? If not, what other steps would you take?
8. Can you explain to the day care center how the enzymes in the detergent work? If yes, how would you do it? Are all enzymes essentially the same in job and effectiveness?

After class discussion and additional research, students add to their concept maps and prepare answers for the day care center. Assessments during this phase include formative assessment similar to the engagement phase. In addition, the students write a letter to the daycare center about the answer to their problem as an authentic assessment. (See Figure 2.)

Application: Lesson Scenario—Part C

The day care center owners are really excited about your answers and wonder where the enzymes that are found in the detergents originate. The owners tell you about an article that they read entitled, "Recombinant Detergent." They read that *Bacillus* bacterium has an enzyme that makes laundry detergent more effective. They want to know if this is true or not. Being the inquisitive biology student that you are, you also want to find out if this claim is true or not.

Students go back to their lab groups to begin investigating this new question. Students look over their concept maps and refer to other sources of information about bacteria. There is class discussion on what the students know, what they want to know, and the problem statement. I have available various kinds of bacteria for the experiments. Each group comes up with a detailed plan. These plans are shared and evaluated. Following class discussion, each group writes a hypothesis, revises the design, prepares data tables, and receives teacher approval to begin the experiment. Then, the students conduct the experiment.

Application: Day 2—Analysis

Students collect their data, analyze the data, and share their results with the rest of the class. In addition, I may ask the following questions to further their analyses:

1. Were the results the same as in the previous experiment? If not, how are they different?
2. Is the digestion occurring inside or outside of the bacterial cell? What is your proof?

Figure 2. Student Letter

Center Grove Daycare Center,

After running several tests, we have decided that Tide Free liquid can best remove Jello stains. The enzymes in the detergent attach on to and then break apart the proteins in gelatin, found in Jello. I would also recommend that the water used in the cycle should be warm and not hot. Extreme heat can change the shape of the enzyme. The shape of the enzyme determines what job it will do and is very specific to that job. Tide liquid seems to have the enzymes best suited for gelatin.

Sincerely,
Sarah
Cowan

3. How are the three substrates affected by the different bacteria?
4. Would you expect all three species of bacteria to digest all three types of organic compounds? Why or why not?
5. Do you have enough information to explain the results and give a sufficient answer to the day care center?
6. Do you have any other questions you might ask about your results?
7. Are you satisfied with your results? If not, what other steps would you take?
8. Can you explain the article "Recombinant Detergents"?

After class discussion and additional research, each student prepares for the day care center either an essay, entitled "A Day in the Life of a Bacterial Enzyme," or a flip chart, demonstrating how an enzyme works in a bacterial cell.

Alignment to Changing Emphases

This enzyme unit is designed to involve my students in inquiry as they learned biological concepts. It illustrates several changing emphases in both teaching standards and in content and inquiry standards.

Having students individually determine what they know and what they need to know helps me recognize experiences students bring into my classroom. This allows me to understand and respond to their needs; I can adapt my questions to guide them in understanding science concepts. By presenting my students with a scenario that contains a problem to be solved, I am able to guide them through the inquiry process and then, through repeated situations, students go on to organize their own inquiry experiences. As students work through the inquiry process they are given opportunities to share with others their experimental designs in order to obtain peer review. In addition, they discuss their data and conclusions in order to learn from each other. This process allows them to re-evaluate the significance of their data.

Assessment of student understanding is a continual process. As I move around the room I am able to interact with each group and learn from their discussions. This formative kind of assessment permits me to redirect my students if there are any misconceptions or problems in understanding the concepts.

Several examples of changes in emphasis from the content and inquiry standards are found within the enzyme unit. Students are provided the day care scenario to give them the opportunity to use inquiry and to bring in their personal perspectives. As students ask questions and seek answers, they do so in a context that can provide scientific knowledge for their personal use.

The emphasis changes that include implementing inquiry as an instructional strategy, investigating and analyzing scientific questions, using multiple process skills such as manipulative, cognitive, and procedural, and using group work to analyze and synthesize data after defending conclusions—these are all implemented in each of the three phases of the enzyme program. Once students focus on their problem statement, which is based on their questions, they will hypothesize a solution and then design an experiment based on their hypothesis. As students travel through the process, they review their evidence, reflect on the problem statement and prepare a response based on their data.

Evidence of *More Emphasis* Conditions

As was mentioned earlier, this unit on enzymes was originally presented to students in a more didactic manner. Students were just given the experiment called "Jello vs. Tide" to demonstrate the enzyme activity as found in detergents. Assessments were in the form of a laboratory write-up and a quiz at the conclusion of the unit. In its present form, the enzyme unit includes an essay that serves as a content assessment, but also concept maps and short response paragraphs to the day care center's questions. To determine whether there has been a significant improvement in using the inquiry strategy, a t-test was performed comparing the quiz scores of the didactic teaching unit to the essay scores of the inquiry unit. A t-value of 2.516 was obtained. With the d.f. = 146, a p value of 0.01 was obtained. This value is significant and would indicate that using the inquiry strategy provides a more positive learning experience for students than a didactic classroom. From interviews and surveys of students who participated in the inquiry experience, results indicated these students learn best in groups, when they can see and touch materials, through teacher questioning, and being allowed to communicate student ideas. Learning from lecture or by reading textbooks was not viewed as favorable in learning biology.

Summary

This enzyme unit demonstrates how students can learn using inquiry and questioning techniques. By providing students the opportunity to share ideas, evaluate problem statements, develop hypotheses, design experiments, and make conclusions, they acquire the skills to be productive in their scientific and technological worlds. Active involvement in their learning definitely helps students learn science concepts. Granted, using this methodology in the classroom takes a great deal more effort on the part of the teacher, but the results of students actively participating and interacting with their peers to become scientifically literate citizens is worth the effort.

References

Andersen, H. O. 2003. Planning, portfolios, and improvisation. *The Hoosier Science Teacher* 28 (3): 72–75.

Armour, S. and R. Fall. 1992. Biotechniques: Enzymes made easy. *The Science Teacher* 59 (8): 46–49.

Demographic study: Center Grove Community School Corporation. *www.centergrove.k12.in.us/demonstrudy.htm*

Enzymes: Classification, Structure, Mechanism. *www.chem.wsu.edu/Chem102/102-EnzStrClassMech.html*

Hayes, C. A. 2003. The story of enzymes. *The Hoosier Science Teacher* 28 (4): 102–111.

Kilmer, E., and M. Thompson. 1997. Now you see it, now you don't. *Microbes in Action*. St. Louis, Missouri: University of Missouri-St.Louis.

Lotter, C. 2004. Nature of inquiry teaching and learning in a high school biology class. Paper presented at the Association for the Education of Teachers in Science meeting in Nashville, TN.

Martin-Hansen, L. 2002. Defining inquiry. *The Science Teacher* 69 (2): 34–37.

McDonald, A. and M. O'Hare. 1991. Enzyme labs using Jello. Princeton, New Jersey: Woodrow Wilson Biology Institute.

National Research Council. 2000. *How people learn*. Washington, DC: National Academy Press.

National Research Council. 1996. *National Science Education Standards*. Washington, DC: National Academy Press.

Zibel, A. 1996. Recombinant detergent. *Popular Science* 248 (1): 35.

Teaching Ecology by Evolving and Revolving

Harry Hitchcock
Clinton High School

Claudia Melear
University of Tennessee

Setting

Five years ago, the senior author started an ecology course at Clinton High School (CHS), in Clinton, Tennessee. CHS (enrollment 1,300) is one of two high schools in the rural, 6,900 pupil, Anderson County School System in East Tennessee. The student body is predominantly white (99%) with approximately 25% of the students on a free/reduced lunch program. CHS has little open space, with only a football practice field and parking lots on campus.

The course was created in response to a need for more elective courses in science, which came about when the school system went from a traditional six-class (55 min.) schedule to a 4 × 4 block with 95-minutes classes, which resulted in a course load of eight classes per year. At that time the only materials available were one set of textbooks (Nebel and Wright 1996) and a study guide consisting of directed reading worksheets aligned with the text.

Goals of Science Education and *More Emphasis* Conditions

The educational philosophy that has guided the *evolution* of the CHS Ecology course over the past five years is rooted in the ideas of Dewey (1938) and Maslow (1992), in which the teacher serves as a facilitator, and learning *revolves* around the student in a trusting environment. The philosophy is articulated for the students in various forms: a class motto, a class slogan, course themes, and a major issue.

The class motto is: *A Learning Place Is a Safe Place*. The job of teenagers is to take risks and challenge authority in order to grow and develop a sense of self as they move along the road toward physical, emotional, and intellectual independence. At the same time, they retain a deep-rooted need to be loved and accepted. They need to both challenge authority and test their own ideas. A safe classroom emphasizes channeling more energy into discussion and debate, rather than protecting self.

The class slogan is: *Think Global, Act Local*. The classroom serves as a microcosm of larger ecosystems, and is ultimately a set of relationships and places where scientific concepts prevail. Students are asked to reflect on applications of scientific processes as well as explanations for relationships and behavioral consequences in their own lives, rather than to simply memorize vocabulary.

Course themes of *energy distribution* and *social justice* provide students a context to integrate the content of their high school education, both linearly over time and horizontally across curriculum. They ask the questions: (1) "Am I a net consumer or producer of energy?"; (2) What are the consequences of my allocation of resources such as time?"; and (3) "How do my decisions affect others in the classroom?" In this way, becoming more literate consumers of scientific knowledge is emphasized. They come to understand an increasingly complex and interrelated global economy and its relationship to the environment, along with personal responsibility.

One of the great environmental issues of today is loss of *biodiversity,* as articulated by E. O. Wilson (1992). Students engage readily with authentic, hands-on experiences of biodiversity. Lesson choices allow students to utilize their own personal learning styles (Coleman, Kaufman, and Ray 1992) for most course activities. Students taste, see, hear, smell, and feel the richness of nature. They become engaged and excited about learning.

The Teacher, Students, and Classroom

Dr. Harry Hitchcock began the CHS Ecology class the same year that the *National Science Education Standards* (NRC 1996) were published. He attended a Woodrow Wilson CORE (COntent-driven Reform in Education) Biology Institute in 2000 and an Eisenhower Workshop on standards-based teaching developed by Dr. Claudia Melear in 2002. These two experiences have guided the evolution of the course toward a student centered-experience. The course is taught using a classroom equipped with a computer and four large monitors, a 50 MB website (Hitchcock 2003), access to a science lab, and a small "butterfly" garden created by previous classes. In addition, a small creek runs by the school and there is a small 1,000 square foot pond. Class size averages 25 students.

Description of Unique Features

The CHS Ecology course began with one set of textbooks and a book of "directed reading" worksheets. In an attempt to engage students with nature, the first ecology class was required to keep a portfolio of class activities. The first class also began a butterfly garden as a service project. From that beginning, and as a result of the teacher's exposure to reform movements in education, many of the *More Emphasis* conditions in the National Science Education Standards (NSES) have been addressed over the past five years.

Teaching Standards, Content, and Inquiry Standards

The class motto, *A Learning Place Is a Safe Place*, guides classroom behavior and management. Students are introduced to the idea that nature has no rewards or punishments, only consequences. Students practice responsibility by moving freely between lab and classroom, accessing the internet and choosing how they wish to engage with content. The teacher provides appropriate consequences in order to maintain safety. In this way, all rules necessary are based on student decisions instead of being viewed as arbitrary and teacher imposed.

The first few days of class are spent analyzing student learning styles. Each student completes a survey to determine whether they rate as a visual, auditory or tactile/kinesthetic learner (Abiator 2003). Students also complete Gregorc's (1984) matrix of learning styles as abstract vs. concrete and random vs. sequential. A discussion follows, based on suggested learning strategies for each style (Abiator 2003). Students are encouraged to critique these strategies and modify them based on their own perceptions of what strategies work for them. What usually results is an awareness among all the participants that a great deal of variety exists in how we learn, and therefore how the content of ecology must be presented and processed in order for all students to be engaged. The teacher then makes a connection to the great variation in nature and why it is adaptive rather than maladaptive. Students find this exercise empowering and take ownership of their individual styles. In addition, we also look at Gardner's concept of multiple intelligences (Coleman, Kaufman, and Ray 1992), which connects variation in student learning to natural variation; i.e., the concept of biodiversity.

The class no longer uses a textbook. Over the past five years, Dr. Hitchcock has developed an extensive website (Hitchcock 2003), often with student input, that contains most of the content to be used in the course. Over 90% of the students have internet access outside of class. The teacher makes access available to the others. In addition, depending on the season, examples of whatever is happening in nature are brought into the classroom. These may be flowers, mushrooms, insects, or fruits. Lessons are presented that are similar to what a field naturalist might present in an interpretive setting. The idea is to study materials, and related science content, that the students can also experience themselves outside of class if they so desire. Consequently, sequencing of curriculum varies with each season. Students keep daily journals in which they record their experiences and questions that arise.

The unifying concept for this hands-on curriculum is biodiversity and its associated relationships. Four questions are addressed: (1) What is biodiversity?; (2) Why is biodiversity important?; (3) What are the threats to biodiversity?; and (4) What can we do to reduce the threats? During the first part of the course, students use interactive CD ROMs, including portions of the *Voyages Through Time* curriculum (SETI 2003), to study diversity of biomes, habitats, feeding and non-feeding relationships. Later, a nine-week composting project continues the inquiry into relationships.

E. O. Wilson (1992) builds a case for collections and museums as a way to preserve biodiversity. In CHS Ecology, an insect collection meeting specific requirements is created by each student. The requirement is that 20 insects from exactly eight Orders are collected with a distribution that maximizes Simpson's Index of Diversity (Maryland Sea Grant 2003). Simpson's Index is then used to quantify diversity throughout the remainder of the course.

Following the collection, an ethnobotany unit is introduced, using ideas in *Cultural Uses of Plants* (DePaye 2000). Each student selects a plant from a recommended list and pursues guided inquiry into its characteristics and cultural uses. This is a guided inquiry in that each student chooses from a number of possible investigations those they will pursue—e.g., dye properties, essential oils, carbohydrate content, medicinal properties, fiber uses, and so on.

In responding to insect collecting, ethnobotany projects, nature walks, and visits to the garden, students are encouraged to use the inquiry language of "I wonder," "what if," and "how does" in their journals. Students share their thoughts in classroom discussions, and they are directed to opportunities for further inquiry. The opportunities are often extensions of the basic activities of the entire class. One striking example involved a student who asked why butterflies are colorful. The next day she came in with an answer attributing it to the scales. She then took a digital microscope picture of the eye spots of a butterfly and placed it in her journal. Thus, projects are not treated as outcomes, but rather as platforms for the students' own inquiry.

Another example occurs during the study of succession. We use clumps of horse manure in paper cups and observe the appearance of various organisms over a two-week period. Many students first think fungal hyphae are spider webs and they are also amazed to see all the nematodes present in manure. Invariably, they develop small experiments that involve a change in environmental conditions of the manure. Some become interested in life cycles, while others might experiment with *Pilobolus* fungi and phototropism.

Journals are assessed each week by the teacher using a rubric (see Table 1). Students have the rubric taped in their journals and are asked to assess themselves periodically. Quite often, students are asked to enter in their journal "two things I learned yesterday." This keeps them involved in the assessment process. It is important to not only assess the students' learning, but for them to also assess their own expectations.

In a class that focuses on prepared labs and lab reports, students are most often guided through the scientific process and come to see it as a set of steps rather than an integrated whole that can be used in all aspects of their life. The CHS ecology class places emphasis on continual observation, using all the senses. Recording of the observations, including measurements when appropriate, are emphasized using journal inscriptions, as described by Lunsford and Melear (2001). Finally, students are asked to compare the observed and the expected in order to refine their views of nature and to examine their personal relationships with the world around them. Some learn to use a classic experimental process. Others simply begin to notice things in the woods that they never noticed before and become better stewards of the earth. Both responses represent authentic learning.

Increasing global population and its effect on the environment is a major concern. The topic is introduced to the students by a slide presentation of the teacher's trips to Haiti. Students are then given the opportunity to write a script for the slide show, thereby engaging directly in

Table 1. Rubrics used to grade nature journals in CHS Ecology class.

Completeness
5: Has entries for 95% of the days and addresses all the activities of the class on those days
4: Misses only a few days, but generally addresses all activities on those days
3: Addresses only 50–75% of the activities
2: Inadequate, less than half of the activities addressed

Daily entries
Depth of coverage: is it more than two or three sentences?

Informative
5: Has detailed procedures and results for 95% the projects
4: Sometimes omits procedures or results or treats them superficially
3: Often omits procedures or results or treats them superficially
2: Usually omits procedures and results

Explanations of procedures and results
Interpret results
Background information

Quantitative
5: Completes tables, calculates means and ranges, compares data
4: Summarizes data but does not compare group means or replications
3: Measures and records data. Doesn't compare or summarize
2: Fails to make complete and/or reasonable measurements

Measurement
Numbers
Graphs
Tables

Variety of Qualitative Modalities
5: Uses scale drawings for project descriptions. Graphs data. Uses color coded illustrations.
4: Uses drawing, tables, and pictures to capture ideas
3: Has microscope drawing and diagrams of lab setups
2: Uses only text to present ideas

Drawings
Photographs
Items from nature
(e.g., dried flowers)

Reflective
5: Considers class activities related to global issues and biological principles. Relates class to personal life.
4: Asks "what if" and generates hypotheses; relates class to life experiences
3: Writes about the application of the lab experiences in their personal life
2: No discernible reflections

Questions
Hypotheses, "what if ?",
"I wonder why… ?"
How does it relate to me
What global concepts are involved

5: Clearly beyond expectations
4: Above minimum expectations but room to improve
3: Meets minimal expectations
2: Inadequate
1: No apparent attempt, but has participated
0: Where have you been ?

---

reflective activities. The class subsequently uses census data to analyze their home county's growth rate, education levels, and birth/death rates, and compare them to global population profiles.

Because of the amount of writing and visual work required in a good journal, the teacher cooperates with teachers in creative writing and art. Students in Art III teach sketching in class and students are encouraged to place nature writing in the school literary magazine.

Assessment Standards

In a class as open ended as the CHS Ecology class, summative assessment of discrete content knowledge is difficult. This is because the class is designed for each student to learn the content that most engages them. Along the way, however, they all practice the same process skills.

Authentic assessment of process skills is easily accomplished by applying rubrics to the student journals. Five areas are assessed: Completeness, Informative, Quantitative, Qualitative, and Reflective. Within these ideas, the rubrics address observation, measuring, recording, comparing, and inferring.

Performance assessment is also possible in extended projects. For example, in the class composting project students work in teams. In addition to recording their process, the compost is judged by their peers. Criteria are smell, texture and appearance, each on a five-point scale. The team must also give a class presentation on how to make compost. A presentation rubric (Table 2) is used for this assessment.

Evidence for Effectiveness

The effectiveness of moving the ecology course from a traditional book-fact-teacher centered course to one of experience-flexibility-inquiry can be viewed from three perspectives. First, because the course is an elective, enrollment is one quantitative measure. In four years the course has grown from 20 to approximately 75 students. We interpret this as evidence that students are being engaged in relevant activities.

Second, the ecology classes represent over one-half of the senior author's student load. In both years when there has been a selection available, the senior classes have voted him the "Teacher I Learned the Most From."

The third, and maybe most telling, mode of assessment is the words of the student themselves in self-assessment. In 2003, two classes were shown the *less/more* dichotomy on an overhead and asked to record their own feelings based upon the ecology class experience. The following are representative responses:

- "This format is better because, honestly, I can't remember facts longer than a year. I cram for tests to remember and forget. By doing activities you always remember what you did if it interests you."
- "Once you see and understand something, that's when you can start learning the big vocabulary for it. And instead of lectures, letting people investigate the situation is more valuable."
- "I can't wait to the next day to see what we're doing. I wish all my classes were this exciting."

Table 2. Rubrics used to grade class presentations in CHS Ecology class.

	Attempted 1	Acceptable 2	Admirable 3	Awesome 4	Your Score
Organization	Audience cannot understand presentation because there is no sequence of information.	Audience has difficulty following the presentation because student jumps around.	Student presents information in logical sequence that audience can follow.	Sequence of ideas is logical and interesting; topic of the presentation remains the focus.	
Subject Knowledge	Student does not have grasp of information; student cannot answer questions about subject.	Student is uncomfortable with information and is able to answer only rudimentary questions.	Student is at ease with answers to all questions, but fails to elaborate.	Student demonstrates full knowledge by answering all questions with explanations and elaboration.	
Visual Aids/ Graphics	Visual aids are sloppy or cannot be seen by audience; student uses superfluous graphics or no graphics.	Student occasionally uses graphics or visual aids that rarely support text and presentation.	Visual aids are well done and can be seen clearly by the audience; graphics relate to text and presentation.	Visual aids or graphics are skillfully done and are used effectively to make presentation more interesting and meaningful.	
Mechanics	Presentation has four or more spelling and/or grammatical errors.	Presentation has three spelling and/or grammatical errors.	Presentation has no more than two spelling and/or grammatical errors.	Presentation is free of spelling and/or grammatical error.	
Eye Contact	Student reads entire report with no eye contact.	Student occasionally uses eye contact, but still reads most of the report.	Student maintains eye contact most of the time but frequently returns to notes.	Student maintains eye contact with audience, seldom returning to notes.	
Speaking Skills	Student mumbles, incorrectly pronounces words, and speaks too softly to be hard.	Voice is low. Student incorrectly pronounces terms. Audience has difficulty hearing presentation.	Voice is clear. Most words correctly pronounced. Audience can hear presentation.	Clear voice. Correct, precise pronunciation of all terms. Audience can hear the presentation clearly.	

Total Points

- "I like doing stuff where I don't have to feel like I'm in school."
- "I like how we work as a class and practically everything in class together".
- "The class taught me to apply the concepts to my own real life experiences, and that helps me retain the knowledge better."
- "I am a concrete-sequential person and I like having things in order. This class has brought me out of my uptight, everything has to be this way and it cannot be changed attitude."
- "If the teacher is having a great day, the students will pick up on that. When the teacher is dull, the class reflects on that and is lazy. It is cool when the teacher admits he/she doesn't know something."

Along with the *Less/More* assessment, each student was asked to list the two most important things they had learned in class. The following are representative responses:

- "The things people spend their money on are the things they value most."
- "How good some wild mushrooms taste. I also like the fact I can walk outside and find some and bring them in and cook them."
- "I never knew that watching a butterfly fly off my finger could be so amazing. It left this enormous feeling of love inside my soul that can't ever be erased. From that experience, I learned to quit looking for God's miracles so hard. "
- "The world is full of lumpers and splitters."
- "Everyone's learning style is different."
- "I never knew there were that many species in the world."
- "There are many wild plants with medicinal uses, but laziness, or busyness, has set into society and we spend incredible amounts of money on prescription drugs."
- "It's hard to say, I have learned so much, but what I think that is most important is my praying mantis project. I never knew that praying mantis's have more than one set of mandibles. *I learned this through watching*." – (emphasis added)
- "There's a whole other world out there with insects in it that we know nothing about."
- "First, I now think of things globally and locally. How things affect me and the world. If you look at something big, for example the color of a plant is not always the dye color."
- "You can compare it to something in your life. Like maybe you're not as happy on the inside as you want people to think on the outside. The more I do in here, the more I find myself comparing my life to things in nature."
- "Plants and shrubs we think of as weeds can be used for medicinal reasons. . ."
- "Viruses and bacteria are always changing to fit its new host. And because of this continuous change, and its inability to find the virus's normal host, we have been unable to find the cure for diseases."
- "How to skin and cure animal skins. How to make scrapers out of rocks." (flint knapping)
- "Respect and responsibility both start with the letter "R," and they work together hand in hand."

- "I have *a talent* for pinning insects." (emphasis added)
- "It's neat that I can now drive down the road or walk into my backyard and be able to tell what kind of plants there are and what things come from that plant."
- "I learned about species and biodiversity. It's easy for someone to overlook the smaller creatures on our planet, but doing projects like (this) helped me understand about looking at the world around me. I look closer and I'm more aware."
- "We humans are one of the smallest species out there. I used to think that we were higher in the species."
- "One thing that made me think about how lucky I am is the number of AIDs cases in Africa. I would never have thought there was that many people in one part of the world that were so affected."
- "Nature has a counter punch to poison ivy. As I did research (on jewelweed) I found out that you can make a soap to use.... I found it very useful."
- "How to take the information we learn in here and apply it to our everyday life. Everything relates to something bigger when we look 'outside the box' to understand it."
- "How even the smallest of bugs/species can be important."

Self-assessments like these can be difficult to quantify; however, one can see a general theme of self awareness, connection to nature, and openness to new ideas.

Summary

The CHS Ecology class is truly a hands-on course. It engages students in personal scientific inquiry and allows them to experience the excitement and richness of nature. It helps enlighten them on the natural laws that govern their relationships with each other and the rest of nature. Students learn to keep journals and practice real science processes such as observation, measurement, recording, and reflecting. Students are evaluated in authentic assessment and participate in their own education and assessment. Most of all, students leave the course better prepared to be stewards of the earth and responsive members of a global community. They also learn about their own nature, by seeing themselves in nature.

References

Abiator's Active Classroom. 2003. *www.berghuis.co.nz/abiator/index.html*

Coleman, D., P. Kaufman, and M. Ray. 1992. *The Creative Spirit.* The Penguin Group.

Dewey, J. 1938. *Experience and Education.* New York: Macmillan.

Gregorc, A. F. and K. A. Butler. 1984. Learning is a matter of style. *Vocational Education Journal* 59 (3): 27–29.

Hitchcock, H. C. 2003. Personal website. *www.drwhwitey.com.*

Lunsford, E. and C. Melear. 2001. Scientific inscriptions as assessment tools: What they can tell us and how they can be used. *Journal of Research in Scientific Teaching.* Submitted paper.

chapter 4

Maryland Sea Grant. 2003. *www.mdsg.umd.edu/Education/biofilm/studnt1a.htm*

Paye, G. D. 2000. *Cultural uses of plants*. Bronx, NY: New York Botanical Garden Press.

Maslow, A. 1962. *Toward a psychology of being*. Princeton, NJ: D. Van Nostrand.

National Research Council (NRC). 1996. *National science education standards*. Washington, DC: National Academy Press.

Nebel, B. and R. Wright. 1996. *Environmental science: The way the world works*. Upper Saddle, NJ: Prentice Hall.

SETI. 2003. *Voyages through time*. Santa Cruz, CA: Learning in Motion.

Wilson, E. O. 1992. *The diversity of life*. Cambridge, MA: Belknap Press.

Biomedical Engineering and Your High School Science Classroom:

Challenge-Based Curriculum that Meets the NSES Standards

Stacy Klein
Vanderbilt University

Robert D. Sherwood
National Science Foundation

Setting

The Vanderbilt-Northwestern-Texas-Harvard/MIT Engineering Research Center in Bioengineering Educational Technologies (VaNTH ERC 2003) (National Science Foundation EEC #9876363), designed seven curriculum modules that incorporate an inquiry-cycle style of instruction into high school level biomedical engineering classes. The Biomedical Engineering Challenge-Based Curriculum has been implemented and field-tested at schools throughout Nashville, Tennessee. Most of the teacher and student participants have come from the Metropolitan Nashville Public Schools. This school system enrolls 70,028 K–12 students (42% White, 46.9% African American, 7.2% Hispanic, 3.5% Asian, 0.2% Indian). Implementation and field-testing have also been completed at the University School of Nashville, an independent K–12 school enrolling 999 total students (77% White, 10.8% African American, 0.01% Hispanic, 6.1% Asian/Pacific Islander, 1.8% Middle Eastern, and 4% Other). The students enrolled in the project represent a broad range of socio-economic groups.

Teachers and Their Classrooms

Five teachers have been primarily responsible for implementing the new curricula: Stacy S. Klein, PhD, at the University School of Nashville, and Doug Finney, M.Ed., Lory Heron, Ed.D., Jeanine Siebold, and Rita Davis, MBA, at the Metropolitan Nashville Public Schools. All five teachers have significant experience teaching in the science classroom, ranging from seven to thirty-five years. Class sizes ranged from very small (five), to much larger, with approximately 30 students. Unfortunately, no race data were recorded in the first year of field-testing. Gender data was only available on 61% of our experimental group that year. Of the group that reported, 58% were female and 42% were male. In the second year of field-testing, the following demographics of the experimental group students were recorded: The group was 47% female and 53% male. The group was also 7% Asian/Asian American, 20% African American, 1% Native American/Indian, 1% Pacific Islander, 66% White, and 5% did not report a race.

Unique Features of the Curriculum

VaNTH's pedagogical design process is guided by research on human learning and its implications for instruction detailed in a recent National Research Council report entitled *How People Learn* (Bransford, Brown, and Cockings 2000). The instruction is designed around "anchored inquiry" of interesting challenges (Bransford et al. 1990, CTGV 1990). These challenges are designed to be pertinent to students' lives, as significant learning takes place when the subject matter is perceived by the students as having relevance for their own purposes.

Student inquiry in the VaNTH modules is guided by an instructional sequence or learning cycle called the "Legacy Cycle" (Schwartz, Lin, Brophy, and Bransford 1999), with *module* defined as a complete, six-step Legacy Cycle. The learning cycle begins with a strongly contextually based "challenge." The challenge statement provides enough background information to access students' prior knowledge, conceptions, misconceptions, intuitions, and to build interest. Careful selection of this challenge is critical to motivating the desired student populations. Students articulate their intuitions and prior knowledge by "generating ideas" and then expand on these ideas by accessing "multiple perspectives" of other students, as well as experts on the topic at hand. Next, they engage in a longer series of "research and revise" exercises where they gain data and information that help them answer the challenge question. Next, students engage in a formative self-assessment of their understanding of key concepts in "test your mettle." The last phase of the cycle, called "go public," requires students to synthesize these ideas into their final answer to the initial challenge question; the synthesis may take the form of a paper, project, demonstration, poster, or any combination of these.

The curricula share a unique feature in so far as they apply biomedical engineering as a means of conveying and integrating basic science knowledge in physics, biology, chemistry, anatomy, and physiology. The curricula also introduce high school students to basic principles of engineering. These challenge-based curricula cover topics that include the electrocardiogram, the biomechanics of the "iron cross" position in gymnastics, LASIK/Optics, medical imaging, the energy systems of swimming, hemodynamics, and the biomechanics of balance.

Accompanied by a sample electrocardiogram, the Electrocardiogram Mosaic of three modules begins with the following grand challenge question, "Suppose one of your teachers visits his doctor and, as a part of a routine exam, he has his electrocardiogram (ECG) measured. The results are shown below. Should your teacher be concerned about these results?"

After initial brainstorming by our students concerning what things they think they know and what more information they would need to answer this question, the mosaic is broken down into three Legacy Cycle modules over a four-week period. Challenge 1 focuses on how the heart beats and why. Challenge 2 focuses on what the normal ECG measures and what information is reflected on the normal ECG. Challenge 3 focuses on how the ECG reflects abnormalities of rhythm and structure. Major topics of the typical physics, anatomy, and physiology courses included are the following: cardiac cycle, cardiac anatomy, the heart's intrinsic conduction system, the cardiac action potential, electric fields, dipoles, basics of the electrocardiogram, and vector projections.

Figures 1 and 2. Students working to understand Einthoven's Triangle and analyzing their own ECG Data.

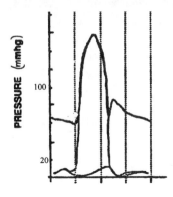

The Iron Cross Module is among the shorter curriculum modules, taking place in a little over a week. This module's focus is primarily on torque. As our students view pictures of gymnasts holding themselves in the "iron cross" position, the challenge is "What muscle strength is needed for an athlete to hold these positions?" Students learn how muscles generate forces and how different muscle groups create different types of movement. They created free body diagrams to represent the situations and calculate, using vector components and toque, whether or not a particular person could maintain the iron cross position.

The Balance Module begins with the following challenge question, "Your grandmother is recovering from a recent right hip injury, and she needs to learn how to use a cane to help her maintain her balance. In which hand should she use the cane and why?" The module then leads the student through a study of forces, Newton's Laws of motion, free body diagrams, equilibrium, and torque. Much attention is paid to the concepts of center of gravity and stability. Our students calculated the center of gravity of their own forearm and of their entire body.

The Swimming Module focuses on the energy systems of the body and their measurement through the context of designing practices and analysis for a high school swim team. The grand challenge reads, "How can a swim team coach best determine the physical condition of his/her team throughout the season? How can he/she modify practices to best meet the needs of the individual swimmers? How can an individual swimmer chart his or her progress during the season?" Specifically, our students learn about specificity of training, glycolysis, Kreb's cycle, oxidative phosphorylation, lactate production and accumulation, and noninvasive measurement of physical fitness. This module involves a high level of independent student research and design.

Figure 3. Finding the center of gravity of forearm and entire body.

The Medical Imaging Mosaic of three modules is one of the longer topics of study. It begins with the grand challenge, "A medical student has palpated a foreign mass in a patient's abdomen. In order to determine the urgency of further medical procedures, the medical student would like to know if that mass is cancerous or not. The medical student would like to minimize the invasiveness of any testing procedures. How could the medical student accurately locate the center of the mass and know exactly where to insert a biopsy needle? Furthermore, could the student avoid using a biopsy needle at all?" Challenge 1 addresses what type of noninvasive imaging systems presently exist and how they work. Challenge 2 focuses on how sound can be used to see into the body. Lastly, Challenge 3 allows students to explore a presently unanswered question in medicine: "Could the student avoid using a biopsy needle at all?" This mosaic includes many topics normally covered in a physics class, including the basic properties of waves (frequency, wavelength, transverse vs. longitudinal, wave speed in different materials, the wave equation, power, intensity, decibels, Doppler effect, and interference), radiation, positron emission, and some magnetism. Our students also learn abdomen anatomy, organ level cellular differences, and the properties of a cancerous cell. Students use an ultrasound machine to find "tumors" (pimento-filled olives) that have been placed in a turkey breast.

The grand challenge for the Optics Mosaic of three modules is, "Your baby brother has broken your mom's glasses (for far-sightedness) for the umpteenth time. She is fed up and would like to consider what she can do so that she never has to deal with them ever again. (She cannot wear contacts!) She looks to her smart kid—you—to help her. So, what is her best option? How does it work? Is it safe?" Individual challenges for the mosaic focus on how vision takes place, the changes that occur to the eye in nearsightedness or farsightedness, and the options one has when considering corrective eye surgery. The materials allow our students to develop their understanding of several optics concepts, such as Snell's Law, lenses, etc., as well as biology related concepts of eye anatomy, vision, etc. A variety of instructional activities are part of the mosaic, including lens laboratories, historical information on eyeglasses and how they are currently prescribed, and the LASIK process itself.

The Hemodynamics Mosaic of three modules has as its grand challenge, "You, as a medical student, are presented with a patient with a heart murmur that can be heard throughout diastole. Listen to the audio file that accompanies this module to hear the murmur through a stethoscope. Pressure measurements made in the heart are shown in the figure. Valve disease is suspected. Which valve and what condition are most likely to be causing this heart sound? Why?" Challenge 1 focuses on the circulatory system as a whole. Challenge 2 investigates principles of fluid dynamics that are relevant in a study of the body's circulatory system. Challenge 3 links these topics together by asking about pressure versus time patterns expected in the major valvular disorders and what is responsible for murmurs. Our students learn about the cardiac cycle as a whole, as well as circulatory system anatomy. Our students compare and contrast arteries and veins macroscopically and microscopically. Assessments include developing an infomercial or brochure to teach a peer about the circulatory system, as well as an informational brochure about hypertension. After listening to audio files on the heart sounds and various murmurs, our students perform auscultation on themselves and take a partner's blood pressure. Additionally, our students analyze cardiac pressure tracings of various valvular diseases and ultimately answer the grand challenge question.

Meeting the Four Goals of Science Education

This challenged-based curriculum meets numerous *More Emphasis* teaching, assessment, content, and inquiry standards. This section briefly outlines some of the standards met and lists these standards under the four goals of science education that they help meet.

The National Science Education Standards (NSES) (NRC 1996) desire to create students who can:

1. Experience the richness and excitement of knowing about and understanding the natural world by:
   a. Understanding and responding to individual student's interest, strengths, experiences, and needs; and
   b. Integrating all aspects of science content.
2. Use appropriate scientific processes and principles in making personal decisions:
   a. Focusing on student understanding and use of scientific knowledge, ideas, and inquiry processes; and
   b. Assessing scientific understanding and reasoning.
3. Engage intelligently in public discourse and debate about matters of scientific and technological concern.
   a. Supporting a classroom community with cooperation, shared responsibility and respect.
   b. Sharing responsibility for learning with students.
   c. Providing opportunities for scientific discussion and debate among students.
4. Increase their economic productivity through the use of the knowledge, understanding, and skills of the scientifically literate person in their careers.

These biomedical engineering modules allow us teachers to meet more readily the numerous *More Emphasis* teaching standards. The curricula allow teachers flexibility within assignments in order to differentiate appropriately for students' strengths and weaknesses. Flexibility within the curricula is allowed, to give each teacher the ability to match the curricula to his or her class' needs and local standards. Because of the interdisciplinary nature of the modules, opportunities for team teaching exist and were utilized by one of our teachers. Each module begins with the generation of ideas by our students and the classroom creation of the topics to be covered in working towards the answer to the challenge question; this active involvement of our students leads to their sharing the responsibility for learning as well as "buying into" the material as a whole. Our students are required to use the scientific process to gain information necessary to answering the challenge question, rather than just simply acquiring information because we are covering a particular chapter. The units vary in length from eight to twenty-four fifty-minute class periods, affording our students the opportunity for in-depth, extended study of a single challenge problem. Because the challenge question is the "guiding light" in each unit, our students constantly refer back to it, relating their new knowledge from each class and debating its relevancy and use in answering the challenge question. Some modules, such as ECG and LASIK/Optics, have class periods devoted to class discussion and synthesis of material as well as to ethical debates. Cooperation, responsibility, and respect are integral parts of these discussions. Because discussion is a fundamental part of the classroom environment, we teachers are more readily able to monitor and assess student progress.

These modules also allow teachers to meet more readily numerous *More Emphasis* assessment standards. Numerous formative assessments in the "test your mettle" and "go public" sections allow both students and teachers to identify and correct misconceptions and missing knowledge. Our students frequently work in teams to complete laboratory assignments and projects, and are responsible for teaching their peers relevant scientific knowledge. No chapter tests are given in these modules. Instead, the assessments are more authentic, and allow our students to demonstrate their knowledge, often by creating products of their choosing (such as brochures, pamphlets, infomercials, PowerPoint presentations, or handouts). Students write journal entries throughout each curriculum module to monitor their own progress toward answering the challenge question and also to consciously relate each learning activity to the challenge question. Our students are also responsible for integrating data and knowledge, both in teams and individually, to reach a scientifically sound conclusion. These assessments all work towards assessing deeper, richer scientific knowledge and understanding, rather than discrete, unrelated knowledge.

These modules also allow the teacher to meet numerous *More Emphasis* content and inquiry standards. These modules decidedly improve our students' ability to conduct scientific inquiry. With the exception of a small number who have worked in laboratories outside of the high school, few students have ever been asked to answer a complex scientific question where research was required. These modules integrate physics, biology, chemistry, anatomy and physiology along with biomedical engineering into each module. Content-specific subject matter is now taught in the context of a problem. Specific scientific and laboratory skills are taught in the context of data and ideas that must be gained in order to answer the challenge question. Communication of ideas and data is vitally important to reaching a scientifically sound conclusion.

Students work together to ask questions, investigate, analyze data, synthesize data, and reach conclusions that they publicize to their peers.

Finally, we ourselves have met *More Emphasis* professional development standards. As teachers, we have infused inquiry into our teaching and students' learning. We have integrated effective teaching methods found in educational research into our classrooms. We ourselves have learned collaboratively and we encourage our students to do so also. We have worked together professionally as a group and strengthened our professional ties and involvement. We have recruited and enthused fellow teachers at our home schools to aid us in more effectively implementing these modules.

Evidence of Success

All but the LASIK/Optics and Hemodynamics Modules (only in their first year) have completed their second year of field-testing for effectiveness in a controlled experiment. Control group classrooms came from physics and/or advanced biology, anatomy and physiology classrooms in the same school as the experimental classrooms, or similar classrooms in other schools. Care was taken to recruit experienced teachers who would be covering similar topics with their classes but without the Legacy Cycle design. Given the use of intact classrooms, a pretest was used as a statistical control, through the ANCOVA analysis method, on the variation in students' pre-existing knowledge about the subject matter under study. Our students in the experimental condition took the pretest exam before they began an instructional unit and a posttest immediately after they finished the unit. Students in the control condition took the pretest before instruction in the general topic that served as the conceptual basis for the experimental unit and the posttest at the conclusion of that unit.

On the segment of the posttest that was identical to the pretest, our students in the experimental condition had mean scores that were higher than students in the control condition on each of the eight units tested. In six of the eight units these differences were statistically significant ($p < .05$), with effect size measures indicating moderate (0.55) to large (1.60) strength of effects. These results indicate that our students in the experimental group generally performed better than control students on this measure of basic conceptual understanding. On the segment of the posttest that was made up of application type items, our students in all experimental conditions again had mean scores that were higher than control students. In six of the eight units this difference was statistically significant ($p < .05$) with one of the two remaining units showing near significance ($p = .067$). Effect sizes were moderate (0.71) to very large (2.12). This result was especially supportive of the contention that our students, who were using these problem-based instructional units, are generally better able to use the knowledge that they have learned to solve new problems. A more complete discussion of the instruments and data analysis may be found in Sherwood and Klein (in review).

An additional analysis was undertaken to see if the race of the student (majority vs. minority) provided additional information about the effectiveness of the instructional technique. The analysis consisted of comparing the students in the experimental and control groups and also classifying them as either majority or minority students. In all of the analyses, except for the swimming module, the main effect of race was not significant and additionally the interaction effect of group (exp. or control) by race (majority vs. minority) was not significant. The interaction effect can be interpreted as indicating that minority students did just as well as majority students in using the experimental materials, therefore the materials appear to be appropriate for a wide variety of students. The swimming unit did have some statistically significant differences between majority and minority students but the number of subjects in this analysis was especially small so the results must be treated with some caution.

Preliminary survey data also show that our students who have participated in this program have statistically significantly more positive attitudes towards science.

Summary

This program features science curricula that meet numerous *More Emphasis* standards through the use of challenge-based "Legacy Cycle" materials. Challenges were based on applications of biomedical engineering topics that allowed our students to learn important concepts in physics, biology, and anatomy and physiology. Extensive field-testing has proven these materials to be more successful in teaching basic science as well giving our students the ability to solve new problems.

References

Bransford, J., A. Brown, and R. Cockings, eds. 2000. *How people learn: Brain, mind, experience, and school.* Washington, DC: National Academy Press.

Bransford, J., R. Sherwood, T. Hasselbring, C. Kinzer, and S. Williams. 1990. Anchored instruction: Why we need it and how technology can help. In *Cognition, Education, and Multimedia,* eds. D. Nix and R. Spiro, 115–141. Hillsdale, NJ: Lawrence Erlbaum Associates.

Cognition and Technology Group at Vanderbilt (CTGV). 1990. Anchored instruction and its relationship to situated cognition. *Educational Researcher*, 19 (6): 2–10.

Schwartz, D., X. Lin, S. Brophy, and J. Bransford. 1999. Toward the development of flexibly adaptive instructional designs. In *Instructional design theories and models: Volume II, ed*. C. Reigeluth, 183–213. Mahwah, NJ: Lawrence Erlbaum Associates.

Sherwood, R. D., and S. S. Klein. (in review). Challenge based biomedical engineering instruction in secondary classrooms: Development and an initial field study. *Journal of Engineering Education*.

VaNTH ERC for Bioengineering Educational Technologies. 2003. *www.vanth.org*.

RIP-ing Away Barriers to Science Education

Inquiry Through The Research Investigation Process

Robert E. Landsman
ANOVA Science Education Corporation

"Schools that implement the Standards will have students learning science by actively engaging in inquiries that are interesting and important to them" (National Research Council (NRC) 1996, p.13). The Research Investigation Process (RIP) is composed of the steps scientists traverse in their critical thinking and in conducting scientific inquiry in their efforts to learn about the world (Carr 1992). The philosophy underlying the RIP is that teaching and learning science as it is really practiced by the scientist should be the hallmark of inquiry approaches in science education. It reflects the premise that students best learn science when they are actively engaged in doing science that has relevance to their lives and interests (Bess 1997; Brandt 1998; NRC 1996). The RIP also recognizes that, although there is not one single correct scientific method that spans the inquiry work of all scientists (Harwood 2004), there are commonalities across their methods that, when followed, guide scientists to their "best guess" when making decisions about hypotheses.

This chapter presents the RIP, an "inquiry" and "critical thinking" model of science education at two high schools: the Academy for the Advancement of Science and Technology (AAST), implemented during the period of 1992–2000; and Halau Lokahi Public Charter School (HLCS), an academically- and economically-challenged school, for 2002–03. Unique characteristics of the program that led to satisfying the NSES More Emphasis conditions are described herein; also discussed are the results of its implementation in the science programs at these two widely disparate high schools in different geographic and demographic areas.

Setting

Halau Lokahi Public Charter School (HLCS) started in September of 2001 to service K–12 students. This school is located in the historic Palama Settlement in the Palama/Kalihi District in Honolulu on the island of Oahu, Hawaii. The socioeconomic conditions of HLCS are especially challenging. The school qualifies for Title I funds, and approximately 80% of the student body receives free or reduced lunch, with the majority of these students receiving free lunch. At least 80% of the student body originates from disadvantaged home environments, and the area of location of the school has been designated by the Honolulu Police Department as the "Weed and Seed District"—reflecting the relatively high rate of drug usage and drug-related arrests. The school building is a small wooden structure consisting of four small rooms: an administrative office, a conference room, a technology room, and a grades K–1 classroom. All other grade levels conduct their classes outdoors due to lack of room availability and funding. The HLCS students do not have an on-site library.

The Academy for the Advancement of Science and Technology (AAST) is located in Hackensack, New Jersey. It can be characterized as a comparatively "highly advantaged" high school. It is a member of the National Consortium of Specialized Secondary Schools of Mathematics, Science, and Technology and of the Coalition of Essential Schools. This school was started in 1992, servicing only ninth graders. The size of the student body at AAST, over the period of time covered in this chapter, ranged from 52 ninth graders in 1992, to 245 ninth through twelfth graders in 2000. Teachers taught their own content area(s) in their own classrooms; there was, in general, some limited team-teaching. No students received free or reduced lunch, and this school did not qualify for TITLE I funding. The AAST student body resided throughout affluent Bergen County in northern New Jersey. The school, consisting of a very large administrative office area and approximately 13 large internet-connected classrooms, comprised one wing of a building within a large technical school. The AAST students had access to the technical school library.

Exemplary Teachers, Student Body, and Nature of Classroom
Halau Lokahi Public Charter School (HLPC)
Exemplary Teachers

At the time of the initial RIP implementation in fall 2002, Mr. Umesh Menon (science and technology support teacher), Ms. Deborah Kojima (general support teacher), and Ms. Hinaleimoana Wong (Hawaiian Cultural Arts teacher) served as noncertified teachers at HLCS. These teachers had two or fewer years of teaching experience and no prior training in teaching science education. Dr. Landsman served as a professional development trainer and teacher mentor for implementation of the RIP.

Student Body

The overall student population at HLCS ranged annually from 117 to 134, with 18–34 high school level students over its first three years. The student population at HLCS is 99% Hawaiian, with 16 classified as special education students. Approximately 90% of the high school students are considered "high-risk, extremely challenged learners." Upon entering the high school, students are appropriately placed in grades 9, 10, 11, or 12. There are two high school grade clusters, consisting of 9th and 10th graders and 11th and 12th graders, with one primary teacher per grade cluster. Primary and support teachers commonly team-teach and are shifted where they are most needed, depending on their strengths, content covered, and/or activity in each class. The school attracted some of the lowest performing students from Hawaii public schools, and a few average to above-average achievers from a private school.

Nature of Classroom

High school classes are typically held outdoors, due to lack of funding and lack of available classroom or covered space. Computer technology and conference rooms are both occasionally available for classroom or science inquiry activities (research) for high school students (Figure 1). There is no ongoing available science equipment at the school.

Science education mission. The overall goal of the science program at HLCS is to meld traditional Hawaiian values, culture, and spirituality with Western perspectives and standards in science education for the purpose of developing students who are interested, life-long learners.

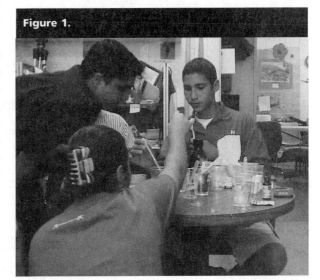

Figure 1.

In their makeshift laboratory at Halau Lokahi, students Varner Allbrett and his research partner practice pipetting daphnia while teacher Umesh Menon observes.

Academy for the Advancement of Science and Technology (AAST)

Exemplary Teachers

Together, Ms. Evelyn Rios, a newly trained technology teacher and former physical education teacher with 15+ years teaching experience, and Dr. Landsman, developer of the RIP, implemented the program into the science curriculum at AAST over a 5-year period, from school year 1992–03 through 1996–97. The RIP Program was continued over the subsequent two years, 1997–98 and 1998–99, by Dr. Landsman and his graduate student, Linda Perrotti. Dr. Don DeWitt, a biology teacher, deserves honorable mention for his advice and assistance during the first two years of implementing the RIP Program at AAST.

Student Body

The student number for each of the five graduating classes covered in this RIP program description and evaluation ranged from 39–67 for the years 1996–2000. The students were of mixed ethnicities, but predominantly white. Students applied to the school and competed for admission based on test scores (with emphasis on math), essay responses to questions, letters of recommendation from previous teachers, and interviews with AAST teachers. The school attracted top students from each district, and a great majority of the students were above average to exceptional achievers prior to entering AAST as 9th graders. Participation in the RIP Program was voluntary, and the academic courses constituted electives in the school's curriculum.

Nature of Classroom

Each classroom was equipped with Internet-connected computers for every student, as well as scientific and teaching equipment. All students and teachers were loaned a computer for home use. The RIP was introduced into the curriculum during the school's second year (1992–93). Two of the classrooms served as RIP laboratories for studying behavior (neuroscience) and cellular immunology (Figure 2). These research laboratory/classrooms were developed and maintained by faculty and students.

Science Education Mission

The goals of AAST were to: (1) promote science literacy through a challenging, research-driven curriculum in a technology-infused, restructured learning environment; and (2) to serve as a working model for innovation and reform in science education.

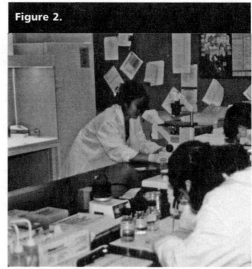

Figure 2.

Students Devika Gajria and Keun Hee Park pipette and count koi T-cells in the high-tech immunology laboratory at AAST.

Unique Features of the RIP and RIP Programs Leading to the *More Emphasis* Conditions

Most of the individual components in the RIP are used for various purposes in science and/or education. The uniqueness of this process is in the arrangement and emphasis of the components. These components can be grouped under five major sections: Introduction, Method, Results, Discussion and Conclusion, and the Next Step (see Figure 3). Inquiry-related skills are developed, practiced, and assessed through various classroom activities *designed by students and teachers*. Examples of activities can be obtained through professional development workshops conducted by ANOVA Science Education Corporation, Honolulu, HI (*www.anovascience.com*). The entire RIP fosters the NSES *More Emphasis* condition of "understanding scientific concepts and developing abilities of inquiry." The following description will highlight some of the unique characteristics of the RIP components and of the two RIP Programs that led to the *More Emphasis* conditions at the two schools.

Unique RIP Component Features

In the RIP Introduction, students use reasoning and decision-making skills while progressing through the components of this section, which sets the stage for the study that they will design and conduct.

Making the Observation

It is often assumed that the research question in a scientific investigation arrives from the observations we make about the world around us. However, since science education textbooks or programs do not usually explicitly present the need to focus on observation, there is insufficient classroom time invested in developing this skill. Observation provides the first opportunity for students to begin engaging in the type of analytical thinking required throughout RIP-based scientific inquiry. Here *observation* refers to the initial event in the inquiry because it triggers the research question that drives the RIP. (It does not refer to the collection of data or to the data collected in the *results* component of the study.) RIP scientific inquiry begins with one or a set of observations that could reflect a problem, an anomaly, or might just stimulate curiosity in the observer. The observation might be processed through the five senses or be a realization of a thought, idea, or memory; any of which can stem from reading scientific literature, hearing a scientific talk, or observing an event in a laboratory, in the field, or in one's everyday environment. *The observation must originate from the student's experience and not the teacher's or another's.* The art of observation serves as the "hook" that invites students to assume ownership of the investigation from the start, leading to interest and relevance that motivates them to learn (Bess 1997;

Figure 3. Flowchart of the RIP.

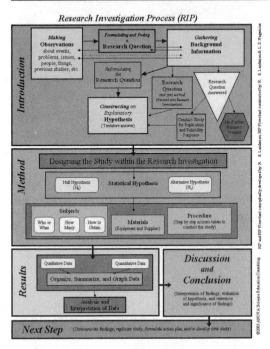

The arrows indicating the order in which the individual components within the Introduction and Method sections are performed may vary depending upon the direction of thought process involved and the content and/or availability of related background information. For example, while the most common flow of direction is from the observation to the research question, some research investigations might proceed from observation to background information (dotted line) and then back to the research question.

The terms "research investigation" and "RIP" refer to the entire scientific inquiry process described here. The terms "study," "research study," and "RIP study" in this chapter refer to the process used to test the hypothesis, which includes all components of the RIP except for Making Observations, Formulating and Posing the Research Question, Constructing the Hypothesis, and the Next Step. (See Landsman 2004, for a detailed description of the RIP components.)

Brandt 1998; Fortier, Vallerand and Guay 1995). For example, a student at AAST observed her grandfather's passing on within months of her grandmother's death, which prompted her to wonder and ask why these two devastating events occurred so close together. This led her to develop a research investigation centering on how depression can affect the immune system and lead to ill health. The RIP thus involves students and teachers "selecting and adapting inquiry-based curriculum." Because observation leads to the research question, teachers can shape the classroom environment or take students to other environments to provide them with the opportunity to make observations germane to the general content area or topic they want their students to address. Based on their observations and research questions, students design the inquiry path they will follow. Development of student proficiency in observation is accompanied by attention to detail and the ability to distinguish objectivity from subjectivity, skills essential throughout the RIP and to success in all aspects of life.

Formulating and Posing the Research Question

"Inquiry into authentic questions generated from student experiences is the central strategy for teaching science." A question to be answered is always at the heart of scientific inquiry. Here, this question originates from students' observations, whether exploratory, (as in "what if?"), directed toward explanation ("why?" and "how?"), location ("where?") or timing ("when?"). In the RIP, *the research question or "problem" is not supplied to the student.* This is in contrast to most approaches to inquiry-based education and hands-on laboratory exercises (NRC 1996; Yager 1997a, b).

An essential criterion of a good question that will lead a student to a successful research study is that *it must be answerable*. Many questions arising from an observation may involve multiple studies or be too general to be answerable within the confines of available time, the students' research capabilities, or the resources of the high school science program. Once a research question is identified, clearly articulated, and posed, students and teachers should assess whether the question should be revised to fit constraints. It cannot be assumed that a particular question should be entirely discarded because it has been determined to be unanswerable. In fact, some of the best thinking experiences in the RIP arise when students are engaged in redefining their questions to make them answerable, yet still relevant to their initial interest in the topic.

Gathering Background Information

The content material for the research investigation is introduced and used for various purposes throughout the RIP. Initially, it is used to learn more about the topic surrounding the student's observations and research question, and to determine whether the answer to the question is already known. The RIP design naturally directs students to "apply science content to new questions." Background information is also used in hypothesis construction and in the discussion of the study's results. The rationale for the hypothesis is based on information the students obtain from many diverse sources, such as articles, books, internet sites, as well as speeches, interviews, and e-mail communications with experts. Students discuss the results of the study they conducted in the context of existing scientific knowledge in the *Discussion and Conclusion* component of the RIP.

In addition to knowing how to use scientific information, knowing how and where to find it are part of mastering the inquiry process in science. Students become creative in developing ways to obtain information relevant to their investigations, a very useful skill that will benefit them in their education, careers, and personal endeavors throughout life. Students become critical consumers of information, not just passively absorbing it as accurate and true. They develop the skills to evaluate the appropriateness of methods and data analyses, and to question and make their own interpretations of findings rather than passively accepting those of the author(s). Students become well versed in evaluating the information obtained from the Internet before using it to justify their thinking and their paths along the RIP (Farah 1995; Iding, Landsman, and Nguyen 2002; Rader 1998).

Textbooks serve as reference material to support the RIP, not the curriculum or learning plan to be followed. They are not expected to be read from chapter to chapter, cover to cover, nor do they serve as the primary or sole source of information for standard-based education. Field trips to public and university libraries enable teachers and the library staff to coach students to become proficient at locating relevant primary sources of scientific literature that contain articles written by scientists (e.g., journals and magazines). Students use RIP rubrics or those they have developed to extract and organize the information from these original articles (Landsman 2004). Additional relevant background information, aligned with the NSES Content Standards, can then be introduced as the student begins to explore what is already known and what still needs to be learned in order to develop a deep understanding of the research subject area, including underlying scientific concepts.

Constructing the Hypothesis

In the RIP, the hypothesis is defined as the student's *tentative answer* to the research question. For example, the tentative answer to the research question, "Is there a difference in pulse rates when collected from the radial and carotid arteries?" might be "No, there is no difference" (Landsman 2002). This tentative answer is also called the *explanatory hypothesis* to differentiate it from the statistical hypothesis (see *Results* component, below). It is creatively constructed, based on the interrelatedness of a number of factors such as critical thinking and reasoning, and on all the evidence available to the student and relevant to the investigation, including background information, other scientific knowledge, and personal experience (Chamberlin 1965; Platt 1964). This process is used again when applying evidence obtained from the study to support or refute the hypothesis that was tested and when explaining how the new knowledge produced by the investigation fits with current science knowledge and ideas. The hypothesis construction and *Discussion and Conclusion* components of the RIP provide students with tools, strategies, and the opportunity to practice "using evidence and strategies for developing or revising an explanation," "science as argument and explanation," and "applying the results of experiments to scientific arguments and explanations." Student understanding of scientific concepts is imperative for this process to be successful, as are the development of creative reasoning and critical thinking skills.

The hypothesis component of the RIP has three criteria: It must be testable; it must be stated in the form "If ... then ... because ..."; and it must address the research question. To be testable, a hypothesis must be stated in such a way that it can be disproved. The "if" defines the antecedent condition, the independent variable in an experiment, or other variable(s) or condition(s) that is/are being investigated; the "then" defines the predicted outcome related to or resulting from the "if"; and the "because" provides the rationale for the predicted outcome. Because the end result of a scientific investigation is not proof, but rather support for or against, the hypothesis must be constructed so that it is testable and can be disproved by a well-designed research investigation (Platt 1964). Rephrasing the above hypothesis into the *testable* form might yield, "*If* the carotid and radial artery pulse rates are compared, *then* the pulse rates will be the same." Students typically require extensive practice in constructing a *testable* hypothesis because it is common for them to provide an "if" that is not practicable within the confines of available resources, or they may frame a "then" that is not measurable or obtainable. This is a check point where the student(s) and teacher(s) should address whether the subjects, and/or materials, and/ or measurements needed for testing the hypothesis are available and that the "then…" pertains to, and is consistent with, the "if…" part of the statement. When initially learning this process, students at HLCS and AAST frequently forgot that a testable hypothesis must constitute a logical, justifiable, or arguable answer to the original research question. The "because" phrase in the hypothesis serves this purpose: "If the carotid and radial artery pulse rates are compared, then the pulse rates will be the same *because* the heart and blood pathways form a closed system and there is no reason to believe that the act of measuring the pulse from either artery would influence the heart rate being measured from that artery." Good science does not mean that the researcher's hypothesis was correct! The RIP introduces the student to the notion of constructing one or more *alternative* explanatory hypotheses that will "cover the bases" in case the results of the study fail to support the explanatory hypothesis (Chamberlin 1965). Creativity, imagination, and critical thinking are essential for entertaining the myriad of possibilities encountered in this process of forming a hypothesis, testing it, and constructing alternative hypotheses that will be able to explain unexpected findings.

Method and Results

The collection and analysis of data constitute one of the most exciting (and challenging) aspects of scientific inquiry. As students design and conduct their studies in the *Method* component of the RIP, they learn the importance of independent and dependent designs and practice their use (Landsman 2004). Students develop the ability to construct statistical hypotheses based on the design of the study and the statistical test they will use to analyze the data. For the *Results* component, groups of students organize, summarize and statistically analyze the data that will be used to support their conclusions (NRC 1996, p. 113). At this time students begin to understand their data and become excited as they draw close to determining the validity of their hypothesis. This in itself is especially motivating and promotes the learning of mathematical concepts relevant to this process. Mathematics plays a critical role in the decision-making process involved in scientific inquiry in biology, chemistry, and physics (Kugler, Hagen, and Singer 2003). If students are to engage in scientific inquiry as it is practiced by scientists, they must understand basic research designs and *statistical hypotheses* (null and alternative) and to some extent the statistics that are used to test them (Kugler, Hagen, and Singer 2003; Landsman 2004; Maret and Ziemba 1997). The *Results* component is crucial for using data to test the statistical hypotheses and, ultimately, to make decisions about the explanatory hypothesis. Similar to the approach described by Kugler, Hagen, and Singer (2003), the RIP emphasizes embracing mathematics as a decision-making tool in inquiry-based science education. Through emphasis on the development of proficiency in application of mathematical concepts, the RIP leads to the NSES goal of "students who are able to use appropriate scientific processes and principles in making personal decisions." Because the consumer of scientifically based health information and medicine can only accurately determine the value of a scientific claim by examining the results of the studies that led to the claim, the educated consumer requires at least a basic working understanding of statistics. A basic understanding of statistical reasoning and its application to decision-making enhances the student's ability to evaluate media claims and even the justification of personal attitudes towards one's self and others. The RIP emphasizes the quantification of error and understanding of its impact on uncertainty in decision-making in science. The RIP approach to data analysis and hypothesis testing focuses on the critical ratio of information to error (Landsman 2004). The greater the error, the smaller the ratio and the higher the likelihood (probability) that the statistical value representing the results is due to chance. How this critical ratio is determined and applied depends upon the ability level of the students and the degree of accuracy desired. Depending on student math proficiency, statistical approaches to data analysis used in the RIP include margin of error (Kugler, Hagen, and Singer 2003) or "eyeball test" (looking for overlap in standard error bars), independent and paired *t*-tests, the correlation coefficient, Chi-square tests for goodness of fit and independence, and analyses of variance (Landsman 2001).

RIP Program Features

De-emphasis of Textbook and Lecture

The RIP-based curriculum at both schools involved student "investigations over extended periods of time" and was not "textbook- and lecture-driven," but rather emphasized field trips to libraries, research sites, or areas of interest pertaining to specific scientific content. For example, students interested in learning about water quality would visit a local stream to make observations, go to the library to gather background information on that site and on water pollution, and then visit the local government agency that handles water evaluation and testing in order to learn about techniques for measuring pollution.

Active and Authentic Assessment

Assessment is key and woven throughout the RIP. Students at both schools were "continually assessed for understanding" of content and process and "scientific reasoning" as their inquiries progressed through the RIP components to their final products, which led into new investigations (Next Step, see Figure 3). Sample literature describing well-done and flawed studies were read and analyzed by students to sharpen their abilities to recognize "good science" and to "encourage the critical analyses of secondary sources" and primary sources. At both schools, research investigation proposals in the form of storyboards were constructed and presented by student scientists to their peers, teachers, and professional scientists for critique and suggestions prior to the start of the study.

It was the responsibility of students at both schools to present scientific content they mastered to their research team and across the class and to assess understanding of scientific concepts underlying their investigation. In-class seminars provided opportunities for students to share their learning gained from articles, books, magazines, and communication with experts; in-class colloquiums enabled students to play the role of specialists presenting aspects of their investigations. Review and feedback from students and teachers, along with that from jointly submitted and published manuscripts and talks at professional conferences—all these provided external professional assessment and evaluation of scientific and education contributions to knowledge. These assessment practices are "consistent with an active approach to learning," and led to the following NSES *more emphasis* conditions for assessment standards: "students engaged in ongoing assessment of their work and that of others"; "accessing what is most highly valued"; "assessing rich, well-structured knowledge"; "assessing scientific understanding and reasoning"; and "and assessing to learn what students do understand."

Teachers as Contributors to Reform

A RIP-based science curriculum features the teacher as a "source and facilitator of change" in science education and as a role model for students by way of contributors to science and science education. In the programs at both schools, teachers conducted their own RIP studies, focused on the impact of RIP features that contributed to student success and facilitated assessment of practices.

Collaboration and partnership support. The RIP Programs at HLCS and AAST developed strong partnerships with parents and with a variety of organizations and companies to support students' and teachers' endeavors in science education (go to *www.anovascience.com* for a list of partners). The partnerships played supporting roles that contributed to the nurturing of positive student attitudes towards science and provided important resources such as professional expertise, equipment, supplies, logistical support, opportunities for students to communicate their scientific contributions to interested professionals, and opportunities for authentic assessment and evaluation of student products.

Impact on Teachers and Students and the Achievement of the *More Emphasis* Conditions

Nature of the Evidence

The indicators of success for the RIP Program meeting the NSES *More Emphasis* conditions include evidence of exemplar student products and performances, positive outcomes from student, teacher, and parent questionnaires, and, for HLCS, positive results from ongoing formative assessments and evaluation of student work.

The impact of the RIP Program on science education at HLCS was evaluated over the period fall 2002 through 2003, during the first year that it was implemented.

The period of impact for the AAST-RIP Program spanned 1994 to the present for the 1996–2000 graduating classes. The most important indicators for this school constitute authentic assessment- and evaluation-based evidence, in the form of publications and research talks, and demonstrate the program's impact on student and teacher contributions to science and science education.

Data from pre- and post-assessments/evaluations for students at HLCS and for randomly selected RIP and non-RIP Program students at AAST were both statistically compared, where possible, using the appropriate test and a $p = 0.05$ criterion for statistical significance. The complete data and statistical analyses for the results discussed here, and those obtained from RIP professional development sessions, can be found at *www.anovascience.com*.

NSES *More Emphasis* Conditions Met and the Four Goals of Science Education

As a science program, the RIP introduces the *More Emphasis* conditions in teaching, assessment, content, professional development, and program recommended by the National Science Education Standards (NSES) (NRC 1996), and is especially closely aligned with those changes that emphasize characteristics directly associated with learning through student-directed, teacher-coached "full" or "open" inquiry (Colburn 2000; Martin-Hansen 2002).

Giving students the ownership in making their *own* observations, asking their *own* questions, and designing and conducting their *own* research investigations to test their *own* hypotheses makes learning relevant and exciting to the student, leading to the NSES *More Emphasis* condition of "understanding and responding to individual student's interests, strengths, experiences, and needs" (NRC 1996, p. 52). The RIP fosters student teamwork. Students and teachers share the responsibility of *selecting and adapting* inquiry-based curriculum (NRC 1996, p. 52) that emphasizes *content with process* and *process with content,* two important approaches to instruction (Chiappetta and Adams 2004). These program features enable students to "experience the richness and excitement of knowing about and understanding the natural world."

"Understanding scientific concepts and developing abilities of inquiry" are realized in the RIP, such as in the use of evidence and reasoning in constructing the hypothesis, in research design and data analysis strategies, and in understanding and recognition of uncertainty in decision-making; this learning enables students to become critical consumers of information, leading them "to use appropriate scientific processes and principles in making personal decisions."

Opportunities for "public communication of student ideas and work to classmates" and beyond—to scientists, other professionals, and partners in education, through talks and publications—not only excite and motivate students as they learn, but also enable students to "engage intelligently in public discourse and debate about matters of scientific and technological concern." Assessments based on such public communication opportunities further lead to the *More Emphasis* conditions of "assessing scientific understanding and reasoning," "communication of science explanations," and "students engaging in on-going assessment of their work and others."

Through "implementing inquiry as instructional strategies, abilities, and ideas to be learned," the RIP facilitates development of student observation, questioning, and communication, together with analytical and critical thinking skills, enabling students to "increase their economic productivity through the use of knowledge, understanding, and the skills of the scientifically literate person in their careers."

Interest and Attitudes Related to Learning about Science and Learning In General

The results from student, teacher and parent questionnaire responses from both schools indicated that: (1) the RIP was instrumental in positive attitude change, fostering student interest and enjoyment in learning science and learning in general; (2) students became engrossed in and took ownership of their learning through their engagement in RIP-based inquiries; and (3) the RIP helped students to learn science. At both schools, student interest in, and motivation for, learning through RIP-based scientific inquiry was exemplified by student-initiated commitment to continue their research investigations beyond school hours—and, on occasion, into the evenings, holidays, and vacations. Learning science became intrinsically rewarding, as evidenced by student devotion to collecting data for testing their hypotheses or improving their studies, rather than for going to science fairs or publishing papers. According to one AAST student, "We were fueled by our desires to learn the answers to our questions, not those assigned to us by our instructors; this made all the difference."

Overall, AAST students felt that their participation in the RIP Program had a strong influence on their future career objectives at the time of high school graduation, as well as a large positive impact on their ability to achieve these objectives. Compared to non-RIP students, significantly more of the AAST RIP students pursued science as a career, chose science as an undergraduate major, and are currently in science careers and/or science graduate school programs. Students attributed much of their interest and enjoyment in learning science, and learning in general, both in high school and later, while pursuing careers related to science, to their participation in the RIP Program.

The RIP also impacted teacher attitudes toward learning science with their students. For example, one exemplar teacher stated, "It was very exciting and intellectually more satisfying learning science through the RIP with my students than by memorizing textbooks and doing labs that already have a known outcome."

Communication Skills

Teachers and parents from both schools felt that the RIP and RIP Program promoted development of speaking and writing skills and confidence, enabling students to communicate effectively (see Figures 4 and 5). These perceptions were corroborated by external sources. For example, Executive Director of Native Science Connections Dr. Mark Sorenson, following HLCS student research talks at the 2002 Conference, exclaimed to the audience, "I don't believe that I was exposed to a scientific talk of this caliber until graduate school!"

To a large extent, AAST-RIP students attributed their abilities to communicate successfully through writing and speaking to their experience with giving research talks and preparing manuscripts of their work for publication in high school—abilities that served them well in college, graduate school, and/or their careers. According to one teacher,

I will never forget when Audrey, Devika, and Keun Hee were presenting their research talks at Long Wood Gardens and Dr. Kate Mc Gill, an internationally respected Clinical Biochemist, approached them afterwards and asked them at which graduate school they were conducting their research!

Dr. Mc Gill later recognized the quality of the students' presentations (constituting authentic evaluation), by statements published in an international trade magazine (Mc Gill 1997):

One of the most interesting presentations I have ever heard, from a professional laboratory scientist's standpoint... As well as the sheer interest value of the talks, I was particularly impressed by the quality of presentation by high school students. The work presented that Sunday morning would hold its own with that of most universities in the UK (p. 51).

Opportunities for Scientific Discussion and Debate among Students

Teachers from both schools agreed that the RIP Program stimulated student interaction and made discussion and debate about scientific process and content an absolute necessity for success. One HLCS teacher commented,

The structure of the entire day changed, so that there were large blocks of time available for extended discussion on topics of interest, without the feeling that we will not have time to cover all the material. Daily seminars are held for students to present background material relevant to their research investigations to each other.

Teachers also noted the importance of providing frequent and varied opportunities for students to interact with peers, scientists, other professionals, and community members to enable students to perform on a level closely approximating that of professionals in the field of science. According to an AAST student,

One of the most important things I developed from the RIP program was the ability to stand on my own in discussing and debating scientific information. The experience allowed me to have the confidence and ability to question what I am reading and to find evidence to build a successful argument for or against it.

Critical Thinking, Reasoning, and Decision-Making Ability

Based on student, teacher, and parent questionnaire responses and comments, the RIP had profound effects on student thinking and on decision-making skills at both schools. AAST students reported that learning using the RIP resulted in a strong positive impact on their ability to use logic and reasoning in making decisions and choices in life, as well as in high school, college, and in their careers. Students' comments cited numerous ways that learning to think like a scientist contributed to their application of logic and reasoning as critical consumers of information. Parents felt that the RIP was extremely helpful in the development of student decision-making abilities, especially in "not just accepting everything at face value." HLCS teachers claimed that the RIP positively impacted student abilities to critically evaluate data underlying "so-called facts." AAST teachers concurred that the RIP developed student abilities to make good decisions and think critically.

Support for a Classroom Community

According to HLCS and AAST teachers, successful learning of science through the RIP necessitated and fostered cooperation and shared responsibility, including accountability for learning, and respect for the classroom community. Following implementation of the RIP, student performance evaluators at HLCS rated students significantly higher in demonstrating shared responsibility related to uniform effort, contribution across individual team members, and in team communication ability. Students frequently mentioned the value of group collaborations and the sharing of responsibility with the teacher in designing and executing the curriculum. They felt these opportunities led to the development of respect for student differences in abilities and personalities, with students unselfishly supporting each other in their scientific inquiry endeavors, and in the safety responsibilities they shared as a whole. Teachers described as being important to the success of this inquiry-based instruction (1) the collaboration among their peers, (2) the ethics components of the RIP such as the responsibility of students to each other for safety in the laboratory, and (3) parent support of student endeavors. The majority of parents felt that the RIP Program clearly provided them with unique opportunities to become participants in the students' education experience.

Impact of the RIP on Student Learning of Science Content, Including Scientific Inquiry

As a result of RIP implementation, HLCS students significantly increased their (1) knowledge and understanding of the scientific inquiry process; (2) understanding of inquiry-based concepts; (3) understanding of and proficiency in using scientific inquiry to learn science; (4) understanding and ability to apply mathematical concepts relating to data presentation, analysis, and the use of statistics, to their decision-making; and (5) ability to learn science following RIP training. They reported that they learned more science through RIP-based inquiry than they had learned previously through traditional lab investigations and predicted that the RIP would help them as a general tool to learn more in school. Evaluators rated students significantly higher in demonstrated proficiency in understanding and being able to explain scientific content to others, including scientific concepts and the inquiry process they used to investigate the concepts. Parents felt that their children were more academically involved since implementation of the RIP program.

In alignment with the NSES, the philosophy of the RIP Program is designed with the belief that students best learn science by doing the same activities that scientists do in learning about the world. Consistent with this philosophy is the belief that evaluations conducted by scientists and other professionals in the field become a very important (and maybe the most valid) indicator of student knowledge about and understanding of science. Some of the more measurable HLCS- and many of the AAST-RIP Program products were in the form of student publications, research talks, and poster presentations, along with their accolades, such as professional and science fair honors, awards, and recognitions. (Figures 4 and 5; See *www. anovascience.com* for complete details.)

The research investigations of RIP students were frequently featured in regional and state newspaper articles (e.g., Longo 1994; McGrath 1994; and Saks 1995), which contained evaluation of the quality of the scientific work by scientists active in the field of the student's inquiry. For example, McGrath (1994), in an article in *The Bergen Record* featuring the research findings of RIP students, wrote the following:

"Here you have a high school student putting to shame some of what you see at a graduate level," said Peter Moller, a professor of biopsychology at Hunter College in New York City and research associate at the American Museum of Natural History. (pp. D1, D3)

Student products were also recognized by internationally known scientists. For example, after attending research investigation presentations by two RIP students and reading their published studies, Mc Gill (1997) wrote in an international publication:

Their research has demonstrated conclusively just how easily the immune response to disease and injury can be damaged in koi, making them especially vulnerable and slow to respond to treatment. They have also discovered that some anesthetics, used in very low concentrations as tranquillizers, can actually boost the immune system, a very important finding with possible impact on future fish handling and treatment procedures. (p.51)

Three AAST students were internationally recognized in three successive years for their scientific contributions to society. The work of these students, evaluated by an international panel composed of scientists and fish hobbyists, received the prestigious *Annual International Platinum Kohaku Award* for the most significant scientific contribution to the understanding of fish health. In its second year, HLCS students were able to enter their investigations and successfully compete at the state science fair and junior science symposium levels with students receiving a number of accolades for their products. AAST RIP students received numerous honors and awards from science fair and symposium participation from 1994–98.

Using the RIP, students were able to contribute new and exciting scientific findings to the scientific literature. The work of students significantly contributed to the development of scientific models (e.g., Lin 1998; Miao and Gupta 1997), practical applications (e.g., Prabhakar 1993), development of research techniques (e.g., Shah, Gajria, Perrotti, and Landsman 1997), and furthering of scientific knowledge (e.g., Park 1997). Students developed technologically based state-of-the-art methods that have challenged scientists for years. For example, students successfully developed a method for quantifying coloration using computer programs and 35 mm photographs to study the evolutionary significance of coloration changes in animals (Silverglate and Bello 1997). Some students were even successful in evaluating the published work of professional scientists and locating errors in methodology or data analysis, resulting in the development of their own research investigations (Gajria 1997). (See *www.anovascience.com* for complete details.)

Figure 4.

HLCS students Jasmine Kamai and Karauna Jennings present their RIP-inquiry product to science teachers and education professionals at the 2002 Annual Native Science Connections Conference at the Waikiki Beach Marriot Hotel, Honolulu, HI.

Students also used their knowledge of science as critical consumers of science products. On one occasion, they discovered an error in one of the formulas used by a statistical program manufactured by the former Jandel Corporation. This resulted in the error being fixed and the establishment of a partnership between the company and AAST's RIP Program. Based on the quality of the students' research investigations, companies solicited partnerships with the RIP Program, featuring student outcomes that used their products (*www.spss.com/sigmastat/ prod_sigmastat_uses.htm*).

During their presentations at professional science and science education conferences and meetings, RIP students spoke about their materials and interacted with scientists with such confidence in, and command of, their content knowledge and communication skills that they appeared to be, and were treated as "seasoned" scientists. For example, Dr. David Crews, a distinguished neuroscientist from the University of Texas, followed up his attendance at an AAST junior's talk at the annual Society for Neuroscience meetings with a written invitation for the latter to join his laboratory and attend the *graduate program* in zoology at the University of Texas!

Evidence of Creativity

The RIP Program at both schools served as an ideal medium for fostering student creativity in the presentation of their research investigations as well as in the design of the RIP study, as exemplified in student products and performances. For HLCS, this creative feature of the RIP supports the school's vision of merging Hawaiian culture with Western standards-based science education. One student, for example, developed an i-movie of her entire RIP-based inquiry set to music on a CD for presentation at a science education conference. This product was subsequently honored in a movie contest. Student performance evaluators rated HLCS students significantly higher in demonstrated creativity in their use of inquiry to learn scientific concepts following RIP implementation.

Most AAST students indicated that the RIP Program provided them with opportunities to develop "new ways" or "many ways" to solve a problem and that the RIP promoted the development of their ability to "think outside the box." Students and teachers frequently described instances involving such creative thinking and creative applications to their research investigations. One teacher commented:

One evening two students and their two student research assistants were beginning their investigations on the immune system of fish after spending an entire day obtaining trout cells from a hatchery. The school immunology laboratory had been preset at great time and supply expense to conduct the investigation. Something went wrong in the transporting of the cells from the

AAST students Sheela Gupta and Charlie Lin present their RIP-inquiry product to professional scientists at the 26th annual meeting of the Society for Neuroscience, Washington, DC, 1996.

field to the school lab and the cells had all died. To save their investigation, the students decided to revise their study by substituting African electric fish immune cells in place of trout cells. This creative decision led to a very exciting evening with the students and their parents being the first to ever observe and record the unique immune cells in these fish.

Impact on High School and Subsequent Academic, Career, and Life Opportunities

Both students and their parents at AAST unanimously felt that participation in the RIP Program enhanced the high school experience. Parents believed that the RIP Program exerted a strong positive impact on the students' success in high school, many referring to the impact of the RIP Program on students' ability to multitask in high school and beyond. Both attributed to the program the high rate of acceptance to colleges of choice. For the 40 RIP students sampled, there were a total of 237 college applications, or six applications per student, to 59 regular and 13 special undergraduate programs. There were 43 special program applications, or one per student. Five of six, or 83% of all applications, and 93% of the special program applications, led to student acceptances. All but one school are considered to be among the best 351 (Franek, Opochinski, Bray, Maier, and Brown 2003), competitive (Thomson Learning 2003), or top tier colleges (U.S. News and World Report 2003).

Compared to non-RIP students, RIP students received significantly more college acceptances per application, a higher proportion of acceptances to their top four college choices, more academic or research/merit aid scholarships per college acceptance, and more college acceptances offering at least one scholarship. Also, significantly more RIP students than non-RIP students with college degrees graduated from or are currently attending post-graduate education institutions.

RIP students and their parents felt that participation in the RIP Program had a strong positive impact on post-high school success, including ability to succeed in college and in college level science courses, and achievement of career objectives. Students described how they were and still are applying components of the RIP and the entire process in science and non-science applications to help make their everyday lives successful, in making career choices and decisions, in fulfilling job responsibilities, and/or selecting college and graduate school majors.

Teacher as a Source and Facilitator of Change in Science Education

Teachers involved in the RIP Programs frequently gave talks at universities and/or science and education conferences (e.g., Landsman, Perrotti, Niedosik, and DeWitt 1996; see *www.anovascience.com*) and published papers explaining the RIP Program and the products that resulted from its implementation (e.g., Chen and Landsman 2000). Teachers also partnered with students in the production of new science and science education knowledge (Ellerbee, Perrotti and Landsman 1997; Menon, Kojima and Wong 2002). Three RIP teachers were awarded the 1994–95 New Jersey State Department of Education's Best Practice Award in Sciences and Mathematics. The uniqueness of the RIP approach to inquiry-based science education at AAST was highlighted in the *New York Times* (Roane 1996); trade publications such as *Mid-Atlantic Koi Magazine* (Burton and Burton 1996) applauded it as a solution in science education reform.

RIP-ing Away Barriers to Science Education in Advantaged and Disadvantaged Schools

The RIP is a research-based approach to inquiry-based science education in which students assume the leading role in their own educational experience, engaging in the same inquiry process that is used by scientists to answer questions about the world. A student's observation is the key to initiating the inquiry, stimulating a research question and hypothesis. Throughout RIP-based inquiry, research is generated and used by teachers and students in the development of science education curriculum, instruction, and assessment that bridges content, skills and process (Haynie 2000). The development and use of communication skills are paramount to student success using this program. Learning through RIP-based inquiry is exciting to the student because it is constructed by the student, relevant to the student, and tailored to differentiated learning. All of the components of the RIP involve critical thinking, reasoning, and creativity in making decisions.

Evidence from both schools provides support for the RIP as a viable approach for addressing and meeting standards-based science education reform through the attainment of the NSES *More Emphasis* conditions and four goals. In general, the results indicate that the RIP works equally well to attain the *More Emphasis* conditions, regardless of whether the school is "advantaged" or "disadvantaged." The RIP Program at both schools promoted the development of positive attitudes toward the learning and teaching of science, along with the application of principles of scientific thought and process to decision-making. At AAST, the RIP Program positively impacted post-high school education and career opportunities and influenced students to pursue advanced graduate degrees and careers in science. Students at both schools developed the abilities to present quality "high-level" talks and publish papers, and like their teachers, contributed to scientific and science education knowledge.

Acknowledgments

The author and exemplar teachers wish to thank Ms. Irene Kamimura, Honolulu District Standards Resource Teacher and Ms. Jonni Sayres, former College Placement Coordinator at AAST, for their support in the compilation of data, continual critique of and suggestions for the manuscript. This project was funded by ANOVA Science Education Corporation, Honolulu, HI.

References

Bess, J. 1997. *Teaching well and liking it: Motivating factors to teach effectively.* Baltimore, MD: The Johns Hopkins University Press.

Brandt, R. 1998. *Powerful learning.* Alexandria, VA: Association for Supervision and Curriculum Development.

Burton, D., and T. Burton. 1996. Science academy focuses its research on koi. *Mid-Atlantic Koi Magazine* 10 (4): 18–21.

Carr, J. J. 1992. *The art of science.* San Diego, CA: HighText Publications.

Chen, D., and R. E. Landsman. 2000. Promotion of science literacy among high school and undergraduate students through affordable, time and space efficient research. *Making Connections,* electronic media, Lockheed Martin and The Park School, MD.

Chiappetta, E. L., and A. D. Adams. 2004. Inquiry-based instruction. *The Science Teacher,* 71 (2): 46–50.

Chamberlain, T. C. 1965. The method of multiple working hypotheses. *Science* 148 (May) 754–759.

Colburn, A. 2000. An inquiry primer. *Science Scope* 23 (6): 42–44.

Ellerbee, A. 1997. Temperature and the koi immune system. *Koi Health Quarterly* 15: 5–8.

Ellerbee, A., L. Perrotti, and R. E. Landsman. 1997. Temperature and fish immunology: assumptions, truths, and new data. *Mid-Atlantic Koi* 10 (11): 5–8.

Farah, B. 1995. Information literacy: retooling evaluation skills in the electronic information environment. *Journal of Educational Technology Systems* 24 (2): 127.

Fortier, M. S., R. J. Vallerand, and F. Guay. 1995. Academic motivation and school performance: Toward a structural model. *Contemporary Educational Psychology* 20: 257–274.

Franek, R., R. Opochinski, T. Bray, C. Maier, and C. Brown. 2003. *The best 351 colleges, 2004 edition.* Princeton, NJ: The Princeton Review.

Gajria, D. 1997. The modern wonder drug: an initial study of the effects of melatonin on the immune system in fish. *Mid-Atlantic Koi* 11 (1): 5–13.

Gora, C., K. Silva, and A. Marcellino. 2003. *Do students use nutritional knowledge to choose their food?* Paper presented at the annual Native Science Connections Conference, Winslow, AZ.

Harwood, W. 2004. An activity model for scientific inquiry. *The Science Teacher* 71 (1): 44–46.

Haynie, E. 2000. Engaging students in science research. *The Science Teacher* 67 (3): 8.

Iding, M., R. E. Landsman, and T. Nguyen. 2002. Critical evaluation of scientific websites by high school students. In *Networking the learner: Computers in education,* eds. D. Watson and J. Andersen, 373–382. Boston, MA: Kluwer Academic Publishers.

Kamai, J., and V. Allbrett. 2003. Kava decreases the heart rate of daphnia. *www.sci-journal.org*.

Kugler, C., J. Hagen, and F. Singer. 2003. Teaching statistical thinking. *Journal of College Science Teaching* 32 (7, May): 434–439.

Landsman, R. E. 2001. *Methods for decision making in science: Procedural steps in statistical thought and analyses for grades 9–12*. Honolulu, HI: ANOVA Science Education Consulting.

Landsman, R. E. 2002. Demonstrating scientific inquiry in the classroom. *The Science Teacher* 69 (1): 56–60.

Landsman, R. E. 2004. *Inquiry through student-directed scientific research: Methods for high school teachers*. Honolulu, HI: ANOVA Science Education Corporation.

Landsman, R. E., L. Perrotti, D. Niedosik, and D. DeWitt. 1996. *Integration of science disciplines in a high school science program through neuroscience research*. Poster session presented at the annual meeting of the Society for Neuroscience, Washington, DC.

Lin, C. 1998. *Catecholaminergic control of the centrally- and peripherally-controlled electric organ discharges in weakly electric fish*. Paper presented at Hackensack University Hospital, Hackensack, NJ.

Lin, C., and S. Gupta. 1996. Norepinephrine alters the centrally controlled rate and peripherally controlled waveform of the electric signal in a weakly discharging fish [Abstract]. *Society for Neuroscience Abstracts* 22: 1337.

Longo, R. 1994. Boy scientist fishing for answers. *The North Jersey Herald News* (Oct. 12): 2.

Maret, T. J., and R. E. Ziemba 1997. Statistics and hypothesis testing in biology: Teaching students the relationship between statistical tests and scientific hypotheses. *Journal of College Science Teaching* 26 (4): 283–285.

Martin-Hansen, L. 2002. Defining inquiry: Exploring the many types of inquiry in the science classroom. *The Science Teacher* 69 (2): 34–37.

Mc Gill, K. 1997. Hands across the pond. *Nishikigoi International* (Winter, 1996/1997): 50–51.

McGrath, M. 1994. Teenage student makes waves. *The Bergen Record* (Nov. 8): D1, D3.

Menon, U., D. Kojima, J. Nagasawa, C. Allbrett, and T. McNeil. 2003. *Using the RIP as a tool to understand culturally-relevant science*. Paper presented at the Native Hawaiian Education Association Conference, Honolulu, HI.

Menon, U., D. Kojima, and H. Wong. 2002. *Learning about culture through the RIP*. Paper presented at the Annual Indigenous Education Conference, Honolulu, HI.

Miao, M., and S. Gupta. 1997. *Epinephrine induces rapid changes in centrally and peripherally mediated electric organ discharge characteristics in a weakly electric fish*. Poster session presented at the annual meeting of the Society for Neuroscience, New Orleans, LA.

National Research Council. (NRC). 1996. *National Science Education Standards*. Washington, DC: National Academy Press.

Park, K. H. 1997. *Are sedated koi healthy koi?* Paper presented at the 16th Annual Associated Koi Clubs of America Seminar, Denver, CO.

Platt, J. R. 1964. Strong inference. *Science* 146 (3642): 347–353.

Prabhakar, A. 1995. Lead alters the waveform and frequency of the electric organ discharge in the electric fish. *NCSSSMST Journal* 1 (1): 28–30.

Rader, H. 1998. Library instruction and information literacy. *Reference Service Review* 26 (3,4): 143.

Roane, K. 1996. School as laboratory: A place where science takes over. *The NY Times* (Dec. 22): 6.

Saks, K. 1995. Research recognition has helped clear a path: His research impresses field. *The Record* (Sept

19): E1, E3.

Shah, M., D. Gajria, L. I. Perrotti, and R. E. Landsman. 1997. Focusing on fish immunology at the cellular level. *Mid-Atlantic Koi* 10 (8–9): 7–11.

Silverglate, S., and D. Bello. 1997. *Food deprivation affects courtship behavior and coloration in Poecilia reticulate.* Poster session presented at the annual meeting of the Society for Neuroscience, New Orleans, LA.

Thomson Learning. 2003. *Competitive colleges 2003-2004.* Florency, KY: Author.

Tomlinson, C. A. 2001. *How to differentiate instruction in mixed ability classrooms.* Alexandria, VA: Assoc. for Supervision and Curriculum Development.

U.S. News and World Report. 2003. *America's best colleges.*

Yager, R. E. 1997a. Contrast of standard and reform classrooms: a consensus regarding reforms. In *Globalization of Science Education,* eds. B-H Yi, H-A Seo, D-H Choi, J-H Kim, M-Y Hong, Y-M Kim, Y-R Lee, S-U Choe, and R. E. Yager, 3–8. Seoul, Korea: Korean Educational Development Institute.

Yager, R. E. 1997b. Science teacher preparation as a part of systemic reform in the United States. In *Issues in science education,* eds. J. Rhoton and P. Bowers, 24–33. Arlington, VA: National Science Teachers Association.

Modeling: Changes in Traditional Physics Instruction

Earl Legleiter
Mid-continent Research for
Education and Learning

Setting

El Dorado (population 12,000) is situated on the edge of the Flint Hills in south central Kansas, approximately 25 miles northeast of Wichita. Founded in 1871, El Dorado became known as an "Oil Town," thanks to one of the largest underground oil reserves in the United States pooled in the ground below it. The Frontier Oil Refinery is still a major industry in the community and one of the largest refineries in the Plains States and Rocky Mountain region.

El Dorado USD 490 is recognized statewide as a leader in school improvement, nurturing innovative learning programs for every student. The district has over 2,000 regular education students and operates seven schools: five elementary buildings (pre-K–5), one middle school (6–8), and one high school (9–12). El Dorado sponsors the Butler County Special Education Cooperative, serving nine other districts and more than 1,800 students. El Dorado High School, where this story takes place, has approximately 600 students that are 91.4% White, 3.9% Hispanic, and 3.2% African American.

Modeling Changes the Emphasis of Traditional Physics Instruction

The Modeling Method of high school physics instruction engages students in the construction and use of scientific models. The course content is structured around an inquiry approach, developing a small set of basic models. The "modeling cycle" is an enhanced version of the learning cycle. Each unit begins with an activity in which students are given a physical phenomenon to investigate and analyze. Student groups are given minimal guidance as they design and conduct an experiment, and as they then formulate their own conclusions. Modeling emphasizes student activities as a means of analyzing a scientific question, instead of activities that only demonstrate and verify science content, as is often the case with traditional instruction.

After student groups complete the lab work, they prepare a whiteboard of the results and present it to the class. During this discussion they are expected to assert and defend a scientific claim. They use evidence from the experiment to propose and justify a model of the physical system they are investigating. A second group then presents a report of their own experimental work, which may collaborate or refute the claim of the first group. Modeling instruction stresses science as argument and explanation, rather than merely exploring and experimenting. Students then apply the model developed in the laboratory to new physical situations in a variety of different ways. Students present this work in whiteboard sessions as they continue to develop and refine their understanding of the model.

Modeling physics achieves a goal of school science as indicated in the *National Science Education Standards*, "engage intelligently in public discourse and debate about matters of scientific and technological concern" (NRC 1996, p. 13).

Teachers and Facilities

Earl Legleiter is an out-of-field high school physics teacher with a Bachelors of Science degree in biology. He was fortunate to participate in the Modeling Leadership Workshop at Arizona State University during the summers of 1995 through 1997 where he learned a reform-based physics teaching method. He has received several teaching awards and has taught for 23 years in rural and small schools in Colorado and Kansas. This report discusses his use of the modeling approach in a regular ninth-grade physics course at El Dorado High School. The students in the course have mastered basic algebraic concepts in eighth grade. Earl is currently a senior science consultant at Mid-continent Research for Education and Learning. The classroom is equipped with a fully mobile computer-interfaced lab, connected through a wireless network, which students use to investigate physical systems.

Modeling in the High School Physics Classroom

The Modeling approach to reform of curriculum design and teaching methodology has been guided by a *Modeling Theory of Physics Instruction* (Hestenes 1987), the focus of educational research by Arizona State University (ASU) physics professor David Hestenes, and other collaborators, since 1980. The National Science Foundation has supported the university's Modeling Workshops with grants from 1989 to 2000 to assist high school teachers in implementing this approach. I was fortunate to attend the first Leadership Modeling Workshop during the summers of 1995 through 1997. This workshop was of enormous value to me because I was an out-of-field physics teacher at the time, and my content and pedagogy background in physics was weak. This workshop addressed both of these issues with an intense immersion into the Modeling approach over a five-week period during two summers at ASU.

The Modeling approach was developed to correct the serious weaknesses of traditional physics instruction, by bringing classroom instruction closer to emulating scientific practice. Students engage in constructing and using models in much the same way that a practicing scientist does, and become fluent in articulating a model using a variety of representations to describe and explain physical phenomena. This approach is a major departure from traditional instruction and implements many of the changes in science instruction that the National Science Education Standards behooves educators to employ (NRC 1996).

Each unit begins with a laboratory investigation that students design to develop a model of a physics concept. Students are presented a physical system to investigate, which is demonstrated by the instructor to the whole class. Students are directed to make observations of the system, which are recorded on the board. They then brainstorm factors that may affect or change the system they are observing. These factors are also recorded on the board for student reference. Students then discuss how they would measure the identified variables. The group thus generates some possible independent variables, dependent variables, and variables to control as they plan their experimental design. The instructor provides very little guidance, so they can draw their own conclusion from the lab work. They also make their own mistakes, from which they learn. Each lab group will often have a different experimental design, and in some cases, a different experiment from other groups. Students soon learn that they are expected to generate a model of the physical system under investigation to present to the class, and to make a scientific claim that they must support and justify with evidence from their laboratory work.

The role of the instructor at this point is to provide the context for model development and to assist students in using appropriate equipment. The Modeling approach makes extensive use of technology. Students conduct their experiments using computer probe-ware to collect data. They also use computer software to analyze and graph results. The end product of the lab investigation will be a lab report prepared with a word processor, which the students submit after having an opportunity to share the results and refine their experimental work. The computerized physics lab at El Dorado High School consists of eight Pentium computers on mobile carts that are interfaced to lab probes with Vernier Labpro. Students analyze data and experimental results using Graphical Analysis, a robust graphing program also supplied by Vernier.

A specific example of this model development stage of the "modeling cycle" will clarify the process of engaging students in content-based open-ended lab investigations. This is an example of a unit that is used in my ninth-grade physics class. Note that this is not a conceptual physics course because an important representation of any physical system that students are challenged to model will include a mathematical representation of that model. Students in this ninth-grade course have satisfactorily completed an algebra course in the eighth grade, or have demonstrated proficiency in algebra concepts on the eighth-grade Kansas State Math Assessment.

As students file into the classroom, they see a set of three pendulums that have been set into motion. Some of the curious come up to "play" with them as they enter the room. When the bell rings and class is called to order, I ask the students to report the observations they have made about the swinging pendulums, which are then recorded on the board. This can start out with some simple observations like, "it goes back and forth," but will eventually progress to more specific observations such as, "the shorter one seems to be faster," or "the heavier one is faster," or the "one with the larger swing is slower." I then invite them to test their observations by planning an experiment to determine the effects that one of the identified variables has on the period of the pendulum, which is operationally defined at this time.

Students work in groups of two or three and plan an experiment in which they will vary one of the variables and control other relevant variables by keeping them constant. There is much discussion as they plan how much they will vary the independent variable, how to keep other variables constant, and how to precisely and effectively measure the dependent variable. Each group must have an approved experimental design diagram (Cothron, Giese, and Rezba 2000) before they are allowed to gather equipment and begin their investigation. Most of the diagrams are approved without recommending major changes, so students learn from an experiment that is of their own making. This entire experimental design process usually requires about one 90-minute block.

During the next time block, students set up the experiment and collect data. By the end of the block they are expected to collect all relevant data and analyze the results. Each lab team performs its own data analysis cooperatively. Graphical Analysis is used to plot the results, and assists in developing a mathematical model. Linear relationships are curve-fitted using $y = mx + b$. Students are expected to propose a meaning for the slope of the graph, as well as the y-intercept when it is significant. If the plot does not yield a linear relationship, students must determine a modification of the results to produce a linear graph that can be curve-fitted in a way that makes sense to them, given the algebra skills that they currently have. The goal of the lab activity is to develop a conceptual understanding of the physical system under investigation, and to articulate this understanding using the model representational tools. Students are expected to be ready to whiteboard their experiment at the beginning of the next period.

Whiteboard sessions are a crucial aspect of modeling that develops understanding as students construct meaning for their investigation. The laboratory activity concludes with the student groups preparing and presenting a detailed postlab discussion. Each group is provided a 32" x 24" whiteboard, which they prepare in their groups for presentation to the class. Students include all graphs, and a complete derivation of the mathematical expression on their whiteboard. Each group is called on in turn to present a detailed report of their findings. They give a full account of the experimental design, how they collected and measured data, and how they expressed the relationship between variables in multiple ways. These include verbalizing the relationship between variables, appealing to the graphical representation to justify their scientific claim, and explaining the mathematical relationship by demonstrating how they derived the mathematical model from their graph.

I reserve all questioning about the results until the student group has been afforded an opportunity to provide a thorough presentation. Presenters are questioned to elicit a full explanation and to probe any inconsistencies that may have any bearing on their claim. Classmates are invited and encouraged to ask questions of the group, and often ask the best questions when the report that they are about to present does not corroborate the model proposed by the first group. I then have other groups follow up with their presentations, and contradictory results are resolved by argumentation and discussion. If contradictory results cannot be satisfactorily resolved, students are encourage to return to the lab. They often want to know which groups' experimental results are correct. I do not provide an answer to that question, but direct them to the laboratory as the ultimate source of information and model construction. The end result is a model that accurately represents the behavior of the system.

To bring closure to the investigation, the results of the students' lab work is generalized into a theoretical statement. This is the only time that my classroom has an activity that could loosely be construed as a lecture. This is when definitions are applied to the model that students have developed. For example, after proposing that the acceleration of a laboratory cart is directly proportional to the force applied to it and inversely proportional to the mass, a generalization to Newton's second law is made. The structure and behavior of the relevant model is extracted from the details of the lab presentations that they have just completed, and the model is extended in a broader sense, such as when they step on the accelerator pedals of their cars.

Students are now ready to move into the deployment stage of the modeling cycle as they apply the model developed in the lab to a variety of new situations. Most of the activities in this stage are like the typical problem assignments in physics, but they also include laboratory activities and a lab practicum. Students are assigned a set of carefully selected and designed problems as homework. In the next block of class time, students working in a cooperative group are assigned one of the problems in the set to prepare for a whiteboard discussion. One member of the group is then randomly selected through the roll of a die to make the presentation in front of the whole class. Presenters are expected to articulate their solutions by applying the model and theory developed in the context of the laboratory investigation.

Students find these discussions exceedingly valuable, and they become skilled at presenting and defending their points of view. They are highly motivated to understand the physics concepts they are learning because each student will eventually be called upon to present a whiteboard in front of their peers. They are on task in preparing the whiteboard, in order to be certain each member of the group understands the problem solution that is about to be presented. When misconceptions arise during the whiteboard discussion, they can be addressed by carefully questioning the student presenter. If the presenter is stumped they may appeal to the rest of their cooperative group for assistance. Early in the year, I direct most of the questioning, but students are encouraged to challenge the presenter, and to ask clarifying questions. As the year goes on, a learning community is developed where it is okay to make mistakes as students work with each other to construct understanding and meaning. Gradually, I assume the role of "physics coach," guiding students by keeping the dialogue moving in a profitable direction. Eventually, I am the guide on the side instead of the sage on the stage, students are responsible for their own learning, and the classroom becomes a community in which learning is largely self-directed.

Modeling and the *More Emphasis* Conditions

Modeling instruction departs from traditional physics teaching, and implements many of the content and inquiry standards visions indicated in the NSES *More Emphasis* listings (NRC 1996, p. 113). A few basic models make up the entire year of the physics course, instead of trying to cover everything in a typical physics textbook. These models are *Particles Moving with a Constant Velocity, Uniformly Accelerated Particle Model, Free Particle Model* (including Newton's first and third law), *Constant Force Particle Model* (second law), *Energy Model,* and *Central Force Particle Model.* Developing depth of understanding takes time. "The ultimate objective is…to have [students] become autonomous scientific thinkers, fluent in the vicissitudes of mathematical modeling" (Hestenes, Wells, and Swackhammer 1995).

Modeling physics implements inquiry as an instructional strategy. Students master scientific concepts through investigation as they design, conduct, and analyze their own experiments, instead of using cookbook style lab manuals that are still widely employed (Legleiter and Adams in press). Inquiry becomes a tool for student learning, rather than just a set of processes to be learned.

Students engage in activities that investigate and analyze science questions. Each modeling unit begins with a physical system to investigate. Students observe the system and propose questions to investigate the system. The laboratory activity is no longer used to demonstrate and verify science content, but as a tool to construct a model and promote students' understanding of physics content.

After the experimental work is complete, students communicate their findings through presentations. This is a structured strategy for them to engage in scientific argument and provide explanation as they propose a model for the system. There is more to their science experience than explorations and experiments as they develop skill in articulating and defending a scientific claim. They apply the results of the experiment to justify and validate the model they propose. The modeling method engages students in a science experience that closely emulates the work of practicing scientists. They discover the science content in much the same way that scientists make discoveries, and feel the excitement of discovering and constructing an understanding of the world around them.

During the deployment stage of the modeling cycle, students apply the results of experiments to scientific arguments and explanations. It is not enough to conclude the inquiry with the result of the experiment. Students must continually refer to the model that was constructed during the lab investigation to justify their solutions to problems. The whiteboard sessions on problem sheets provide a public forum for them to communicate ideas and work to classmates. Modeling physics implements many of the inquiry standards' visions of the changing emphasis, which leads to unparalleled student success in mastering physics concepts.

Effectiveness of Modeling Instruction

The effectiveness of the Modeling approach in enhancing student learning in physics began when the program was developed, and it continues today. The *Force Concept Inventory* (FCI) (Hestenes, Wells, and Swackhammer 1992) was developed for this task, and has evolved into a standard instrument for physics education researchers. The FCI assesses the effectiveness of a mechanics course (motion of objects and Newtonian theory). It is a multiple choice test with 30 items that was very carefully designed, taking into account the naïve beliefs that students often have about the physical world.

Baseline data was established by sampling 7,500 high school physics students. The average pretest FCI score is 26% which is only slightly higher than the 20% score a student could achieve through random guessing (there are five choices per question). Students who had traditional high school physics instruction have a small gain on the FCI, with an average post-test score of 42%. The post-test score for students of beginning modeling instructors is 52%, and for expert modelers (two years in the project) 69%. "Thus student gains in understanding under expert modeling instruction are more than double (40 percentage points gained), compared to traditional instruction (16 percentage points gained)" (ASU website). These results have now been substantiated with a total of more than 20,000 students. "By comparison to traditional instruction, under modeling instruction high school students average about 1.5 standard deviations higher on standard instruments for assessing conceptual understanding of physics" (ASU website).

The United States Department of Education designated the modeling method in high school physics as one of two exemplary science education programs out of 27 programs submitted to the agency in 2001. Modeling also received recognition as one of the seven best education technology programs out of 134 programs for its effective infusion and use of technology in 2000 (U. S. Department of Education website 2001).

Although all these results and national accolades are very impressive, my main concern is how effective modeling is in enhancing the achievement of my students at El Dorado High School. There is, however, no database to compare my ninth-grade students with other ninth-grade physics students, since physics is traditionally taught at the junior or senior level. I thus decided to measure the achievement of my freshman against upper-level students, thus raising the bar for them. Table 1 shows the results of the FCI scores for the four years that physics has been taught to ninth graders at El Dorado High School.

Bear in mind that the nationwide average post-test scores for mostly senior physics students under traditional instruction is 42%. The scores of my freshman group are comparable to senior students with traditional instruction, and have increased as my skills with working with freshman have improved. The average pretest score of my freshman students is only 22%, which is lower than the national average pretest score of 26% for seniors. Seniors taught in the traditional manner have an average gain of 16% (26% pretest to 42% posttest). My students posted an average gain of 23.1% (22.5 pretest to 45.6% posttest), indicating that they learned more from modeling instruction than traditionally taught seniors.

Table 1. FCI test score average per year. Since the modeling method has been introduced into the physics classroom, scores have steadily increased year by year.

School Year	FCI Post Test Score
99–00	37.4%
00–01	43.5%
01–02	43.5%
02–03	54.0%

With these impressive gains on the FCI, I decided to put my freshman students to another test that requires them to apply the physics they learned. Each spring the *Worlds of Fun* amusement park in Kansas City, together with Dr. Allan Pringle, a physics professor at the University of Missouri-Rolla, hosts a Physics Olympics competition at the park (Pringle 2003). Students make measurements on a few select rides that are evaluated by the nearness of the results to accepted values. They also have a rigorous one-hour multiple-choice exam, with 36 questions to be completed by students working in groups of three. Talented physics students from a four-state area, which includes students from regular junior/senior level physics courses to advanced placement courses, compete in the Physics Olympics. To my and Dr. Pringle's knowledge, there have previously never been freshman physics groups entered into this competition. My intention was to compare my ninth-grade students to the best high school physics students in the area.

I was thrilled when the results indicated that one of my freshman teams was recognized in the honorable mention category in the competition. I contacted Dr. Pringle, who provided the results of all my groups. All of the ninth-grade physics students were above average in this event, which pitted them against senior and A. P. physics students! This success is affirmation for the teaching method because El Dorado High School is the only school in the area that participated in the Physics Olympics competition that uses the modeling approach.

Summary

The modeling approach to high school physics instruction is a curriculum design that engages students in constructing a few basic models of physics. Model development begins with students working in cooperative groups, designing experiments, analyzing results, orally communicating them to the rest of the class, proposing a model, and justifying a scientific claim. The model is extracted from the experimental setting and continually refined to ever increasing levels of sophistication in the model deployment activities. A key element of instruction is the use of student-size whiteboards that are completed in cooperative groups and presented to the class using a variety of model representational tools to communicate understanding of the physical system.

The modeling approach incorporates much of the vision of the *changing emphasis* of NSES. It was recognized in 2001 by the U. S. Department of Education as one of two exemplary programs in K–12 Science Education. Extensive nationwide research, as well as my own research, documents that student gains in understanding physics concepts through modeling are substantially better than students who have only experienced traditional physics instruction.

References

Arizona State University, Tempe. How effective is modeling instruction? Available online at *http://modeling.asu.edu/modeling/Mthdfx.pdf*.

Arizona State University, Tempe, Modeling Instruction Program. Available online at *http://modeling.asu.edu*.

Arizona State University, Tempe, Promising Program Modeling Instruction in High School Physics. Available online at *http://www.ed.gov/pubs/edtechprograms/modelinginstruction.pdf*.

Cothron, J. H., R. N. Giese, and R. J. Rezba. 2000. *Students and research: Practical strategies for science classrooms and competitions* (3rd ed.) Dubuque, IA: Kendall/Hunt.

Hestenes, D., G. Wells, and G. Swackhammer. 1992. Force concept inventory. *The Physics Teacher* 30: 159–166.

Hestenes, D., G. Wells, and G. Swackhammer. 1995. A modeling method for high school physics instruction. *American Journal of Physics* 63: 606–619.

Hestenes, D. 1987. A modeling theory of physics instruction. *American Journal of Physics*, 55, 440-454.

Legleiter, E. and Adams, P. (in Press) Survey of Kansas High School Physics Teachers. *The Kansas Science Teacher.* Emporia, KS: Emporia State University Press.

Pringle, A. 2003. *2003 Worlds of Fun Physics Competition.* Available online at University of Missouri-Rolla Physics department website: *http://web.umr.edu/~pringle/physics/oly/*

National Research Council (NRC). 1996. *National science education standards.* Washington, DC: National Academy Press.

U.S. Department of Education. 2001. U.S. Department of Education Expert Panel Report, *Promising and examplary programs in science.* Available online at *http://www.ed.gov/office/OERI/ORAD/KAD/ expert_panel/math-science.html*

Guided by the Standards:

Inquiry and Assessment in Two Rural and Urban Schools

Julie A. Luft
University of Texas at Austin

Teresa Potter
Rio Rico High School

Steve Fletcher
Sunnyside High School

Setting

Prior to our discussion, a description of the environment in which Teresa and Steve work is needed. Both are at schools near the border of Mexico. Teresa's school is just ten miles north of the border and is the only high school in her district. As a recently built high school in a rural area, the design of the school is modern, inviting, and influenced by the surrounding Hispanic community. The brick buildings that comprise the school are perched on a ledge that overlooks the dry Santa Cruz River bed. Between buildings are spacious patios with plants, benches, and even a fountain. A majority (90%) of the 800 students are Hispanic and almost all students (96%) will graduate with a diploma. The overall socioeconomic status is quite low, with 40% of the students qualifying for free or reduced lunch.

Steve's school is located on the south side of Tucson, a region of the city that traditionally has been home to industry. The school sits on a large tract of land, with large, windowless brick buildings arranged in a nonlinear fashion. Breezeways between the buildings lack plants and benches. In the middle of the school is a large mural that spans the entire face of a building and depicts the importance of a high school diploma. For the 1,200 students at the school, the mural offers a connection to their cultural heritage—85% are Hispanic, and the message conveys the importance of an education—even though only 57% will graduate. Roughly half the students qualify for free and reduced lunch and about a quarter of the population are classified as English as Second Language learners or Limited English Proficiency.

Guiding Instructional Decisions

The NSES provide important guidelines for Teresa's and Steve's instruction. When designing lessons, they first consult their school district standards, and then they cross-reference these standards with the NSES. Fortunately, their district standards are closely aligned with the national guidelines. As a result, both documents suggest an instructional approach that utilizes the content standards of Science as Inquiry, Life Science, Earth and Space Science, Physical Science, Science and Technology, Science in Personal and Social Perspectives, and the History and Nature of Science. Even more importantly, state assessments measure student knowledge in these domains, thus reinforcing their importance.

The driving goal of each lesson for Teresa and Steve is to allow students to construct their own knowledge. Such an environment involves constructivist teaching and constructivist learning. As teachers, they plan lessons that allow for ongoing assessment in order to determine how the students are comprehending the topic, and they create an environment that allows them to question and seek explanations from the students. In this setting, Teresa and Steve are often working with students in small groups, questioning and interacting with the students, and constantly examining student work. In creating a constructivist learning environment, students frequently elicit their current beliefs about the topic and confront those ideas through inquiry-based explorations. Students are constantly predicting what will happen in a laboratory or demonstration, and providing an explanation as to how they came to this prediction. When their expectations don't match the experienced outcomes, the students have to reconcile their observations with their predictions. Depending upon the event, their predictions may be modified to accept a more scientifically correct answer. Ultimately, both positions come together to create an environment in which the teacher is, as Driver et al. (1994) state, "a tour guide" for the student to the world of science.

By combining the NSES and a constructivist position, Teresa and Steve have developed a general instructional format that is student- and knowledge-centered. In this format, inquiry is the primary instructional strategy employed in order to address specific science concepts. Students are also provided ample time to interact with materials and each other during lessons in order to build a cognitive framework related to the designated knowledge. Technology is frequently utilized to facilitate the collection and analysis of data. When possible, a connection to the history of science in made in order to demonstrate the tentative and diverse aspects of science, or the topic investigated focuses on a specific local issue that requires students to make personal decisions, and engage intelligently in debate regarding matters of scientific and technological concern. As a result, students in Teresa's and Steve's classes have opportunities to develop their own knowledge in specific areas of science, to understand the process of how science progresses, and to practice being responsible, scientifically literate citizens who make important decisions in their communities.

Steve and Teresa's Classrooms

Julie has worked extensively with Teresa and Steve over the years. She initially met Teresa during an in-service program on "science as inquiry," while Steve was a student in a Master's program at her university. Both Steve and Teresa could appreciate the learning environment that Julie envisioned for students in science, and often explored their own instruction with the goal of trying to implement inquiry-based science. The length of both programs—lasting over a year—allowed Teresa and Steve to examine their own assumptions about science instruction and to attempt more standards-based approaches.

In visiting Teresa's and Steve's schools, Julie has come to appreciate the unique culture that exists on each campus. While both schools have a student body that consists predominantly of Hispanic students, Teresa works in a rural school and Steve works in an urban school. The rural school environment has resulted in a close student community. Students and their families interact in several different venues, which gives their learning relationships a context outside of school. The community influence is apparent as students joke with one another about extracurricular events, which include working on local farms, attending church functions, or visiting family and close friends. In class, students work together to help each other and there seems to be little differentiation of status among students. It's a pleasant and comfortable school, with small classes, and a place in which students and teachers clearly appreciate one another.

Steve's school, which is urban, is certainly impacted by the city. Set in a campus that is located on a side of town that is growing, some students come from established families in the area and some students have recently arrived from Mexico. While all of the students are Hispanic, the community is not prevalent in the school. Instead, the "hip hop" culture prevails in terms of attitude and dress, with baggy jeans for boys, nylon mesh tops for girls, and gold jewelry for both. Students try hard to not be labeled as "school boys or school girls," as such a title would indicate outstanding academic achievement. The culture that exists at the school is unsettled, but dedicated. Teachers enjoy working in the school with the students, but the diverse backgrounds of the students often creates a classroom climate that is not cohesive or directed towards learning stated content.

Using a standards-based approach is not always easy in either school. First, students are often reluctant to engage in instruction that requires their active cognitive involvement. Students historically have engaged in curriculum completely developed by the teacher and consisting of assignments that are easy to complete in one class period. Student-centered assignments entail more student involvement and often last longer than one class period. Second, administrators and other teachers are still learning the specifics of standards-based instruction. Teresa and Steve often have to devote time explaining their instructional focus to colleagues and administrators, which takes time from designated planning periods. Yet, even given the existing constraints, when Steve or Teresa engage in such lessons, they can see the potential of implementing a standards-based format in the classroom and become more committed to a standards-based curriculum.

Examples from Teresa and Steve's Classrooms

Teresa and Steve's classroom instruction represents several "changing emphases" areas in content and inquiry standards. Specifically, they place more emphasis on studying a few fundamental science concepts through activities that investigate and analyze science questions. In addition, they use science process skills in context through investigations over extended periods with groups of students analyzing and synthesizing data. The results of their investigations are then applied to represent scientific arguments and explanations. In all of their extended investigations, they have students publicly communicate their results to their peers and/or experts. The following discussion will provide examples from their classrooms that highlight these changing emphases.

An area that is emphasized from the content and inquiry standards is "studying a few fundamental science concepts." Steve and Teresa place less emphasis on "covering many science topics," which is also know as "covering the book." Instead, they identify major underlying themes and principles of the content area in each of their courses and address these in depth. For both, the NSES are an excellent source for locating salient themes and essential principles that are developmentally appropriate. Once identified, students' interests, strengths, and experiences are carefully considered. Triangulating each of these important aspects in unit plans facilitates student engagement and the learning of the selected content. Furthermore, Teresa and Steve have found that by delving deeply into a few fundamental topics, students tend to understand and retain the concepts beyond major assessments.

In Teresa's class, for example, a major principle that is covered addresses the properties of different forms of matter. Over several weeks, Teresa has students explore how gases are different from liquids and solids at the macro- and microscopic levels. Instead of a quick lecture to cover the different properties, Teresa has students engage in different explorations that allow students to examine gases, liquids, and solids in different conditions. Throughout the investigations, students develop their own working models related to the macro- and microscopic level of matter. They constantly challenge their models and revise them as more evidence is collected during investigations. Students who have experienced this depth of instruction initially express concerns, as they feel like they are not covering the book. Eventually, when they understand Teresa's philosophy, these are less concerned about covering the book and more focused on understanding the topics addressed in class. In addition, they recognize that they understand the concepts more deeply, and that they can apply the learned concepts to their daily life.

Both Steve and Teresa strive to create a learning environment in which students constantly investigate and analyze science questions. For them, an important aspect of science entails the identification and development of scientific questions, a process which is often bypassed in science classrooms. In most science classes, students are typically presented a question to investigate, as opposed to developing their own questions. That said, it's not enough for students to simply develop a question concerning some phenomenon, it's important that the question be scientifically oriented. Such a question should address the phenomenon that is being explored, seek to advance the student's understanding, and clearly depict how the topic will be studied. A quality question, for example, would seek to understand an aspect of photosynthesis, as opposed to finding the chemical formula for photosynthesis or confirming the existence of the process.

Students in Teresa's class frequently develop their own questions while exploring natural phenomena. A few years ago, when she was teaching an anatomy and physiology class, she had her students develop a guiding question for the entire semester, with more specific and targeted questions framed periodically. To initiate the guiding question, she had students discuss their experiences as they related to anatomy and physiology. Students shared their experiences in various types of physical activities and sports. This discussion progressed to students contemplating questions that scientists would study in this area. With Teresa's guidance, the class developed driving questions that asked, "What nutrients does your body draw upon during physical activity? Are sports drinks the best mechanism to replenish your body during exercise?" Throughout the semester, students completed investigations (in which they also developed questions) that added to their emerging knowledge of anatomy and physiology within the context of supplements and fuel sources.

As Teresa and Steve conduct their classes, it is clear that science process skills in context and investigations over extended periods of time are essential in the design and enactment of their curricula. The importance of these areas derives from the teachers' own experiences in science and the amount of time they have dedicated to contemplating the scientific endeavor. As a result, they both view science as a process that seeks to understand and make predictions about natural phenomena; both view science as an endeavor that provides different explanations over time. The teachers' broad view of science is also supported by an understanding of the role of society in science, and of the importance of looking at science historically. In the classroom, Teresa and Steve are guided by their views in conducting a class that allows students to engage in science processes over extended periods of time—from three days to a semester.

The commitment by Teresa and Steve to implement such lessons has resulted in each adopting a way of thinking about instruction that emphasizes the process of science in a context that is important to the student. One of Teresa's favorite investigations addresses safety (see Potter 1999). At the beginning of the school year, she has students spend a week studying the importance of safety in the laboratory. Students devise experiments in which they observe harmful chemical reactions, compare neutralization processes, and hypothesize about potential events that could be unsafe in the laboratory, to list a few. For example, in one investigation, students explore how acids can denature proteins and then make conclusions about how to handle acids carefully. In a different context, Steve often has his students study various local insects in order to understand their unique ecological niches. Using terrestrial isopods, or "pillbugs," as they are commonly called, students design experiments that investigate their function in the local soil ecosystem. Over the course of several weeks, students ultimately become responsible for developing hypotheses, making observations, and organizing their data. From their investigations, the students begin to develop basic explanations about pillbugs and the soil ecosystem. More importantly, they realize that understanding in science takes time and that with every question asked, there are more questions to be pursued.

An essential aspect of Steve's and Teresa's classroom investigations has students representing the results of their investigations as scientific arguments and explanations. In analyzing their data, students craft conclusions that allow them to develop and defend a reasoned argument about the observed phenomena. The arguments developed by students should be constructed from evidence and logically interpreted in an accurate representation of the experience. Students often struggle with creating logical arguments and tend to discuss the results they had hoped to observe. Learning how to create reasoned statements from evidence takes time and practice for students.

In Teresa's chemistry class, students frequently collect and analyze data, and then share their conclusions. During her unit on the gas laws, students frequently conduct experiments to understand the relationship between temperature, pressure, and volume. After a series of experiments, the student groups share their results in a large group setting. When students share the conclusions of their experiments in class, there is always lively discussion. They question one another on the methods used and the actual results obtained during the investigation. Some students question if the stated claims could be made, given that the data to support such claims is absent. For example, one group discussed how a soda can, which had been heated with a small amount of water, collapsed when it cooled. They added that a can filled with water could collapse to an even greater degree. They continued their discussion with a description of the movement of the water molecules in the can. Several of the students in the class pointed out that the group had failed to experiment with a can of frozen water and that the results may actually be different from what they reported. Not only did the students learn about creating an argument from evidence, they also learned that it is important to be able to defend your argument, based upon your observations.

The roles of students in the class and their relationships to the community are a unique feature of Teresa's and Steve's classes. Both are advocates of cooperative learning (see Johnson, Johnson, and Holubec 1994) and both acknowledge the importance of the relationship of the classroom to the community (Reyes, Scribner, and Scribner 1999). These orientations prepare students to learn to work with one another and with members of the community towards designated outcomes. As a result, in their classrooms you frequently see groups of students analyzing and synthesizing data, and in extended investigations, they have students publicly communicate their results to their peers and/or experts.

In Steve's class, a strong connection to the community is created through several different approaches. During the school year, students participate in extended projects that consider local issues, and students participate in service-learning projects that show them the importance of science in the community. "Water in our Town" is one example of such a project with local significance. The semi-arid region in which Steve's school is located certainly brings the issue of water to the forefront of local discussion. Water is a limited resource; local households are frequently asked to consider how they can conserve this resource. During the water project, local experts on water come to his class to discuss the status of water use in the area. Students were initially surprised to hear that agriculture takes a great deal of water (about 85%), with houses and golf courses taking much less. The students, in groups, were then asked to explore how they and their families used water in and outside of their homes. The projects initially began with the monitoring of individual family water use, and then expanded to looking at how the community drew upon the local water table. In understanding the uses of water, students learned about the recharge of water, water tables, how water flow in the region changes over time, and what factors contribute to this change. They made predictions about the longevity of the local water table, based upon current water use. This project culminates with an interactive forum in which students meet with local water experts and members of their community to share their findings.

Looking in the Classroom: Assessing Teacher and Student Performances

The NSES call for change in regard to assessment in the science classroom. Historically, students were evaluated in ways that valued knowledge, and teachers were often the object of assessment instead of being actively involved in the process. In spending time in Teresa's and Steve's classrooms, Julie has observed new modes for teacher and student assessment that are aligned with NSES. This has resulted in the assessment of student thinking and reasoning in order to assist students and to direct the curriculum, and in the assessment of teacher practice in order to achieve an equitable environment that ensures the an opportunity to learn for all students.

In their classrooms, Steve and Teresa have moved away from assessments that primarily assess the knowledge level of the students. Instead, they use rubrics that are designed to capture the process of student thinking and reasoning. Rubrics are often presented in conjunction with the activities that are inquiry-based and are developed with consideration of the NSES (see Luft 1997). For example, in Steve's class extended inquiry lessons are always assessed with a "science as inquiry" rubric that examines the quality of the research question, the process that was used to answer the question, the analysis of data, and the sharing of findings. As students complete the extended inquiry lessons, each student is assessed in order to provide the student feedback on his or her learning and to allow Steve to understand the impact of his curriculum. During the terrestrial isopod investigation, Steve noticed during his assessment of the question generation phase that students were not able to construct a scientifically oriented question. Based upon his assessment with the rubric, he designated more days in his class to the process of identifying a researchable question so that students could develop an understanding of the process of identifying a scientifically oriented question and to determine if their questions were configured in such a fashion.

As teachers, Steve and Teresa are constantly assessing their own practice to determine if they are enacting lessons that ensure all students have the opportunity to learn in their classrooms. This type of assessment considers the practices used by Teresa and Steve and it explores student achievement. While Julie was visiting Teresa's class, she observed a salient example of this practice. Teresa began her class by posing a problem that her students had to solve. Teresa provided the students with a rubric that described how she would assess the problem solving process of the students. The students began the task and within 15 minutes Teresa had realized that her students were not able to identify the different variables they would need in order to solve the problem. Teresa decided to change the assignment, using a scaffolding process in order to ensure that students learned how to identify such variables. Her quick change in the lesson came when she was able to determine that most of her students were unable to complete the problem. Her rubric considered aspects of the problem solving process, and when students were not achieving, she was able to modify her practice to best meet the needs of her students.

While Steve and Teresa monitor the progress of the entire class, they also monitor individual students. They frequently make changes at the student level to allow for individual learning. Steve, for example, was working with a student when he realized he needed a new approach in order to help a student analyze her data. While the rest of the class was engaged in a descriptive assessment of their collected data, this student was struggling with identifying the mean of her survey population. In realizing her constraints, Steve worked with the student individually so that she could analyze her data and eventually state her results to the class. Teresa and Steve are not typical teachers in terms of monitoring their students and their practice. Their clearly articulated standards assist them in understanding the progress of their students and the adequacy of their instruction. In addition, their assessments allow students to understand what will be assessed and require that students reflect upon the articulated goals so that they meet the standards put forth. While this type of assessment takes time to craft, the benefit to the teacher and the students certainly exceeds the time commitment.

Summary

The NSES are foremost in Teresa's and Steve's teaching. They continually set goals for themselves based on the Teaching Standards, particularly in relation to inquiry-based science instruction. By adopting an inquiry position towards the teaching of science, students learn to take responsibility for their own learning as they interact with scientific phenomena, and the teachers constantly examine how they create an effective inquiry environment for all of their students. More importantly, this type of instructional approach ensures that the students are at the center of their instruction.

Teresa and Steve work in schools in which a "science as inquiry" position towards teaching and learning has just recently been accepted. While they see the potential for this framework of instruction, their peers and their students are just beginning to understand its power. In years to come, the teachers hope that all of those in the school community will see the potential and need for science in an inquiry format, especially in terms of working with students who historically have not succeeded or participated in science. All students can succeed from such a form of instruction, but students who have not participated fully in science stand to gain the most at this time. The unique acknowledgement of the student can account for community and cultural influences which impact student learning. Clearly, there is a need to extend the NSES into the classroom and in the broadest perspective that accounts for the individual differences of each student.

References

Driver, R., H. Asoko, J. Leach, E. Mortimer, and P. Scott. 1994. Constructing scientific knowledge in the classroom. *Education Researcher* 23 (7): 5–12.

Johnson, D., R. Johnson, and E. Holubec. 1994. *The new circles of learning: Cooperation in the classroom and school*. Alexandria, VA: Association for Supervision and Curriculum Development.

Luft, J. A. 1997. Design your own rubric. *Science Scope* 20 (5): 25–27.

National Research Council (NRC). 1996. *National science education standards*. Washington DC: National Academy Press.

Potter, T. 1999. Safety in the science classroom. *The Science Teacher* 66 (4): 24–27.

Reyes, P., J. Scribner, and A. Scribner, 1999. *Lessons from high performing hispanic schools: Creating learning communities*. New York: Teachers College Press.

National Science Teachers Association

The View from One Classroom

Carmela Rivera Minaya
Hanalani Schools

Setting

I began teaching in August of 1992 at Hanalani Schools, a private institution in Hawaii. Hanalani is a college preparatory, Christian school with an average enrollment of over 600 students ranging from grades preK–12. This moderately sized student body occupies three large classroom buildings, one gathering hall, and an extensive Student Activities Center on six acres of land on the island of Oahu in a suburban town called Mililani, which was voted the "Best City in the United States" in 1983. The town is comprised of 29,000 lower- to upper-middle class families of diverse ethnic, cultural, and occupational backgrounds. However not all those enrolled at Hanalani are from the Mililani area. There are busloads and vanloads of commuter attendees from many other areas of the island such as Ewa Beach, Waianae, Waialua, Wahiawa, and the North Shore.

Where Do We Begin?

What can a teacher do when a full classroom of students gaze blankly toward the chalkboard? What can a teacher do when the traditional transmission method is used because it is familiar, albeit ineffective? Does this describe your humdrum classroom? It doesn't have to be that way. Things can change for the better.

Any teacher has the ability to research tried and proven teaching methods, to use them immediately, and to inject life and passion back into the classroom. Physics, Physiology, & Technology (PP&T) is one such program. It began in 1976 as the early high school phase of the middle school Foundational Approaches in Science Teaching (FAST) program. Since then, there have been several drafts of the curriculum, in which the focus has shifted from a survey approach of science to classical Newtonian physics, with physiological applications to mechanics.

I stumbled across PP&T as I was attending a Modeling Instruction meeting. Modeling Instruction is a national science program that has been tried and proven. In this chapter, I will describe both programs in detail, highlighting their respective strengths and degrees of alignment with the *More Emphasis* conditions of the National Science Education Standards (NSES) (NRC 1996). I will explain how both programs were merged in my classroom to create a truly unique academic experience. The United States Department of Education chose several programs for national recognition. FAST and Modeling Instruction were the only two designated with the highest honors as "exemplary" programs. I did not even realize this fact until I began using both in my classroom.

During my early career, I began by teaching physics, chemistry, and Earth science, as well as Spanish. I eventually exchanged some of those courses for others like health, Advanced Placement chemistry, biology, and physical science. In the beginning, I was exclusively a traditional transmission teacher (McDermott 1993): I mainly lectured, demonstrated phenomena, did example problems on the board or overhead for students to duplicate, and handed out prescribed labs for them to follow step-by-step. I thought I was pretty decent at teaching until I looked out into my classroom and noticed a room full of glassy-eyed, daydreaming students. At that point, I knew I that I was in a state of denial; something had to be done, and soon. In those dark times I became extremely discouraged as a teacher—so much so that I actually considered an alternative career.

Teaching Standards: Two Effective Approaches

Consequently, I began searching for something to revitalize and improve my teaching. This urgent search led me to the University of Hawaii in the summer of 2000. I enrolled in the Chemistry Modeling course in the biology department. That gave me the jumpstart I needed to return to a new school year energized. It was the method that was emphasized in the course. Consuelo Rogers from Maryknoll High School in Honolulu was the instructor who pioneered one of the first attempts to apply Modeling Instruction to a scientific field other than physics, where it was already well established. I was then introduced to the Masters of Natural Science in Physics program at Arizona State University (ASU), and to which I subsequently applied.

The story behind the Modeling Method is quite touching, filled with deep, heartfelt conviction. Malcolm Wells was a graduate student at ASU, pursuing a PhD in physics and astronomy. He had been teaching for many years using learning cycles and inquiry (Lawson, Abraham, and Renner 1989). However, his students' Force Concepts Inventory (FCI) test results revealed that something was missing in his teaching. He sought to find missing links during his thesis research.

Eventually, he found that the missing pieces were Socratic dialogue and the use of models as a framework for student learning. He and Dr. David Hestenes from the physics and astronomy department at ASU articulated the Modeling Method and received a National Science Foundation (NSF) grant to conduct seminars training teachers in Modeling Instruction. Before

Malcolm Wells could write anything formal about this methodology, he was diagnosed with Lou Gehrig's disease; the illness eventually took his life.

He chose to spend the remainder of his time training others in Modeling rather than publishing his results. His colleagues eventually paid tribute to Malcolm as they carried on his legacy (Wells, Hestenes, and Swackhamer 1995). In the meantime, the widespread demand for training programs inspired ASU to create a masters of natural science program in physics, which trains educators in Modeling pedagogy, provides opportunities for curriculum development in other scientific disciplines, like physical science and chemistry, and catalyzes science education reform on a national level by supporting and encouraging teachers to do their individual parts as leaders in their respective communities.

In a nutshell, the Modeling Method can be subdivided into three sections: the paradigm or prelab, the lab experiment, and the postlab. During the paradigm or prelab, students record personal observations as they witness a phenomenon, which leads them eventually to design a lab experiment. They collect and analyze data during the lab experiment phase of the method. Afterward, they share their findings with their peers in the postlab time.

The paradigm or prelab could be a simple apparatus or a discrepant event. Students are not specifically told exactly what observations to make; it is an open-ended exercise for them. They could describe the object itself or the behavior of the object, but they must be specific and clear. They are given a few minutes to share their personal observations with the two other members of their group. Each member must record in his or her notebook all observations made by fellow group members.

Each person then writes one unique observation on the chalkboard to share with the entire class. The teacher reviews each observation one-by-one, asking for operational definitions or clarification of ambiguous phrases. One observation might read: "The container is transparent." I would ask that student, "What do you mean by transparent?" The student could reply: "It's see-through." I might then ask the class, "Could we all agree that transparent means see-through?" If they are in agreement, I say, "Please write that operational definition down in your personal lab notebooks."

Students are asked which of the observations can be quantified or measured. Students point these out, giving the name of the property and the unit to be used. For example, if the observation is, "It feels hot." The student would say, "That describes temperature, which we would measure in degrees Celsius." Another observation might read, "The object takes up space." A student could comment, "That refers to volume, which is measured in milliliters." After all the observations that can be quantified are exhausted, the teacher reveals the two variables upon which the students will be experimenting.

Students formulate a problem question, a hypothesis, a list of materials, numbered directions for the procedure, and a blank data table to prepare for the lab experiment. I look over each group's procedures and question them if I notice potential problems in design. I lead them to a solution using Socratic questioning (Hake 1992). For example, if they are timing something only once, I would say, "Is there a way to average times so that we don't rely on only one time?" Hopefully, that group decides to measure several times, obtaining an average after eliminating the highest and the lowest values. Now they have the green light to run their experiment.

During the lab experiment, students independently collect data and graph their data using a graphing program on the computer. They are allowed to use the computer only after they demonstrate accurate manual graphing at the beginning of the school year; they also calculate the slope, determine the validity of the y-intercept, and defend the percentage accuracy of their data. Students are expected, whenever possible, to portray their data in four different ways: graphically, mathematically, pictorially, and verbally. The graph leads them to an algorithm. They are asked to express the algorithm pictorially, through diagrams such as particle diagrams, vector diagrams, or energy diagrams. During the oral presentation, they defend their data and position, as well as field questions from their peers and the teacher.

Assessment Standards: "Where Are Students Currently in Their Thinking?"

Once students obtain a graph, they write their results on a whiteboard, including any relevant diagrams. The students are subjected to questioning by their peers and teacher when they orally present their results. At the onset of the school year, an atmosphere of minimal criticism is promoted so that students are not fearful of making mistakes before their classmates. I question lines of thinking rather than publicly correcting an individual or group, and the students also eventually follow suit and do the same with one another. More individuals benefit by adjusting their own mental models when information is mutually shared in this manner. Model formation is an essential key to *modeling instruction*. These mental models provide a useful framework for student learning. Rather than a set of lonely learners, we have a collaboration of active participants.

The students receive constant feedback, providing many opportunities to correct their own mental models. After these presentations are completed, students apply the principles learned by solving application problems, by doing a practicum, and by writing a lab report as though they were submitting a paper to a scientific journal. Information gleaned from the presentations become public domain and may be referenced provided proper credit is given. Modeling is the method that I incorporate no matter what the curriculum. Much of the actual curriculum I use comes from both the modeling materials I have collected over the years and from PP&T materials. The chemistry materials are still evolving, as they are currently under development by a variety of teachers across the country.

Content and Inquiry Standards: "What Are Students Learning?"

An application explored in PP&T is mechanics in physiology. The University of Hawaii's Curriculum Research and Development Group (UH-CRDG) provides training for PP&T. Dr. Frank Pottenger oversees this project, which includes the elementary curriculum of the *Developmental Approaches in Science and Health* (DASH), Foundational Approaches in Science Teaching (FAST) for the middle school years, the *Fluid Earth/Living Ocean Marine Science* course, and PP&T, both for underclassmen (Raloff 2001). I use modeling methodology to segue from one activity to another in PP&T. For example, at the beginning of the school year, the introduction to acceleration is *reaction times*. Students try to catch a dollar bill with two fingers as the teacher drops it from directly above their hands. We make observations of this introductory activity, leading to work on the variable of distance. Students then do a "ruler drop" activity, designing parameters to quantify their reaction times with respect to distances.

The introduction to *constant velocity* consists in observations of an electric car and its behavior. This leads the students to design a lab demonstrating the relationship between distance and time—adding one more dimension to distance alone—for an object moving at a constant velocity, and using these same electric cars. They also do an acceleration lab, causing them to see patterns in changing velocities, using a steel ball rolling down a ramp, which is introduced with a marble race on two differently bent metal tracks. From the acceleration lab, they derive the equation $d = \frac{1}{2} a_g t^2$. This is followed by an activity where they use the equation to determine the placement of a cup on the floor, predicting where the steel ball will drop after leaving the ramp. To relate it back to *modeling,* this portion is the actual lab experiment, where the different introductions serve as paradigms.

At the end of this series, students use an apparatus to determine that the average reaction time for most people is about 0.2 seconds from the moment they recognize the stimulus until they perform the reactive response to that stimulus. Knowing all this, they revisit the reaction distances obtained at the beginning of this series, convert the distances to time using the equation, and adjust the time, taking into consideration their own average reaction times. They also learn about nerves and the integral role they play in contributing to reaction time. Later, when electricity is studied, neural travel time is compared to the time it takes for electricity to travel through metal wires. Students conclude that nature is quite efficient in reacting to stimuli. This latter part of the process, which includes analyzing data and applying physical ideas, is the postlab portion.

Conclusion: *More Emphasis*

All of the activities and labs are student-centered and most are student-designed. The teacher serves as a mentor or guide and uses Socratic dialogue to move the discussion forward, rather than explicit commands or public correction. Although it seems like the teacher is passive, the responsibility of direction falls solely on him or her. It is imperative that teachers immediately assess where students currently are in their thinking, unobtrusively guide them where they need to go, and cleverly help them to determine how they need to get there. Teachers actually need to be doubly prepared.

Guiding students without spoon-feeding them is a tedious skill to master. Socratic dialogue is like building a road for the students to travel. When they arrive at the final destination, they claim ownership of their own learning. Building the road itself requires greater effort than being a tour guide. It may seem simple, but in reality it is quite difficult to keep a hands-off, questioning approach when you have invested extensive preparation time. Much restraint is involved in allowing students to articulate, correct, and adjust their own thinking with seemingly minimal intervention. It also requires great patience in order to give them enough time to process information. Thoughtful investment in the art of restraint yields unparalleled returns in the lives of students.

Through the unique merging of both of these excellent programs, many of the *More Emphasis* conditions outlined by the NSES are addressed, specifically the teaching standards. (See the *More Emphasis* table at the end of this chapter.) The greatest challenge to a teacher using both methods is in maintaining a balance between being an academic guide and a disciplinary authority in the classroom. Without that authority, there is great potential for chaos. Although students enjoyed unlimited freedom of discovery through directed inquiry, they knew not to become unruly. That would utterly defeat the purpose of their freedom. They lived with the possibility of losing their freedom if they misbehaved. As long as they were actively participating, they kept their well-earned rights. Thus far, I have not had to return to the traditional method due to student misbehavior. Although outwardly there is a level of necessary learning "noise," it has never become unmanageable. Students generally guard their freedom and handle it responsibly.

The whiteboard is an indispensable tool to meet the NSES assessment standards (Yost 2003). Thought processes are revealed on the whiteboard. For example, particle diagrams under various conditions expose many student misconceptions. When the volume of a gas expands or contracts, many students believe the actual atoms are expanding or contracting, while in reality it is the space between atoms that changes and not the size of the atoms themselves (Lin, Cheng, and Lawrenz 2000). Energy diagrams are extremely useful in making students accountable for energy exchanges, while at the same time forcing them to demonstrate the first law of thermodynamics (Dukerich and Swackhamer 2003).

Both programs also address content and inquiry standards. Due to the innate design of both programs, the public communication of ideas provides ample opportunities for students to adjust and change their thinking about certain phenomena. Time and again I have witnessed students thinking a certain way and then changing their minds because of their data and results, or because of the Socratic dialogue during the presentation time. It was extremely rewarding, seeing the persistence of these ideas when challenged later. Students knew that acceleration due to gravity was 9.8 m/sec^2, even after several months passed, or even during the next school year, because they discovered this value themselves by dropping balls from the second floor of one of the campus buildings, coming up with actual measurements ranging from 10 m/sec^2 to 16 m/sec^2. Students that were off by a great deal could account for that by explaining their specific procedures and how they would redesign to increase accuracy.

The degree program at ASU for *Modeling Instruction* and training programs at UH for PP&T meet many of the staff development standards for NSES. Both universities provide continual support and accountability for participants. At ASU, summer courses create the venue for intensive interaction between teachers from all over the country. There are also two listserves, one for modeling instruction and the other for chemistry modeling, where modelers have a medium to express their thoughts on a variety of science educational issues. At UH, a yearly winter follow-up meeting allows course attendees to discuss implementation and improvement. PP&T teachers also meet monthly to evaluate the lessons done, to train for future lessons, and to develop curriculum.

The *Force Concepts Inventory* (FCI) provides compelling evidence of student success in learning (Halloun and Hestenes 1985). Halloun found that his college modeling class surpassed the

Table 1. Modeling and the More Emphasis Standards

Less Emphasis On	More Emphasis On	Example Activities/Lessons
Teaching Standards		
Presenting scientific knowledge through lecture, text, and demonstration.	Guiding students in active and extended scientific and extended scientific inquiry.	Modeling Instruction provides the frame to guide students in the inquiry process.
Asking for recitation of acquired knowledge.	Providing opportunities for scientific discussion and debate among students.	Oral presentations give students ample opportunities for true scientific discourse.
Maintaining responsibility and authority.	Sharing responsibility for learning with students.	Students are active participants therefore they claim ownership for their learning.
Assessment Standards		
Assessing to learn what students do not know.	Assessing to learn what students do understand.	Diagrams allow students to create a picture of what and how they are thinking.
End of term assessments by teachers.	Students engaged in ongoing assessment of their work and others.	Students readily correct their own thinking as they share their ideas with their peers.
Development of external assessments by measurement experts alone.	Teachers involved in development of external assessments.	**Matter Concepts Inventory(MCI)** for chemistry was developed by a team of high school teachers who researchedstudent misconceptions in the current literature and field tested those misconceptions to formulate distracter questions.
Content and Inquiry Standards		
Getting an answer.	Using evidence and strategies for developing or revising an explanation.	Socratic questioning during the process allows students to develop and revise defenses.
Doing few investigations to leave time to cover large amounts of content.	Doing more investigations to develop understanding, ability, values of inquiry, and knowledge of science content.	Depth is preferred to width; the ratio of labs to lecture is 4:1 as compared to 1:4 in former, traditional, transmission classroom; labs are the teaching tool and not simply a reinforcing tool.
Private communication of student ideas and conclusions to teacher.	Public communication of student ideas and work to classmates.	An atmosphere of minimal criticism and mutual learning is promoted and encouraged within the setting of constant group presentations.
Staff Development Standards		
Individual learning.	Collegial, collaborative learning.	Both at ASU and UH, group project work.
Fragmented, one-shot sessions.	Long-term coherent plans.	ASU supports teacher participants as leaders in their respective communities. PP&T monthly meetings provide opportunities for long-term interaction among colleagues.
Teacher is an individual based in a classroom.	Teacher is a member of a collegial professional community.	Partnerships formed between college professors in both programs and high school teachers and between high school teachers from across the country.

traditional class by 12% on a common problem-solving exam. All of Halloun's students passed the course with a C or better, while 80% of the traditional students failed to achieve a C or better, even though the grading system was common for both classes. According to research done by Wells and Hestenes, modeling students did nearly 21% better than traditional students on pre- and post-FCI tests. The *Matter Concepts Inventory* (MCI), a tool developed by teachers based on current research and field-tested misconceptions, is another external tool for assessment. My chemistry modeling students over the past three years have had modest gains in pre- and post-MCI tests, but since the curriculum is not fully developed, these results are inconclusive. Effective Socratic questioning, framing concepts with models, and group collaboration contribute to these gains. Both Modeling and PP&T rely heavily on this learning cooperation among group members. PP&T students also had gains of 12% on FCI pre- and posttests. However, like the chemistry modeling results, the PP&T program has been in place at our school for too short a time period to draw decisive conclusions. With consistent repetition of these results, we could assess learning in these programs more confidently. It will take more time and effort to effectively assess the extensions of these programs in my specific classroom.

Nevertheless, students in these programs see themselves as young, adventurous scientists utilizing available technology, rather than passive participants blandly studying the discipline of science. They do many of the things that real scientists do. A good many students who go through these programs in high school choose science, math, medicine, or engineering as their field of study in college. One of my former students is a chemist with the Hawaii Biotechnology Group. In a letter supporting me for the 2003 Shell Science Teaching Award, her mother gives her daughter's high school chemistry education program credit for her pursuit of that profession. Information on official graduation programs reveal that of last year's graduates, about 31% are currently pursuing a major in science, math, premed, or engineering. That is a significant ratio, considering that nine years ago a mere 13% of our graduates pursued those fields. We can conclude that more of them feel confident in choosing those majors. Most, if not all, gain the skills they need to be discerning and logical thinkers, allowing them to contribute to and improve society by making informed decisions.

Our students hold their own in statewide academic competitions. We have participated in math meets, math bowls, and science bowls over the past five years. Our math teams consistently place in the top three, while our science bowl team has placed second, fourth, seventh, and tenth in the state. When their skills are tested against their peers, they perform in stellar fashion. This is due to the efforts of both the science and math departments, since collaboration often occurs between individual teachers. In addition to the hands-on science students experience in class, our algebra and calculus teacher helps immensely in preparing them for the math in the competition, since the award money from the Science Bowl goes to both departments.

Current students make favorable comments about the entire inquiry process. One student, upon seeing the white boards in my classroom, expressed gratitude for the opportunity to share information with her peers, using that tool in this positive environment. She also shared how challenging her first group was to work with and how rewarding the last group had been. We talked a bit about how those experiences might help her later when she becomes an adult and is obliged to work with all types of personalities. No matter their eventual professions, they come away better equipped to handle the demands and rigors of adult life.

As a teacher involved in these programs, I see myself as a trainer of future professionals in science, math, medicine, and engineering. Teachers associated with these programs have received national recognition. The National Science Teachers Association's *Shell Science Teaching Award* is given yearly to the top teacher in the country. Three of thirteen recipients were *modelers*. In fact, Malcolm Wells' good friend, Wayne Williams, who originally served as the experimental control because he used the traditional method in his classroom, eventually became trained in *Modeling Instruction,* and went on to receive the 1995 Shell Award. I was also a humble recipient in 2003. I credit *Modeling Instruction* and PP&T for giving me the tools to be seriously considered for such an award. Teachers from both programs have earned the National Science Foundation's prestigious *Presidential Award for Excellence in Math and Science Teaching* (PAEMST), as well as generous GTE Gift Grants, among other NSF and NSTA awards and grants.

I do not claim that these two programs exclusively improve a classroom, but I do submit that they do a wonderful job, addressing many of the issues that accomplish just that. I remain confident that there exists a wealth of other programs that also address many of the NSES *More Emphasis* conditions as effectively as *Modeling Instruction* and PP&T do. Through this NSTA Monograph series, many educators will become acutely aware of these available programs and will be thoroughly challenged to think about how to implement them in their own classrooms, thereby improving the quality of science education for generations to come. That thought inspires me to keep doing what I love to do in my own classroom on a tiny island in the middle of the Pacific Ocean.

References

Dukerich, L. and G. Swackhamer. 2003. A coherent approach to energy. Paper presented at the summer meeting of the American Association of Physics Teachers, Madison, Wisconsin.

Hake, R. 1992. Socratic pedagogy in the introductory physics laboratory. *The Physics Teacher* 30: 546–552.

Halloun, I. and D. Hestenes. 1985. The initial knowledge state of college physics students. *American Journal of Physics* 53: 1043–1055.

Hestenes. D. 1987. A modeling theory of physics instruction. *American Journal of Physics* 55: 440–454.

Karplus, R. 1977. Science teaching and the development of reasoning. *Journal of Research in Science Teaching* 14: 169–175.

Lawson, A., M. Abraham, and J. Renner. 1989. *A theory of instruction using the learning cycle to teach science concepts and thinking skills.* Manhattan, KS: National Association for Research in Science Teaching.

Lin, H., H. Cheng, and F. Lawrenz. 2000. The assessment of students and teachers' understanding of gas laws. *Journal of Chemical Education* 77 (2): 235–238.

McDermott, L. 1993. How we teach and how students learn—a mismatch? *American Journal of Physics* 61 (4): 295–298.

Mestre, J. 1991. Learning and instruction in pre-college physical science. *Physics Today* 44 (9): 56–62.

Raloff, J. 2001. Where's the Book? Science education is redefining texts. *Science News Online* 159 (12): 1–9.

Rice, R. 2003. Physics first at Clayton high school. *modeling@asu.edu*

Wells, M., D. Hestenes, and G. Swackhamer. 1995. A modeling method for high school physics instruction. *American Journal of Physics* 63 (7): 606–619.

Yost, D. 2003. Whiteboarding: A learning process. *DoYost@aol.com*

For more information about *Modeling Instruction,* contact:

Dr. David Hestenes, Director
Jane Jackson, Co-Director
Modeling Instruction Program
Box 871504
Department of Physics and Astronomy
Arizona State University
Tempe, AZ 85287
(480) 965-8438

For more information about *PP&T, DASH,* or *FAST* contact:

Dr. Frank Pottenger, Director
Valerie Hashimoto, Assistant
University of Hawaii—College of Education
Curriculum Research and Development Group
1776 University Avenue
Honolulu, HI 96822
(808) 956-6918

Sing and Dance Your Way to Science Success

Cindy Moss
Charlotte Mecklenburg Schools

Setting

This research was conducted to determine whether creating a different kind of classroom learning environment could help at-risk students achieve success in Biology. After conducting research for two years to determine which factors in the learning environment led to increased test scores, an intervention was attempted. In this intervention, at-risk students were placed in a classroom that attempted to model the National Science Education Standards (NSES) and to meet the students' learning environment needs. This work was done at Independence High School in Charlotte, North Carolina. The Charlotte-Mecklenburg School system is one of the 20 largest systems in the United States and faces all the problems of large urban school districts. The Charlotte region is growing rapidly, with more than 2,000 people moving into the area each week, and this influx of citizens creates problems for schools and teachers. Many of these newcomers to the Charlotte area come for service industry jobs requiring little in the way of education or skills, and that requires them to work more than one job. That also means they are unable to be involved in their children's education, and are usually not educated beyond high school themselves.

Independence High School is a microcosm of urban education. The school is approximately 60% non-White, with students from more than 50 countries. There are programs for all levels of students, including: English as a Second Language, International Studies, a Biomedical Academy, an International Business Academy, an Air Force ROTC program, and an International Baccalaureate program. There is also a high degree of student mobility between the 18 high schools in this district, and approximately 30% of the student body qualifies for free/reduced lunch. The high achieving students in this school outperform the rest of the country, but our at-risk students fail miserably relative to the other schools in our district and the state of North Carolina.

Purpose and Methodology

This research was conducted to deal with the frustration of the teachers in attempting to help their students learn enough Biology to pass the North Carolina End-of-Course exam as well as the course itself. Students are required to pass Biology as a graduation requirement and approximately 50% of the students require more than one year to fulfill this requirement. The factors contributing to this high failure rate include below grade reading ability, no exposure to science in the past, and no interest in the content. Because the End-of-Course exam is a multiple-choice exam, there is also pressure by many administrators to delete all lab work and teach in a "stand and deliver" fashion. Currently in elementary schools in North Carolina the students must pass End-of-Grade exams that cover reading and math abilities, so science is not taught there. In the middle schools the students are scheduled for science classes, but those teachers end up doing remedial math and reading lessons to prepare the students for the End-of-Grade tests. Therefore, high school biology is the first time North Carolina students are really required to take a science course that counts. The biology teachers are also under pressure to improve their students' test scores because bonus money for the entire school is dependent upon student scores on biology, algebra, ninth-grade history, and English. Many teachers and administrators have completely ignored the National Science Education Standards because they see no way that changing the way education is delivered will improve the test scores of their students. This combination of poorly prepared students and pressure from peers and administrators to improve test scores has contributed to high rates of teacher turnover and frustration. It also results in young, inexperienced teachers in the schools with the most at-risk students, many of whom are being advised by older teachers to continue in the "stand and deliver" tradition. Sadly, many of these eager, young teachers are strongly discouraged from using any innovative strategies, including those recommended by the National Science Education Standards (NRC 1996). In the Charlotte-Mecklenburg School system, new teachers are given a pacing guide and with the amount of required content this leads to lecturing as the predominant means of instruction.

The research began with the administration of the "What is happening in this class?" (WIHIC) learning environment questionnaire to more than 600 Biology students over two years. The students took an "actual" form and a "preferred" form to determine the differences in the environment they would choose, and the one experienced in their biology classrooms. This questionnaire has been used widely in many parts of the world, but not in the United States, so it was given for two years to validate the results with different versions of the test. The teachers were not evaluated in any fashion by this questionnaire; it was to help the researcher determine which factors were correlated to the state test. Graphs were prepared for each class to show the teacher the differences in the preferred and actual learning environment for males versus females, and African American versus non-African American students (CMS schools required teachers to record the number of African American and non-African American students in each class and work towards decreasing the gap between the groups). Possible reasons for these differences were discussed in meetings of the biology teacher team. For most of the teachers involved this was the first time they had ever been involved in a collegial study group, and they enjoyed the opportunity to work with other science teachers. They were also surprised that this is a recommendation of the National Science Education Standards (NRC 1996). This WIHIC questionnaire covered the scales of: Student Cohesiveness, Teacher Support, Involvement, Investigation, Task Orientation, Cooperation, Equity, and Attitude toward Science. Equity was included to deal with diversity issues, and Attitude toward Science was included to determine if the teachers could increase the percentage of students taking three years of science in high school. The scales were chosen based upon the work of Fraser, et al., using the WIHIC in schools from many parts of the world. The North Carolina End-of-Course exam is given in three different forms that emphasize different areas of biology, so it was with great interest that the correlation between learning environment factors and test scores was determined for the EOC over two years. The research indicated that Student Cohesiveness, Involvement, and Investigation were positively correlated to student achievement at the class level and that all these factors were more strongly correlated to positive attitudes towards science. At the individual level, Task Orientation, Equity, and Teacher Support were important to low-achieving students. However, the results showed no significant difference in classroom learning environment preferred among African American, non-African American, male, and female subgroups. According to the data, each classroom had its own particular preferred environment, but these environments were not gender or ethnically determined. The fact that Involvement, Investigation, and Student Cohesiveness were found to be positively correlated to test scores also tied in to the National Science Education Standards (NRC 1996) putting *more emphasis* on learning science through investigation and inquiry. The biology team teachers were surprised that Investigation had any impact on test scores, because the North Carolina EOC examination has relatively few questions on laboratory work. Since lab work is not as easily assessed using multiple-choice questions, the biology team had many spirited discussions as reflective practitioners. They also developed innovative ways to encourage students to develop leadership skills in this inquiry experience, and to communicate their ideas and work clearly to their peers and teacher.

The third year of the research was an intervention to determine if creating the prescribed learning environment would truly improve test scores. After the first five weeks of school, the biology team met to discuss the intervention. The teachers were given the opportunity to remove students from their class that they would classify as at-risk or as "definite failures." The teachers were told to use their professional judgment to make this determination, so many of these students were placed in this category because of poor attendance and behavior problems. With a continuous influx of students into Independence High School there are constant schedule changes, so these students were never told they were placed in the Intervention classes because a teacher had designated them as a "definite failure." During the first day of their new "Intervention" biology class, these students were given a learning styles inventory and their own personal learning style was explained to them. They were also given the WIHIC Preferred questionnaire immediately and the Actual form several weeks after they were placed into these Intervention classes. The actual versus preferred graph for the regular class is shown in Figure 1, indicating these students needed more teacher support, cooperation, and equity.

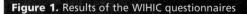

Figure 1. Results of the WIHIC questionnaires

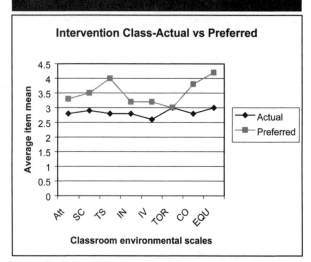

Figure 2. Perceptions of the classroom learning environment by race

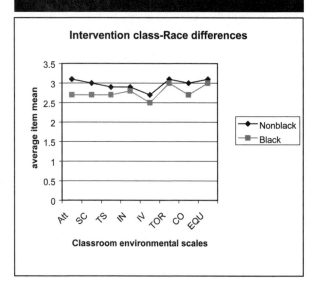

They were given diagnostic reading tests and the majority of the students in the three classes were found to read at the fifth-grade level or lower. The students were told that their teacher was involved in a doctoral program and was working to help them succeed, and their parents were informed that their son/daughter was in the intervention classes. The students and parents were informed that this classroom would be structured in a different way from traditional science classrooms and that there would be lots of inquiry learning, and integration of skills would be expected. There were a total of 67 students in this intervention year, 20 in a regular (lowest track) and 47 in two preIB (International Bacalaureate) classes (rigorous track that is self-selected).

The graph in Figure 2 shows that there was relatively little difference in the perceptions of the classroom learning environment between the African American and non-African American students. This was consistent with the findings from the previous two years of study with more than 600 students in Biology 1 classes. This is also consistent with other work done by Fraser, et al., using the WIHIC in various countries around the world.

The graph in Figure 3 showed that overall, the females viewed the classroom learning environment more favorably than the males. It also indicates that the males wanted more investigation and more cooperation in the classroom, while the females wanted more teacher support. These graphs were discussed by the biology teacher team and shared with the students in the Intervention classes so that they would understand the types of activities and lessons they would be experiencing during the year. This information was also used by the teacher-researcher to plan strategies to use with these classes.

With the information from the diagnostic reading tests, the learning styles inventories, and the WIHIC questionnaires, the biology team met to discuss ways to help these students achieve. Of the strategies that were developed and used, the majority involved innovative ways to help these students learn to read for meaning. Other research studies have shown that most biology courses are more vocabulary-laden than foreign language classes, so vocabulary acquisition is extremely important to success. These strategies involved peer coaching, using songs and stories to convey content objectives, cooperative learning, and lots of hands-on, minds-on laboratory activities. The National Science Education Standards (NRC 1996) were also stud-

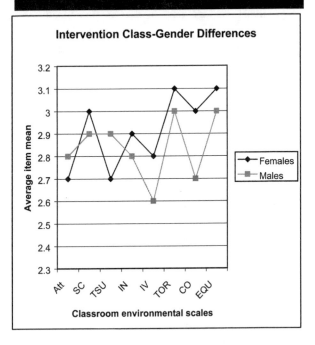

Figure 3. Perceptions of the classroom learning environment by gender

ied by the biology team to determine if it would be possible to implement some of the suggested changes in emphasis in teaching methods and content into this intervention class.

Another key component of this program consisted in involving parents. With 74% of these students on free/reduced lunch, we knew the majority of these parents were working more than one job or had transportation problems. When parents of only two students showed up for the parent night we realized we needed a different solution. We enlisted the help of a local African American minister, and with his pulpit announcements and the use of his church for a meeting location, we were able to bring in 80% of the parents to the second meeting. The parents were informed about their sons' and daughters' learning styles. They were also shown how to use the internet (and how to get an account at the local public library) to check the class assignment and communicate with the teacher, and they were included in several field trips taken by the classes. They were also invited to come in to discuss the future career paths available to their child, and 88% of the parents of the Intervention students ultimately scheduled a meeting to discuss their sons' or daughters' future. After this meeting, the communication between teacher and parents increased in scope and frequency.

Given the extremely poor reading ability of most of the Intervention students, the methods for delivering information were changed. The teacher became the coach and not the deliverer of information. Many members of the biology team were concerned that this method would not work with low ability students, because it would require them to take more ownership for their learning. This strategy reflected the National Science Education Standard change in emphasis from teacher responsibility for the students' learning to students accepting responsibility for their own learning. To help the students develop reading comprehension skills, they read information from their texts in class at least once a week, with a partner, and with some sort of guided reading material. These "Levels Guides" (Hal Herber) and word card activities (Dunn and Dunn) place students in groups of three with at least one student of higher ability paired with two others. These activities enable the teacher to circulate and deal with individual reading difficulties. They also allowed the teacher-researcher to understand and respond to the individual student's interests, strengths, experiences, and needs because she had the time to give them individual attention. The students took notes in class only rarely; the information was contained in stories to introduce or wrap-up a unit, and in songs containing the meat of the content. Students who were too intimidated to read aloud were willing to assume the identity of a character in a play or sing the words of a song, and this improved their confidence in their own reading ability. The concert readings (stories read to baroque classical music) were used to introduce each and every unit to give these students the "big picture."

The reasoning for using these types of exercises was explained to the students, so that they understood how the teacher was working to accommodate their learning styles. With nearly 90% of these students scoring as extremely right-brained learners, this type of learning became integral to their success. They also benefited from the practice of doing hands-on, minds-on activities nearly every class period. They began to understand that they could learn the vocabulary and concepts through inquiry activities, in which they were able to do investigations to answer their own questions.

The students were involved with their peers in collegial and collaborative learning and conducted several long-term labs that required them to plan and communicate with their group members. They also had ample opportunity to present and discuss their findings in front of their peers. The students also learned methods to organize their notebooks, and keeping a planner was routinely modeled for them and required. They were encouraged to form study teams and after school "study buddy" help sessions were offered on Tuesdays and Thursdays. The parents were encouraged to help their children with these organization skills by checking the agendas posted on *www.schoolnotes.com*. The School Notes site was also used to praise individual students for their successes in class, so parents and students checked the site often, looking for mention of their achievements.

Sample Unit

A typical two-week unit in these intervention classes would proceed in the following manner. A unit on biochemistry will be used as an example.

Day 1	Concert	Reading Willy the Wacky Water Molecule and MTV
	Song	Water Molecule
		The students would sing the song, highlight the most important phrases and discuss any new vocabulary.
	LAB	Chemical and physical properties of water

Each lab group chose 2 chemical and 2 physical properties to measure and then presented their findings to the class during the next class period

HW   Complete questions from the lab activity, reflect on your learning and be Prepared to present to the class

Day 2   Review   Sing the Water Song
                   Class presentations of inquiry learning from last class
          Quiz   Chemical and physical properties of Water Levels Guide (guided reading) Basic Chemistry (approximately 20 pages of text, read with 2 partners
          LAB   Constructing molecules
          HW   Worksheet on Basic Chemistry

Day 3   Review   Word cards: Basic Chemistry Terms
                   Students cut out cards and play a partner matching game with definitions
          Quiz   Basic Chemistry
                   Organic chemistry song—students will highlight important terms and color macromolecules
          LAB   Chemistry of carbohydrates
                   Students will test foods for reactions with indicators to determine which indicators work for carbohydrates. They were given the opportunity to bring in foods to test and have several possibilities provided for them
          HW   Complete lab questions, reflect on your learning and prepare presentation

Day 4   Review   Organic Chemistry
                   Class review of Chemistry of Carbohydrates lab
                   Organic Chemistry Song
          LAB   Chemistry of fats and proteins
                   Students will test foods for reactions with indicators to determine which indicators are best for fats and proteins
          HW   Complete lab questions, reflect on your learning and prepare presentation

Day 5   Review   Organic Chemistry
                   Class Review of Data from Carbohydrate lab
                   "Think and Learn" partner sharing activity
                   Organic chemistry song
          LAB   Enzymes: Planning Day
                   Students will use enzymes from avocado and liver and conduct some basic tests to determine information. With their partner they will design a lab to be completed next class about some aspect of enzymes.
          HW   Write up their proposed lab procedure

Day 6   Review   Organic Chemistry
                   Organic Chemistry Song
          LAB   Enzymes: Carry out their own lab
          HW   Write up results, reflect on your procedure, possible errors, and suggestions for improvement. Be prepared to present to class

Day 7   Review   Organic Chemistry
                   Organic Chemistry Song
                   Present Lab Results and suggest improvements to their lab
          HW   Chemistry review sheet

Day 8	Review	Organic Chemistry
	Levels Guide	Organic chemistry
	Speaker	Hospital nutritionist (30 minutes)
	Review Activity	Word cards
	HW	Construct a concept map with the word cards you made in class
Day 9	Review	Sing Organic Chemistry and Water Songs
		Put together "Chemistry Review Puzzle" with a partner
		Complete test exercises (Educational kinesiology)
	Take test	Biochemistry

In this biochemistry unit, one that is typically difficult for beginning biology students who have not taken chemistry, these students were able to construct their own knowledge about inorganic and organic chemistry as it related to biology. They manually used lab equipment, acted as real scientists in designing an experiment to answer a question they formulated, and shared their results with their peers. These activities worked to create the classroom learning environment found to be correlated with higher test scores on the North Carolina EOC exam (investigation, involvement and cooperation) at the class level, as well as the scales of equity, task orientation, and teacher support found to be important at the individual level. The students were also able to see how this information is integral to a well-paying job in our local area. At each step during the year, their confidence in their abilities increased. They were engaged in ongoing assessment of their work and that of others, and were learning to be members of a learning community that cooperates, shares responsibility, and respects one another.

Assessment

The Charlotte Mecklenburg School system creates and administers Quarter Assessments for each of its high-stakes tested content areas. At the end of each quarter all biology students in the district take a multiple-choice test and these results are to be used to provide the teacher with information for remediation. Teachers and schools can compare their results with those of the other schools in the district. After only five weeks in this intervention class, these students tested very poorly on the 1st Quarter Assessment (35% for the regular class and 58% for the preIB classes) but improved each quarter. The biology team teachers analyzed these results each quarter for their own individual classes and for the students in the intervention classes.

As the teacher of the intervention classes, I spent a large percentage of time convincing the students that they had the individual skills necessary to succeed, and that their own future was worth the effort. Even though completion of biology is necessary for graduation, many of these students had only experienced failure in the past, and chose not to try. They needed constant encouragement and individual attention. To further reinforce the idea that science could lead to future careers, community members working in fields that required scientific backgrounds were brought in to speak with these students. These speakers were successful business owners, engineers, medical professionals, and public officials. They were people of various ethnicities, with backgrounds similar to these students, so their message was well received. The community speakers also established relationships with many of the students, offering them after-school jobs, and checking on their academic progress throughout the year.

Another aspect of at-risk students is their feeling of powerlessness. These students often expressed frustration because they felt they were stuck in poverty situations, no matter how hard they would try. To help them gain a sense of self-worth I engaged them in the local Groundwater Guardian program. In this program the students went to local fourth-grade classes monthly to teach the younger students lessons about water. Clean water is a current environmental issue in Charlotte, due to the constant influx of people into the area and the strain on the water supply. The biology students worked in groups of three to four, practiced their lessons, and developed relationships with the younger students.

These lessons involved teaching the elementary students songs, involving them in lab work, and helping them understand chemical and biological aspects of water. The elementary students looked forward to their special classes with the high school students and looked up to them as role models. For low income/disadvantaged high school students this was an extremely empowering experience. The high school students received certificates from the mayor of Charlotte and the Governor of North Carolina, thanking them for their contribution to their community. They also met many of the fourth graders' parents at a Saturday Water Festival hosted at our school, and many of these parents expressed their appreciation to the high school students for their work with the younger students. We wrote a North Carolina Learn and Serve Grant and received funding to pay for the materials we used, the supplies for the Water Festival, and training for the high school students who acted as teachers. The Intervention students were able to go to a local waterfront camp on a teacher workday to learn about the technical aspects of water and how to teach elementary students. They were also able to participate in team-building activities such as low-ropes and high-ropes courses. With local fund-raising we were also able to select two of the Intervention students to receive $1,000 scholarships for their work in this program.

During this intervention year the high school biology team teachers met weekly to discuss any problems in their own classes and to provide support for the intervention teacher. Because the other teachers were not required to try any innovative strategies and because the intervention students' test scores would not reflect upon them, they were open and eager to discuss possibilities. During the course of the year, most of the biology team teachers did eventually try many of the strategies that were suggested and attempted during the intervention. When they saw the success these students experienced, they became believers in many of the various strategies used. The biology team teachers also experienced the joy of being a member of a collegial professional community. Most said they learned more from this experience than from all the professional development workshops they had attended during their entire careers, and with the Intervention teacher creating the activities and setting up the activities, the other teachers were willing to use them in their own classrooms. The biology team also grew professionally from their discussions of the National Science Education Standards (NRC 1996) in teaching, assessment, content and inquiry, and professional development. Their main frustration was that with a high-stakes state written final assessment, there was little latitude in choosing a few fundamental science concepts to study well.

Success Markers

Evidence of success from this research was prevalent from the first week. The students' attendance improved tremendously because they had experienced success. The majority of these students had missed at least 20 days of school the previous year and after the intervention began most missed fewer than three days throughout the rest of the year.

When the 1st Quarter Assessment scores came back to our school, the biology team members chuckled to themselves that these kids were definitely "at risk," but each quarter, the Intervention students showed amazing gains, as evidenced in the graphs below. These graphs (Figures 5 and 6) show the regular class (lowest track) and the two preIB (International Baccalaureate) classes (self-selected rigorous track) and their results.

Overall, 64 of these 67 students passed the End-of-Course exam and 100% of these students passed the biology course (compared to 50% of the Biology students in this school). These students also stayed in this school, which is an unusual occurrence in this district. Many of the low-income students move frequently because their parent/guardian are unable to pay the rent or lose their jobs. The parents and guardians saw the impact of this program on their sons and daughters, and did everything in their power to keep them in this class and school. Their overall grades in all classes improved during this Intervention year. When the intervention started at five weeks into the year, 74% of the students were failing three or more classes. By the end of the year only 7% of the students failed even one course. This effect carried over into the next two years as well, with 90% of them remaining at this school to graduate. Further, 85% of the students in this intervention ended up taking 3 years of science before they graduated, and 78% of them went on to college. This is unusually high, because only 67% of the students graduating from this school go onto higher education of any sort. These students maintained contact with this biology teacher during the next two years and their parents also sought out the advice of this teacher for school related problems during the next two years.

This research shows that even at-risk students can succeed when they have a committed teacher using research-based strategies to help them succeed. Using many changes suggested by the National Science Education Standards (NRC 1996), the teacher was able to change the type of education experience these students had in biology. These changes involved restructuring how instruction was delivered and empowering the students to succeed. These students were not only able to achieve in this class, but went on to complete two more years of science successfully. Their parents were willing to be involved, but needed the school to make their involvement possible, and teach them how to help their children. The teachers involved as observers and members of the biology team needed to see that simple activities designed to meet the needs of the students could produce the desired results on the multiple-choice test, and the teachers needed convincing that inquiry learning could actually impact a test score. Most of the teachers expressed the opinion when we began that the National Science Education Standards could only be used with wealthy and privileged students who would read the book at home. They were convinced that these intervention students would never be able to learn in that manner. They were all soundly convinced after witnessing this intervention that these strategies worked with the most at-risk population.

The importance of this research is that many of our current science students are not experiencing science because their teachers are under pressure to teach to a multiple-choice test. Many administrators do not understand or see the correlation between hands-on laboratory learning and multiple-choice testing, so we need to educate the administrators and decision makers about the efficacy of inquiry learning. The classroom teachers need financial support for laboratory equipment and supplies, as well as psychological support in providing these types of learning experiences for their students. Many science teachers need additional training so that they are comfortable with laboratory activities. Teachers need to be empowered to develop their own learning community with other caring professionals in their location. With the advent of "No Child Left Behind," there will be an increased pressure on teachers in all parts of our country to cover the content, sometimes at the expense of true learning. However, this research shows that even our lowest ability students can achieve on a high-stakes multiple-choice exam and still have a quality learning experience in science. It shows that implementing the changes suggested by the National Science Education Standards can have a positive impact on student test scores even when those tests do not assess the variety of learning experiences the students had during the year. In conclusion, this research shows that when teachers follow the National Science Education Standards as much as possible in their local situation, the teacher feels empowered as a professional, the students feel empowered to take responsibility for their own learning, and the students' test scores improve.

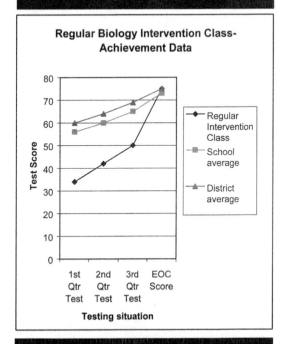

Figure 5. Regular Intervention class test scores

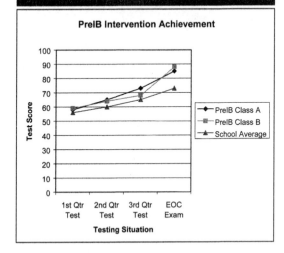

Figure 6. PreIB Intervention class test scores

References

Baker, Gwendolyn Calvert. 1994. *Planning and organizing for multicultural instruction*. Menlo Park, CA: Addison-Wesley Publishing.

Fisher, D. L., ed. 1993. *The study of learning environments, vol. 7*. Perth: Science and Mathematics Education Centre, Curtin University of Technology.

Fisher, D. L., D. Henderson, and B. J. Fraser. 1997. Laboratory environment and student outcomes in senior high biology. *American Biology Teacher* 59: 214–219.

Fraser, B. J. 1984. The effects of classroom climate on student outcomes: A replication in two developing countries. *Singapore Journal of Education* 6 (2): 60–63.

Fraser, B. J. 1986. *Classroom environment.* London: Croom Helm.

Fraser, B. J. 1991. Two decades of classroom environment research. In *Educational environments: Evaluation, antecedents and consequences, eds.* B. J. Fraser and H. J. Walberg, 3–27. Oxford: Pergamon.

Frase, L. E. and W. Streshly. 2000. *Top 10 myths in education: Fantasies Americans love to believe.* Lanham, MD: The Scarecrow Press.

Higginbotham, E. 1996. Getting all students to listen: Analyzing and coping with student resistance. *The American Behavioral Scientist* 40 (Nov/Dec): 203–11.

Irvine, J. J. 1988. Urban schools that work: A summary of relevant factors. *Journal of Negro Education* 57 (3): 236–242.

National Research Council (NRC). 1996. *National science education standards.* Washington, DC: National Academy Press.

Sizer, T. R. 1973. *Places for learning, places for joy: Speculations on merican school reform.* Cambridge: Harvard University Press.

Wood, G. H. 1992. *Schools that work: America's most innovative public education programs.* New York: Penguin Books USA.

Student Inquiry at the Illinois Mathematics and Science Academy

Judith A. Scheppler, Donald Dosch, Susan Styer
Illinois Mathematics and Science Academy

Steven Rogg
DePaul University School of Education

Setting

Located in Aurora, Illinois, the Illinois Mathematics and Science Academy (IMSA) is an internationally recognized, pioneering educational institution created by the State to develop talent and stimulate excellence in teaching and learning in mathematics, science, and technology (Marshall 2002). IMSA's advanced residential college preparatory program enrolls 650 academically talented Illinois students in grades 10–12. Students come from across the state of Illinois, applying as freshmen to enter the Academy in the sophomore class. The student body is 50% female and 50% male. Of the 2003–04 student profile, 69% of students were from the Chicago/Metropolitan area and 31% were from other areas of Illinois. Ethnic demographics for this group were 49% White, 35% Asian, 8% African American, 4% Latino, 3% bi-racial/multi-ethnic, and fewer than 1% Native American. IMSA utilizes an accomplishment-based selection process that incorporates performance on projects as well as participation or leadership in extracurricular activities, together with more traditional indicators of achievement, such as test scores and grades. Typically, 10–15% of the entering class will be eighth graders, although younger students have been admitted occasionally.

The *More Emphasis* Conditions

Student inquiry (Illinois Mathematics and Science Academy 2000) encourages students to be in charge of their own investigations, thus engaging them in a rich opportunity to emulate a practicing scientist (Table 1). This approach allows them to learn scientific concepts in the context of inquiry, and not as isolated, unconnected facts. Since the inquiry investigations are focused on a question of the students' choice, students investigate a few fundamental scientific concepts in depth. As students work on their investigation, the scientific skills they learn are in the context of their question, so there is an inherent reason for them to learn the subject matter. Since investigations take place over a year, students reflect about how real science is done, rather than classroom science. The goal is for students to build a rich experience, to integrate their scientific learning into their conceptual understanding, and to learn important skills such as critical thinking, skeptical inquiry, and finding and evaluating information. Students employ skills in their investigation that are more complex than simple observations or inferences. When they design and conduct their own research, they draw conclusions based on generated evidence. Investigations do not necessarily come up with "correct" answers and frequently lead to more questions. Advisors and students share in the responsibility for learning, and advisors are continually assessing students' growing scientific understanding and reasoning. As the students become more experienced, they self-assess their understanding and take on more responsibility for their learning.

Table 1. The Student Inquiry Program at IMSA.

Started in 1998, the Inquiry Program (which actually encompasses all disciplines—mathematics, history and social science, foreign language and culture, fine and performing arts, as well as in the sciences) has steadily grown and investigations in the sciences have increased. The total number of investigations is cumulative of inquiry and senior research across all disciplines and junior/senior research in science. The number of investigations reflects unique investigations, some of which have more than one student working collaboratively on a project. Science investigations are inclusive of experimental studies, observational studies, computer science, the biographies writing project, and science education curriculum development; social science investigations were not included. Note that more females than males are pursuing scientific investigations.

School Year	98–99	99–00	00–01	01–02	02–03
Investigations	30	48	45	66	74
Total Students	50	96	102	133	127
Student in Science Investigations	19	36	53	66	76
Students in Nonscience Investigations	31	60	49	67	51
Male	42%	44.8%	47.1%	45.1%	44.9%
Female	58%	55.2%	52.9%	54.9%	55.1%

Teachers, Students, and Inquiry at IMSA

Students conducting inquiries are advised by Academy faculty and staff members, who do so on a voluntary basis. Of the entire IMSA faculty, all have a minimum of a master's degree, with 38% holding a doctorate. Of the fourteen science faculty, seven hold doctorates, five are NBPTS certified, and most have research experience. The Coordinator of Student Inquiry holds a doctorate in science and oversees the entire program; she does not teach any formal classes at the Academy. She directs the Grainger Center for Imagination and Inquiry (GCII), which is approximately three thousand square feet of space designated for student investigations in the laboratory as well as general inquiry support. For most students, inquiries are pursued during their unscheduled time and on "inquiry Wednesdays," a day at the Academy without scheduled classes. The exception to this schedule pertains to students who are enrolled in the Junior/Senior Research in Science course. They have time allotted for this work in their schedules and are expected to pursue their work on inquiry Wednesdays as well. Investigations begin in August, when students return to the Academy, and culminate in a public presentation of their work in late April.

Student Inquiry in Science at IMSA

Student Inquiry in Science at IMSA is an in-depth and actively pursued study of topics reflecting student interests. The self-directed student plan of inquiry is a progression of learning experiences that is designed and conducted in response to a student's (or a group of students') questions. Students pose a specific question or problem and strive to answer it through carefully focused study. The knowledge generated helps students gain a deeper understanding of the topic of their interest.

The role of the *advisor* is to support and guide the student in pursuit of the inquiry. The advisor, an IMSA staff or faculty member, is usually experienced in the particular subject area, or interested in the topic, so that he can thoughtfully guide the student in content specifics as well as process.

The investigation begins by formulating a *proposal* or plan of inquiry. The inquiry advisor and the Coordinator of Student Inquiry review the student's proposal, which includes discussion of sufficient depth to explain the investigation, as well as discussion of the potential ethical implications of the work. The investigation that is carried out is documented through a journal or notebook. A formal progress report or abstract of the work is written each semester to assess progress of the study and to allow for reflection on the investigation. Public communication of work for peer review and discussion is an important part of every inquiry. Presentation Day at IMSA, each spring, provides a forum where all those completing Student Inquiry and Research offer their work to the IMSA community, guests, and parents via a formal fifteen-minute oral presentation, including questions. A final report and reflective discussion with the inquiry advisor completes the inquiry investigation.

Students may pursue an Inquiry investigation through three different pathways. These options are the *Student Inquiry Program*, *Senior Research* (SR), or *Junior/Senior Research in Science* (JSR). Most students successfully completing an inquiry investigation receive notation on their IMSA transcript, but do not receive a grade or graduation credit.

Senior Research is an inquiry investigation that has continued into its second year. Only seniors who have successfully completed one year of inquiry are eligible. It counts as 0.5 credits per semester and students complete the same requirements as for the student inquiry program. Senior Research receives a pass/fail grade, but SR does not count in the course requirements for graduation. Some students who have reached course enrollment limitations will pursue a second year of investigation as student inquiry rather than senior research (with successful completion noted on their transcript).

Junior/Senior Research in Science is a one-year long, credit-bearing course offered for the first time in the 2002–03 school year. The requirements are the same as for student inquiry and SR. A major difference, however, is that students have time allotted in their course schedule, and an instructor, as part of his teaching load, has been designated to work with the students. Students receive a letter grade for JSR and it can count toward graduation requirements.

Inquiry Proposal

The *inquiry proposal* serves to plan and focus an inquiry investigation. Key to the inquiry is a *focusing question* that the student develops and commits to pursuing. This question is developed by the student in response to passion, curiosity, and interest, and is based on what is known about a particular subject. Marbach-Ad and Sokolove rank questions from "simple" to those that are "academically grounded" and admit of being investigated (Marbach-Ad and Sokolove 2000). We are striving for questions that are formed and answerable using multiple sources. While students may want to make or build something, such as a fuel cell or terrarium, "Can I make … ?" or "Can I build … ?" is not a sufficient question because it doesn't encompass a scientific investigation—and it has a "yes or no" answer. Rather, a question such as "What components are critical to constructing an efficient fuel cell?" is better, and the resulting investigation contains elements that can be modified and changed for experimental data collection.

The *project description* serves to document background knowledge and to describe, in detail, the strategy for implementing the inquiry in the context of what the student knows. The description should declare what is known about the subject of the inquiry and how one got to the point of wanting to carry out the work.

The background research for the inquiry is documented by a *bibliography*. The listed bibliography may also include materials that have been identified for use as the inquiry progresses; it will change and grow depending on the path the inquiry takes. As the inquiry develops, the bibliography should reflect use of more primary sources as knowledge deepens and as the inquiry grows and becomes more meaningful and sophisticated.

The inquiry proposal includes a *research plan*. This is a timeline that includes biweekly benchmarks for accomplishment. This plan will help the student define the work to be accomplished in order to answer the focusing question. It should help determine whether what the student intends to do can actually be accomplished. It will also help to determine whether the project's intended goal (and perhaps its focusing question) is changing based on the work. The research plan documents a regular schedule for meetings with the inquiry advisor for substantive discussion of the investigation. The plan will also expose potential safety issues at the start of the investigation.

Research studies have the potential to affect the human condition and society. Analysis of the *ethical* and *societal* aspects of the work assists the student in moral growth, places a social perspective on the work, and helps ensure that no one is harmed. Students should fully and carefully state and discuss the work they are undertaking, and how the topic has affected society in the past or may affect society in the future.

The Investigation

Students determine the course of their investigations. They must find time in their schedule to do the work and meet with their advisors. It is expected that they will meet with their advisor at least every "inquiry Wednesday" to discuss what has and has not been done. This meeting may be brief if little has been accomplished or if work is "routine." It may last for several hours if data is being analyzed and discussed or if roadblocks have been encountered. Inquiry Wednesdays are also used for the actual hands-on laboratory work in the GCII and other facilities, as well as field observation and consultation with other experts in the area. Laboratory work is rarely completed on a single day, so students also work after school and during class breaks in the regular school day.

Inquiry Journal

Documentation of one's work and the journey that was taken to arrive at a particular conclusion or final product is important in constructing the meaning of the work. It assists in providing a basis for replicating, developing, and polishing further efforts. A journal provides a way to keep a record of specific work accomplished or to record the

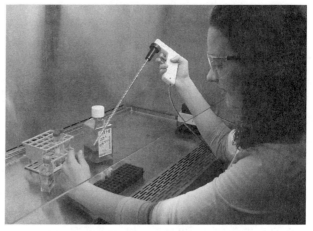

Students perform hands-on laboratory work during "Inquiry Wednesdays."

path of failure; both can be built upon. Additionally, an inquiry journal can be used to record reflections and thoughts of possible paths that may not be pursued immediately. A good journal will include notes from discussion with an advisor or other individual who has helped the investigation, notes and excerpts from the literature that serve to guide the inquiry, protocols followed, and results, observations, data analyses, and questions for further thought and investigation.

Progress Report

Near the end of the first semester of an inquiry, students document and reflect on their projects by preparing a progress report. One page is usually sufficient to discuss what has been accomplished and where the inquiry is going. It should include a brief discussion of problems that have been encountered and where the investigation has gone. Has the focusing question changed?

Additions to the bibliography should be included. The report should include any data, analysis, and observations that document successes and challenges. A well-maintained inquiry journal should facilitate the writing of the progress report.

Presentation of the Investigation

Public presentation and discussion of one's work or work-in-progress is standard in the academic community. The discussion that follows the presentation is beneficial to the academic community as a means of constructing understanding. Work that is conducted is certainly valuable to the investigation, but inviting scrutiny by peers and the community shares what has been learned and allows others to use it as well and to offer critiques. Critique is a useful means to gauge learning and a springboard for further productive investigation. IMSA offers Presentation Day in the spring, when students participating in Student Inquiry and Research present their work orally.

Each year, IMSA publishes a Presentation Day *abstract* book. Individuals attending presentations use the book to determine which talks they would like to attend. The abstract, therefore, should provide a summary of the key accomplishments and information that the listener will hear about in the presentation.

Oral Presentation

Students at IMSA are expected to speak with power, economy, and elegance (Illinois Mathematics and Science Academy 1999). The oral presentation of their inquiry investigation demonstrates these skills while communicating highlights of what has been accomplished and learned. Students are allotted fifteen minutes on Presentation Day to exhibit their work to others, with talks moderated by IMSA faculty and staff. The talk is organized so that the student speaks for ten to twelve minutes and allows three to five minutes for audience questions. Because we plan Presentation Day for the end of April each year, some students will not complete their investigation in this time period. Even so, they must still present their work-in-progress, discussing accomplishments, learning, and the next steps.

One week prior to Presentation Day, a formal, required practice day is scheduled. This gives students the opportunity to test and use presentation equipment while practicing their presentations. Staff moderators use practice day to provide feedback to the students on both presentation content as well as the students' speaking skills. Practice day is critical to good oration and forces students to plan instead of leaving the preparation to the last minute. This gives students another week in which to polish their talk and modify content. Many will practice again with their advisor.

Final Paper

A final paper, in the form of a scientific report, is expected of each investigation. Draft papers are collected about two weeks prior to Presentation Day. This process assists students in preparing their oral presentations and serves as a formative assessment. The advisor provides comments and feedback for improving the final paper, which is due about two weeks after Presentation Day.

One aspect of the final report asks the student to consider and reflect, in a metacognitive fashion, on the inquiry experience itself. What did the student learn about learning? How is this different from science class? Where did the investigation start? Where did it go? What answers were found? What answers were not found? What did the student learn and accomplish? How is that learning valued and valuable? What was learned about inquiry and directing one's own learning? These are the questions that one should consider when reflecting on the inquiry investigation.

Reflection with Advisor

Following Presentation Day, and after completing the requirements for inquiry, the student and advisor also discuss the process of the investigation and what has occurred during the course of the Inquiry. This is a critical examination of the learning experience, where both student and advisor reflect on accomplishments and on how improvements could have been made. It is intended to provide for growth in further learning. Any deficiencies or lack of quality in requirements are addressed, and determination made as to whether the deficiencies (if present) are serious enough to drop the inquiry from the transcript, with no penalty to the student.

Student Learning

Communication, discussion, and defense of one's learning are powerful ways to demonstrate authentic learning through inquiry. For this reason, students are required to present their work on Presentation Day to IMSA staff, guests, and peers. We do not want students to fail on Presentation Day and neither student nor advisor wants to be embarrassed by a poor presentation, so the formative assessments (progress report, abstract, journaling, discussions) are very important to a successful inquiry. Some self-selection by the student about accomplishment and learning occurs prior to presentation and some inquiries are dropped during the year. The advisor and Coordinator of Student Inquiry also speak throughout the year about what the student has been doing and accomplishing, and intervene if work is not being done. Sometimes students are encouraged to drop the inquiry, primarily because the student has taken on too many other activities or responsibilities in addition to the rigorous academic course requirements of the Academy. Sometimes the student is just not doing the work needed, or has lost interest in the inquiry. The advisor plays the largest role in determining whether the student has accomplished sufficient learning, but advisor expectations can differ, making the determination subjective. One makes an assumption that all of those students presenting on Presentation Day have met minimal program requirements.

Objective demonstration of learning is most clear when students are able to present or publish in peer-reviewed venues, as has been the case for some students in inquiry. Fifteen students each wrote a biography of a living American scientist, based on personal interviews and background research. Prometheus Books published *Portraits of Great American Scientists,* edited by L. M. Lederman and J. A. Scheppler, in 2001. (Fourteen students are writing a second book.) A few students have authored or co-authored journal articles (Agarwal 2001; Malina and Young 2002; Scheppler, Sethakorn, and Styer in press).

Scientific meetings are important presentation venues, both those that are strictly for students as well as those for professionals. Our students regularly present at the Illinois Junior Academy of Sciences (IJAS) and the National Consortium of Specialized Secondary Schools in Mathematics, Science, and Technology (NCSSSMST) Student Research Symposium. IJAS and NCSSSMST provide an opportunity for students to present to, and interact with, peers external to IMSA, as well as to speak about and to defend their work before an audience of knowledgeable professionals. We also look for safe and nurturing opportunities where students can present at professional conferences. These opportunities have occurred at the national meetings of the American Society of Microbiology, the National Association of Biology Teachers, and the Society for Integrative and Comparative Biology. Regional meetings, such as the Illinois Section of the Mathematics Association and the Illinois State Academy of Sciences have proven appropriate presentation venues for our young scholars. Siemens Westinghouse Science and Technology Talent Search and the Intel Science Talent Search are two well-known competitions to which IMSA students often submit work.

Presentations at professional conferences, reviewed publications, and juried venues provide good standards for student work. In reality, this happens for a small, but significant, number of students each year. What about the rest of the students and their work? This has been something that we have grappled with for the entire five-year history of the inquiry program. "I know it when I see it" is a common phrase heard in discussions of inquiry quality and student learning. Part of the difficulty lies in the wide variety of investigations that students pursue. There are also many different advisors involved in the program, and both the students' abilities and the advisors' knowledge vary. Part of the assessment consists in whether students have completed all of the requirements: proposal, discussion of ethical and societal implications, progress report, abstract, presentation, and engagement in the work in a satisfactory way.

To better define a reliable assessment of student inquiry performance and learning, standards for inquiry have been drafted (Table 2). It is expected that these standards will guide focused discussions between students and staff in helping to assess learning. The standards are centered on planning, investigating, analyzing, and communicating the investigation. We emphasize, however, that this process is not a linear one. For example, students are expected to continually review scientific literature for research that relates to theirs. They may move back and forth many times between investigation and analysis, modifying protocols or selecting alternative ones. A conclusion may lead the student along an entirely different path than originally intended, resulting in the development of a new focusing question and the need to delve into different scientific literature.

We undertook a retrospective analysis of the past two years' worth of science inquiry investigations. These years were chosen because the inquiry program is continually evolving. Investigations were assessed (Table 3) using a framework for evaluating inquiry tasks (Chinn and Malhotra 2002), designed to determine the degree of similarity between school inquiry investigations and authentic science.

As discussed earlier, all investigations, even writing investigations, must have a research question; also, the students' work must be academically grounded in the professional literature, so these two characteristics were present in all investigations.

Table 2. Inquiry Standards—Plan, Investigate, Analyze, Communicate

For the purposes of developing standards, an Inquiry investigation was broken down into planning, investigating, analyzing, and communicating. One should note, however, that Inquiry is not a linear process. As the Inquiry progresses, you will return to primary and secondary sources, looking for new connections or newly produced research by others. You will move back and forth between investigation and analysis as you progress in your work, using what you have done to refine your focus and your work, and to move forward. You will continually plan, work safely, and determine whether you need more materials. Discussion and communication with your advisor and colleagues is ongoing.

PLANNING

A. Students engaged in inquiry construct viable inquiry questions
  • The question exhibits a focus for the student's curiosity
  • The question is compelling and complex for the student

B. Students engaged in inquiry conduct scholarly background research
  • The student uses multiple and appropriate primary and secondary sources
  • The student evaluates the credibility of the source material
  • The student creates a bibliography

C. Students engaged in inquiry organize and plan their investigation
  • The student states potential outcomes
  • The student schedules and plans work
  • The student addresses safety issues where appropriate
  • The student acquires all necessary materials

D. Students engaged in inquiry address implications of the investigation
  • The student addresses ethical implications of the investigation
  • The student discusses societal implications of the content of the investigation

INVESTIGATION

E. Students engaged in inquiry use appropriate procedures and methods
  • The student assesses risk of the procedures and works in a safe manner
  • The student makes multiple observations/examines varied evidence
  • The student selects variables/critical parameters
  • The student develops controls/calibrate instruments, where appropriate

F. Students engaged in inquiry document the inquiry in a journal
  • The journal contains a record of data and observations
  • The journal contains a detailed record of the methods used
  • The journal contains a record of sources and an annotated bibliography
  • The journal documents discussions of the inquiry with advisor and others
  • The journal documents the student's thinking

G. Students engaged in inquiry meet face-to-face, at least weekly with the inquiry advisor
  • The student discusses and demonstrates progress
  • The student discusses difficulties and possible solutions

ANALYSIS

H. Students consider relationships among components of the inquiry
  • The student identifies the components
  • The student organizes the components into coherent and cohesive form
  • The student averages and graphs data if appropriate
  • The student performs statistical analysis where appropriate
  • The student conjectures relationships where appropriate

- The student constructs arguments based on information
- The student compares the inquiry to work by others
- The student builds systematic arguments or synthesis

I. Students engaged in inquiry draw and defend conclusions
- The student considers the limitations of the methods
- The student discusses uncertainty, if appropriate
- The student considers the contribution to the field
- The student reconsiders ethical and societal implications

COMMUNICATION

J. Students engaged in inquiry orally communicate their investigation to the public
- The student uses good oratory and presentation skills
- The student conveys concise summary and significance
- The student uses appropriate visual aids
- The student balances evidence and discussion
- The student fields questions well

K. Students engaged in inquiry communicate their investigation in written format
- The paper is grammatically and mechanically correct and discipline appropriate
- The paper is complete and thorough—see discipline specific paper guidelines
- The paper contains an abstract
- The paper contains appropriate visual resources
- The paper contains complete appropriate bibliography, references, or footnotes
- The paper contains an appendix or addendum as needed

Not all investigations will contain all of the characteristics of authentic inquiry, and this framework is most applicable to investigations where experiments are conducted. For example, our students often pursue writing projects, develop science education curriculum, and do engineering and technology design, so in these investigations students do not select variables, develop controls, observe intervening variables, and so forth. These investigations are still important to students gaining real-world science experiences.

Summary

The Student Inquiry Program at IMSA provides students with opportunities to conduct long-term investigations of their own design. Many of our students have preconceived expectations of science from their course work. The fact that students pursue their work on Inquiry Wednesdays, during free time, and utilizing the GCII, deliberately places their work in a different context from the classroom, therefore it is closer to "real" investigation, and students think about it differently. Acceptable investigations cover a wide range of scientific work, including the writing of scientists' biographies, field observations, and technological design, as well as experimental research.

Students are capable of carrying out high quality work, especially when the work is exciting and interesting to them. Educators must, therefore, set a high standard and create the conditions for student success. The Student Inquiry Program at IMSA provides one way in which students can conduct authentic inquiry investigations, striving for the high quality and real science experiences that the National Science Education Standards demand.

Table 3. Science investigations with features of authentic inquiry

Science investigations from 2001–02 and 2002–03 were evaluated as to whether the investigation exhibited the features of authentic inquiry, described by Chinn and Malhotra (Chinn and Malhotra 2002). The 52 investigations were conducted in the groups: inquiry, senior research, or junior/senior research in science.

Characteristic	*% of projects (52 total) with characteristic*
Generating research questions	100 %
Selecting variables	61.5%
Developing simple controls	51.9%
Developing relatively complex controls	11.5%
Making multiple observations	55.8%
Observing intervening variables	9.6%
Using analog models	46.2%
Simple transformation of observations	63.5%
Complex transformation of observations	5.8%
Consideration of methodological flaws	44.2%
Developing theories and mechanisms	23.1%
Multiple studies of the same type	61.5%
Multiple studies of different types	9.6%
Studying expert research reports	100 %

The Student Inquiry Program allows students to develop a proposal, perform a long-term investigation, present their findings to faculty and classmates, and write up a formal scientific report.

Acknowledgments

We greatly thank all of the IMSA staff and students for participation in the Inquiry Program over the past five years. We thank Rich Shavelson for his discussion of assessment and Ray Dagenais for critically reading our manuscript.

References

Agarwal, P. 2001. If I could make a school. *Learning and Leading with Technology*. 29 (3): 28–41.

Chinn, C. A., and B. A. Malhotra. 2002. Epistemologically authentic inquiry in schools: A theoretical framework for evaluating inquiry tasks. *Science Education* 86 (2): 175–218.

Illinois Mathematics and Science Academy. 1999. *IMSA's learning standards.* Aurora, IL: Illinois Mathematics and Science Academy.

Illinois Mathematics and Science Academy. 2000. *Student inquiry and research program*. Aurora, IL.: Illinois Mathematics and Science Academy.

Lederman, L. M., and J. A. Scheppler, eds. 2001. *Portraits of great american scientists.* New York: Prometheus Books.

Malina, P. and C. Young. 2002. Raise your hands for science. *Learning and Leading with Technology* 29 (8): 50–52.

Marbach-Ad, G. and P. G. Sokolove. 2000. Good science begins with good questions. *Journal of College Science Teaching* 30 (3): 192–195.

Marshall, S. P. 2002. The Illinois mathematics and science academy: A commitment to transformation. In *Science Literacy for the Twenty-first Century,* eds. J. Marshall, A. Scheppler, and M. J. Palmisano. Amherst, NY: Prometheus Books.

Minstrell, S. P., and E. H. van Zee, eds. 2000. *Inquiring into inquiry learning and teaching in science.* Washington, DC: American Association for the Advancement of Science.

National Research Council (NRC). 1996. *National science education standards.* Washington, DC: National Academy Press.

National Research Council (NRC). 2000. *Inquiry and the national science education standards.* Washington, DC: National Academy Press.

Scheppler, J. A., N. Sethakorn, and S. Styer. 2003. A modification of the Kirby-Bauer disc diffusion assay for inquiry in the science classroom. *The Science Teacher*.

Teacher Action Research on Interactive Lectures:

Engaging *All* Students in Verbal Give-and-Take

Ruth Trimarchi
Amherst Regional High School

Brenda Capobianco
Purdue University

Setting

Amherst Regional High School is a public school located within a five-college community in western Massachusetts. There are close to 1,400 students in the high school, 71% of whom are White, 10.2% African American, 9.9% Asian, 7.5% Hispanic, and 1% Native American. About 24 different first languages are spoken. Approximately 16% of the high school students are on the federal free and reduced lunch program. There is also a middle school of 700 students, and four elementary schools serving an additional 2,200 students.

Standards

Interactive lectures meet some of the *More Emphasis* conditions in each of the four standards. Specifically, in the Science Teaching Standards the techniques developed here increase a teacher's ability to

- understand and respond to individual student's interests, strengths, experiences, and needs;
- select and adapt curriculum (based on the above enhanced understanding);
- focus on student understanding and use of scientific knowledge, ideas and inquiry process; and

- continuously assess student understanding.

While the teaching standards call for *Less Emphasis* on lecture, this pedagogical tool remains an important part of science classes, and the techniques discussed in Interactive Lectures solidly meet the standard to guide students in active and extended scientific inquiry.

In the Professional Development Standards, the techniques developed here increase a teacher's emphasis on

- inquiry into teaching and learning;
- the teacher as an intellectual, reflective practitioner;
- the teacher as a producer of knowledge about teaching; and
- the teacher as a source and facilitator of change.

In the Assessment Standards the techniques developed here increase the ability of a teacher to

- assess scientific understanding and reasoning of her students;
- allow students to engage in an ongoing assessment of their work and that of others.

In the Science Content and Inquiry Standards the techniques developed here increase students'

- understanding of scientific concepts and abilities of inquiry;
- implementing inquiry as instructional strategies, abilities, and ideas to be learned;
- activities that investigate and analyze science questions;
- using evidence and strategies for developing or revising an explanation;
- exploring science as argument and explanation;
- applying the results of experiments to scientific arguments and explanations; and
- public communication of student ideas and work to classmates.

By consistently implementing Interactive Lecture techniques in the classroom, the teacher can better meet the NSES goals to educate students who can

- experience the richness and excitement of understanding the natural world;
- use appropriate scientific principles in making personal decisions; and
- engage intelligently in public discourse and debate about matters of scientific and technological concern.

Most of the work outlined in this document springs from a course on Collaborative action research (Car). Conducting *action research* allows teachers to develop changes that measurably benefit students. However, sharing this research with other practitioners (*Collaborative* action research) has proven itself an effective vehicle (hence a Car) for reflecting on *why* these changes are beneficial to students, and so for continuing to develop new ideas.

Car has profoundly changed the way I teach. I now not only implement interactive lecture techniques regularly, but continue to use the Car approach to explore, reflect upon, and critically analyze my teaching practice. My students understand that I am continually refining the curriculum to best meet their needs, and that I ask for and gratefully receive their requests for specific changes. This pedagogical dialogue between teacher and students is a quiet undercurrent to the actual content of the courses.

The National Science Education Standards call for *Less Emphasis* on "presenting scientific knowledge through lecture," and *More Emphasis* on "guiding students in active and extended scientific inquiry." The techniques to be presented here show that these need not be mutually exclusive goals.

While it is important that teachers use a wide array of tools to engage students in active learning, lecture continues to be widely used in science classes. It has been said that teachers like to use lecture because it is a familiar teaching tool for us, and because we don't like to learn new tricks, such as student-centered investigative activities. In less than a decade "lecture" has become a four-letter word! However, there are important reasons why teachers steadfastly employ lecture for at least a portion of many classes: the information given out is accurate (student presentations sometimes are not, and it can be difficult to interrupt and clarify misconceptions at that point); concepts are clearly and thoroughly presented; and students are all learning the same curriculum at the same time. Investigative projects often allow students to become "experts" in one area, but diminish the breadth of the curriculum that students can examine. If students are asked to research one area in a unit and teach it to others, each group seems to learn its area well, but other areas only marginally. Teachers need to ensure that a solid curriculum is mastered by all students. In short, lecture continues to be used by teachers everywhere because it is highly effective. The question becomes, how can this effective pedagogical tool be improved so that students find lectures personally engaging, challenging, and helpful to them in retaining concepts?

Interactive lectures was first put forth in "Drawing Out the Quiet Voices" (Trimarchi 2002). Interactive lectures are defined as "a method of conveying concepts, ideas, facts, and information that invites—and sometimes demands—active learning by students. Any technique that can momentarily slow down the pace, and thereby increase student participation in a lecture, without significantly lengthening the time needed to cover a unit of material, is an interactive lecture." (Trimarchi, p. 32). The idea was further developed in a workshop: "Short Activities to Accompany Interactive Lectures," presented at the NSTA Convention in Philadelphia in March 2003. Examples of interactive lecture techniques follow, but the reader is encouraged to develop additional techniques based on the definition above.

While most students need some help in learning through lecture, a driving force behind development of these interactive lecture techniques was the observation that certain groups of students are too often quiet during lectures. While there were many exceptions, low-income students, students of color, second-language learners, and girls in science classes seemed frequently marginalized during lectures. A series of anonymous surveys drew out specific reasons why each of these groups found lecture a difficult way to learn: students from economically disadvantaged backgrounds say they find even the nonscience vocabulary of lectures unfamiliar; students of color say that cultural differences may make analogies useless; ESL students say they frequently struggle with the rapid pace of a lecture; and girls say they are sometimes intimidated by the seemingly greater familiarity that boys have with the content at hand (Trimarchi, p. 31). All of the students surveyed showed a need to learn how to access learning during lectures. Since students will continue to encounter lectures throughout their academic careers, it is imperative that they become comfortable with this teaching technique.

How to Turn a Standard Podium Lecture into an Interactive Lecture

Since all of these techniques demand personal accountability by students listening to a lecture, it keeps each student engaged and focused.

Reflective Responses

During an interactive lecture the teacher can increase the odds that quieter students will participate if she increases the "wait time" in one way or another. During reflective responses the teacher frequently asks students to write a response to a thoughtful question directly in their notebooks. For example, following a lecture segment contrasting Darwinian and Lamarckian theories of evolution, the teacher asks students to design an experiment that would test first one then the other theory. Students will come up with suggestions, such as dyeing rabbits' tails blue and breeding them to look for inheritance of acquired characteristics, and checking bird populations in a year following a significant change in their food source to look at survival of the fittest. Writing out their answers before they speak allows students to practice what they want to say before running the risk of speaking in front of their peers. If the teacher walks around and looks over students' shoulders while they write, this will additionally allow her to call on quiet students whom she knows have good answers.

Quick Check-Ins

This has become my favorite interactive lecture technique. Periodically hand out slips of paper during a lecture and ask students to write answers to a probing question directly related to the lecture. Tell students not to write their names on the slips. Give students a few minutes to focus their thoughts, write, and then collect the slips. Immediately begin to scan the paper slips and read aloud examples of correct answers, as well as examples of misconceptions. Since the writings are anonymous, this reduces student stress when they hear their idea either complimented or corrected. This is a risk-free way for students to assess their understanding of the lecture as it progresses, as well as to hear a wide variety of their peers' ideas concerning a single pithy question.

Teacher Letter

Prepare a fill-in-the-blank letter that reads: "Dear Teacher, Here is what I understood to be the MAIN IDEA of today's class; these are a few *important points* I learned about this main idea; and these are things you talked about today that *I did not get*." Use a full page, leaving plenty of space for students to write responses to each of the three statements. Hand these blank letters out in the last five minutes of class following a lecture, and tell students they may use their notes to write responses. Have them sign and date the letters, read them for your own homework, and begin class the next day by reading selected responses. With this technique, the teacher knows who needs help with what, but the students' responses are still anonymous to their peers.

The Morning After (or Lecture Leftovers)

How to enhance continuity in a series of unit lectures: The day after a particularly challenging lecture, it can be useful to ask students to take a few minutes while the teacher takes attendance and finishes other starting business, to write a summary of the previous day's lecture. Allow students to use their lecture notes. Call on a frequently quiet student to begin the summary. Follow this by asking if there is more to be said about yesterday's lecture. Pick up on the last student's response to segue into the new day's lecture, or weave together comments each student makes to build a launch pad for the new day's lecture.

No-Count Quizzes

When you feel students may have missed some of a lecture, design a short quiz with a few key questions to start class the next day. Write the questions on the board or overhead. Tell the students that it's a No-Count Pop Quiz, but walk around while they are writing their answers. Read over their shoulders as they write to determine who has a good answer to each question (and to be sure they're taking you seriously and not writing love notes!). Call on these students to contribute answers, compliment them, and allow time for everyone to write down "good" answers to these key lecture questions.

Example: What is the Hereditary Material, Protein, or DNA?

This interactive lecture is a variation on the spontaneous use of reflective responses and quick check-ins above, and instead has a preset series of questions and overheads to accompany them. The goal is to present students with descriptions of classical experiments in molecular biology and ask them to predict the outcomes; then ask them to analyze the results scientists obtained to the experiments and draw their own conclusions about the experiments. This challenges students to consider data in the same way that scientists do, and to try their hand at concisely writing an appropriate conclusion without claiming that an experiment shows more than it actually does.

Question series (students are to write responses in their notebooks to each of these questions, along with taking notes on the lecture): Remind students that Darwin speculated that there had to be some way for hereditary information from parent organisms to be transferred to their offspring but he did not know what it was. Remind them also that while most students today know that this hereditary information is DNA, scientists had to conduct a long series of experiments to discover this. Ask them to temporarily suspend their knowledge of this fact and put their minds back to an earlier era so that they can follow this line of scientific reasoning.

Question #1: Since scientists knew that DNA is made of four building blocks (ATGC nucleotides), and protein is made of twenty building blocks (the twenty common amino acids), which of these two molecules—DNA or protein—do you think most scientists predicted was most likely to encode information for building and running a living organism? Explain your reasoning. (Students write a response in their notebooks.)

Teacher's Task: Present an overhead, illustrating Frederick Griffith's classic 1928 experiment series demonstrating that a "transforming molecule," passed between strains of Streptococcus pneumoniae bacteria, could change benign into lethal bacteria, resulting in the death of infected mice.

Question #2: How can you explain Griffith's results? (Students write a response in their notebooks.)

Teacher's Task: Next present an overhead of Avery, MacLeod, and McCarty's classic 1944 experiment, using the cell extract DNA alone to repeat Griffith's experiments.

Question #3: What can you conclude from this experiment? (Students write a response in their notebooks.)

Teacher's Task: Finally, explain the phage lifecycle and present an overhead of Hershey and Chase's 1952 experiments, showing that when bacterial viruses (bacteriophages) infect and subsequently transform a bacterial cell, only the DNA enters while the viral protein coat remains outside.

Question #4: Based on your knowledge of the phage life cycle, and of DNA and protein chemical composition—i.e., that DNA can take up radioactive phosphorous and protein can take up radioactive sulfur—what would you predict the outcome of this experiment was? Alternatively, if students have trouble making this leap, ask, "Where do you think each of these radioactive molecules will be found—inside or outside of cells?" (Students write a response in their notebooks.)

Whether through a standard or an interactive lecture, most students can reach an understanding that DNA carries hereditary information. However, students always far prefer being drawn into these experiments by being asked to reason as these scientists did, rather than by listening to a standard lecture on these discoveries. Additionally, they are gaining practice in analytical reasoning in a "brains-on" way.

Short Activities to Accompany Interactive Lectures
Short activities to punctuate interactive lectures allow the teacher to change the choreography enough to maintain student interest, but still keep all students focused on the same curriculum at the same time.

Analyzing Cartoon Differences
This can be used early in the year to introduce the idea of observation as the first step of the scientific method. Collect and laminate cartoon puzzles of the type that asks you to find several differences between two or more nearly identical pictures. Word-find puzzles can also work. You will need one for each student in the class, so prepare 30 or so to allow for loss.

Have each student pick up one puzzle as s/he enters the room. As the class is getting settled, let students examine these puzzles and try to solve them. (Solutions can be pasted onto the back of the puzzles).

Allow students to discuss what they were doing as they tried to solve the puzzles. After they explain that they had to look carefully at the puzzles to solve them, tell them that observation is the first step in the scientific method. Explain that careful observation of differences and similarities (Step #1: Observation), often lead scientists to reflect on the patterns seen (Step #2: Hypothesis), eventually perhaps to perform some tests (Step #3: Experiment), and finally to understand something about the initial observation (Step #4: Draw Conclusions). It is the careful attention to patterns, and differences in patterns, that is the first step of the scientific method mimicked in this short activity. Let students know that they will be called upon to make careful observations while doing experiments all year long.

Yardstick Beaks

This is a great icebreaker to introduce the idea of adaptation of the fittest in an evolution unit. Ask for two volunteers. Give one student two yardsticks and the other a pair of tongs. Place a pile of markers, pens, and pencils on a bench or desk, and two one-liter beakers on each side of the pile. Tell the students that they are birds, the markers, pens, and pencils are their food, the yardsticks or tongs are their beaks, and the beakers represent their mouths. Give them a set amount of time to "eat," and ask the class to interpret what they see happening. Occasionally, examples of altruism or cheating arise, which add to the discussion of adaptive advantages.

Then ask the class to imagine what the outcome would be if the area became flooded desk-high with water, and fish swimming underfoot were their food source. A long-beaked bird that could scoop or stab a fish would perhaps have the advantage over one with a short beak, even a tong beak, in this newly changed environment. Students readily see that what is a liability in one environment can become a selective advantage in another.

Word Splash

This technique (credit to Suzanne Panico) can be used in an early lecture of a unit to give definitions of science vocabulary while probing what students already know about a topic.

Write a key word, such as "photosynthesis," or "cloning," in the center of the board. Ask students to call out words related to this topic and write them on the board "in a splash" around the central word. Then ask students to choose three of the words and write the best sentence they can for each of them. Sometimes the words can be clustered and assigned to small groups of students. As they read their sentences aloud, ask for discussion, and correct misconceptions along the way. All students' work need not be read aloud; the point is to draw out what students already understand, or perhaps misunderstand, to lay the groundwork for your lecture, which follows this short activity. Refer back to individual student's contributions from this preliminary discussion as you subsequently lecture on this topic.

Listen Carefully, Then Write

When introducing a complex topic, such as the nature of the gene, ask students to put down their pens for five minutes while you just tell them about what they'll be studying. Let them get the "lay of the land." Then ask them to try to recall as much as they can about what you've said and write about it for five minutes. Let them discuss their writing with other students sometimes before addressing questions that the writing activity produced.

Evidence

One piece of data to support my contention that interactive lectures increase student participation is a self-assessment by students of their participation before and after six weeks of interactive lectures (Trimarchi 2002, p.34). Results of this self-assessment show that all students—including specific subgroups of ESL students, girls, students of color, and low-income students—said that they participate more often in interactive lectures as contrasted with standard lectures.

A second piece of data was collected by an independent observer recording each response students made during both standard and interactive lectures. The observer sat in the back of the room with a blank seating chart. She noted each time that a student spoke and coded the type of response they gave in each blank square of the seating chart. The observer used this key:

1. Student gave *a one-word answer* when called on.
2. Student gave *a simple answer* when called on.
3. Student asked *a simple question.*
4. Student offered *an insightful answer.*
5. Student asked *an insightful question.*

Responses 1, 2, and 3 are considered low quality responses; 4 and 5 are considered high quality responses.

The observer followed the same class of 24 students for six days, including three standard lectures, followed by two interactive lectures, and then one final standard lecture. The class averaged 10.5 responses/day during the four standard lectures, and 25.5 responses/day during the two interactive lectures. More importantly, the *quality* of responses improved, with zero high quality responses during standard lectures and an average of 11.5 high quality responses/day during interactive lectures. (See Figures 1 and 2.) Together, these assessments indicate that both the frequency and quality of student participation during lectures increases with the consistent use of interactive lectures.

Note: By necessity, this data was collected in the beginning of the school year, when an independent observer was available for six days. As students became more comfortable with interactive lectures their responses increased in both frequency and quality. It is now May and nearly all of these same students routinely participate in interactive lectures on a daily basis.

Figure 1.

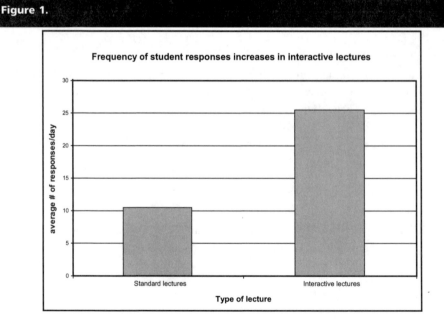

Frequency of student responses increases in interactive lectures

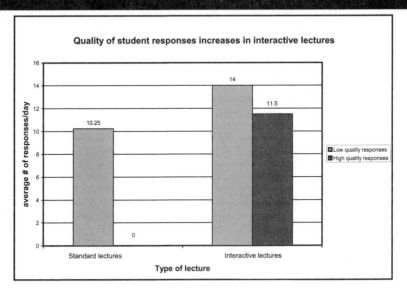

Figure 2.

Quality of student responses increases in interactive lectures

This writer believes that while interactive lectures provide a highly effective and engaging way for students to learn, lecture by itself is insufficient for engaging students. Teachers must also use long-term hands-on projects. One example of a long-term project involves exploring a single concept in biology (namely, that all living things change) is outlined in a photography project detailed in the article "Life is Change" (Trimarchi 2003). One way to challenge students to defend their scientific understanding in public is highlighted in the article "Says Who" (Trimarchi 2002), in which students take their opinions regarding an environmental proposal to an actual Town. These articles provide a variety of instructional approaches to supplement lectures and offer additional ways to support and enhance students' participation in the science classroom. In addition to these two examples, an avalanche of investigative activities for high school science teachers to explore arrives each month in *The Science Teacher.*

References

Banner, J., and H. Cannon. 1997. *The elements of teaching*. New Haven and London: Yale University Press.

Capobianco, B. 2001. *Making science accessible for all students through collaborative science teacher action research*.

Capobianco, B., R. Horowitz, D. Canuel-Browne, and R. Trimarchi. 2004. Action research for teachers. *The Science Teacher,* 71 (3): 48–53

Dewey, J. 1944. *Democracy and education*. New York: The Free Press.

Gardner, H. 1999. *The disciplined mind*. London and New York: Penguin Books.

Goleman, D. 1995. *Emotional intelligence*. New York, Toronto, London, Sydney, Auchland: Bantam Books.

Joyce, B., M. Weil, and E. Calhoun. 2000. *Models of teaching*. Needham Heights, MA: Allyn and Bacon.

National Research Council (NRC). 1996. *National science education standards*. Washington DC: National Academy Press.

Schlechty, P. 2001. *Shaking up the schoolhouse*. Hoboken, NJ: Jossey-Bass.

Trimarchi, R. 2002. Drawing out the quiet voices. *The Science Teacher,* 69 (1): 30–34.

Trimarchi, R. 2002. Says who? *The Science Teacher,* 69 (5): 45–47.

Trimarchi, R. 2003. Life is change. *The Science Teacher,* 70 (5): 28–31.

Stop Talking, Start Listening:

Turning Didactic Science Teaching on Its Head

Peter Veronesi
State University of New York

Karl Biedlingmaier
Churchville-Chili High School

What does education often do? It makes a straight-cut ditch of a free, meandering brook.
—*Henry David Thoreau*

Introduction

It could easily be argued that a visitor to most science classrooms today would see a science teacher at the front of a room, with students sitting in rows, listening and writing notes. Didactic modes of teaching keep a strong foothold in public education, due to such factors as the inertia of an outdated system, to assessments that do not match the critical analysis encouraged by reform movements, or to the myriad other barriers to teaching and learning science in the most effective ways. This work hopes to demonstrate how one chemistry teacher looked at his teaching behaviors, at reform movements aimed toward increased critical thinking, and who then set about changing his actions as a science teacher.

In this chapter, we hope to illustrate science instruction that focuses on real-world problems and features the science teacher performing a variety of research-based strategies during any given teaching segment (See Figure 1, page 137).

It is a major goal of this chapter to describe how a relatively new chemistry teacher is able to focus on and achieve almost every National Science Education Standards (NSES) *More Emphasis* tenet while drastically moving away from the *Less Emphasis* aspects of science teaching. Specifically, this chapter will attempt to explain how students solve their own real-world chemistry problems with the advent of what we will call the SLICK: Student Led Investigations in Chemical Knowledge.

Because effective science teaching is a fluid and complex endeavor, it is difficult at best to portray the described teaching methods and teacher/student actions in graphic or text form. However, if compared to a classic vision, it is hoped that a reasonable understanding of the methods of teaching described in this chapter can be achieved.

Research-Based Rationale

Learning theory supports the idea that people learn differently (Bransford 2000). The differentiated instruction movement supports the concept of offering various methods of instruction to maximize learning by all students (Burke 1985, Tomlinson 1996). These authors have provided a fantastic base that supports a student-centered method of instruction.

Brainstorming, cooperative learning, demonstration, guided practice, inquiry, instructional technology, memorization, note-taking/graphic organizers, presentations, exhibitions, problem-based learning, project design, research, Socratic seminar, teacher questions, work-based learning, and yes, lecture—these are all well-defined teaching methods for various objectives and learning styles (ICLE 2000). Integrating these teaching methods (particularly student-led inquiry) in a meaningful way to help the greatest number of students is the primary goal of this project.

The National Science Education Standards and Project 2061 make it clear that research supports inquiry-based projects to increase student learning in a subject area. Inquiry-based projects allow students to propose questions and to investigate those questions through experimental design and literature research (NRC 1996; AAAS 1994).

A large problem associated with inquiry-based projects in the classroom is the time needed for the students to design and complete the experiments. It is hardly fair to ask students to inquire about a natural phenomenon, and then tell them when they can inquire about it. The very nature of inquiry is open-ended, and so students are allowed to design their own laboratory work.

In a practical sense, students may choose an investigation that might take five consecutive class periods of set-up and data collection. Other students may choose projects that require data collection that only takes a few moments, but need to take that data on a weekly basis for three months. In thinking about integrating a full-inquiry project, it didn't take long to realize that a traditional course design would not allow an appropriate level of freedom for student inquiry design.

Setting

Churchville-Chili High School is a suburban school southwest of Rochester, New York that serves grades 10–12. The graduating class is typically 400 students. Regents chemistry is an optional course generally taken after Earth Science and Living Environment courses. The class represented in this chapter has a population that is generally about 40% sophomores, 40% juniors, and 20% seniors. Class size is limited to twenty-four students, but the average is much closer to twenty-two. Classes are blocked in a four-day rotation so that students have a great deal more time to focus on real science study. These chemistry students have the opportunity to learn in the context of two 85-minute meetings and one 40-minute meeting during a four-day cycle.

> *"From my experiences with colleagues around the state, I have found that most science teachers must go through radical personal belief changes toward teaching and learning science for a classroom with* More Emphasis *tenets to be incorporated. For example, the science teacher must change from saying, 'I can't do this in my classroom!' to ' I can't wait to try this in my classroom.' "*

— Karl Biedlingmaier

Figure 1. A visitor's observation on any given day in two very different science classrooms. This graphic compares teacher and student positions and actions in a typical 50-minute period.

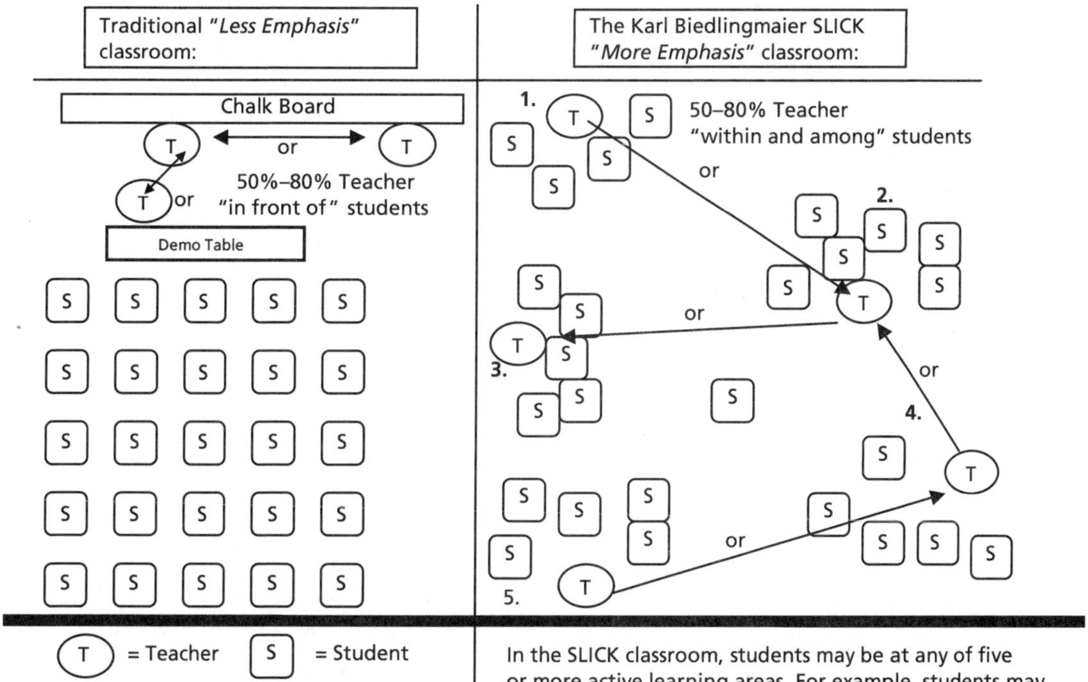

Traditional *"Less Emphasis"* classroom:

The Karl Biedlingmaier SLICK *"More Emphasis"* classroom:

Chalk Board

50%–80% Teacher "in front of" students

Demo Table

1. 50–80% Teacher "within and among" students

or

2.

3.

4.

5.

T = Teacher   S = Student

The *Less Emphasis* classroom traditionally has the science teacher-as-lecturer model. The "one" who holds the knowledge to be given to the students in the fastest, most efficient manner. Students are mostly passive.

In the SLICK classroom, students may be at any of five or more active learning areas. For example, students may simultaneously be (1) at a previously recorded, videotaped lecture about a chemistry concept, (2) on the internet, (3) pulling out support challenge problems or doing labs, (4) be involved in a mini lecture with <5 students, or (5) holding a one-on-one conversation with the teacher. No matter what learning situation the students involve themselves with, the teacher is free to venture there and hold informal discussions. Trust, high expectations, and informal structure rule the day.

Meeting the Conditions of *More Emphasis*

In this section, we address how four goals of the monograph are achieved:

1. Experience the richness and excitement of knowing about and understanding the natural world;
2. Use appropriate scientific processes and principles in making personal decisions;
3. Engage intelligently in public discourse and debate about matters of scientific and technological concern; and
4. Increase their economic productivity through the use of the knowledge, understanding, and skills of the scientifically literate person in their careers.

Discussion of More Emphasis 1

Anything related to the SLICK program automatically deals with understanding of the natural world. As an example, Jenny's work is shown here. It includes an example of a serendipitous discovery and the excitement that comes from it. A major goal and purpose of SLICK is to meet the objective of richness and excitement.

Jenny's Discovery. The SLICK Project in Chemistry involved choosing a topic that interested me. After racking my brain for an idea, I remembered the Crayola markers that you could use to write secret messages in, and then discover what was written by using a colored "decoder" marker. I decided to do invisible ink. After getting a feel for what the project was really about, my topic changed to disappearing ink. For the experiments, I wanted to answer several questions: What is it made out of? How does it disappear? Can I make disappearing ink? (Even though at that point I had no recipe to make it.) The first two questions were connected to the third, because I thought that if I was able to answer the first two they could help me in answering the third. I discovered that the air affected the disappearing ink, not the light. To discover the components, I tried to perform chromatography. After several unsuccessful experiments, I discovered that the carbon dioxide in the air was causing the change in color, from blue to colorless. From there I discovered that the disappearing ink that was bought from the store was actually a combination of a base and an indicator. From there, I was able to experiment to make my own disappearing ink.

Discussion of More Emphasis 2

The SLICK is to be designed by the student in such a way that they make all of their future decisions based on their previous evidence and data. Since they have the results of one experiment, they decide what the next experiment will be, based on these results. They are not forced in any direction by the teacher. Rather, they move in a direction that evolves from their initial question and the resulting data they produce (i.e., Nature of Science). Typically, it is viewed by the teacher as the choose-your-own adventure books of the 1980s, where the reader decided what was to happen next and then proceeded to a specific page based on that decision. Thus, many people could read the same book and end up reading vastly different stories. In concurrent years, two students in different classes started with the same basic idea or concept, but after one or two experiments they ended up in totally different places with different conclusions. It is indeed hoped that the processes involved in doing the SLICKs will lead each student to better understand events in their own lives, both in and out of school, and act on these events from an informed, scientifically literate, point of view.

Discussion of More Emphasis 3

Public discussion and debate is closely associated with Phase II of the course. That is, students routinely discuss their work with classmates at appropriate times. While there is no formal science conference constructed, there are many times available when students address each other in small group settings where they share information and obtain constructive feedback from their peers. For example, students debate over "how to do something" or "which way is best" to solve the problems associated with the next question. In piloting the various phases of this course structure, this "constructive sharing" is a much more formal part of the class. Formal presentation in a large group setting is avoided, as these events tend to lead to bored students.

The best debate was found to occur between groups of peers who watched each other work. For example, one student asked, "Why do Rice Krispies snap, crackle, and pop?" This question put four teenagers together to see where they could take that one question. Arguments ensued over equipment (beakers, or bowls if we want to simulate real life) what type of milk, the temperature of the milk, the age of the Rice Krispies, etc. These informal discussions are most rich and age appropriate, and they cause deep thinking. And, while they do not involve the entire class, the small group debates focus attention on analytical thinking.

Discussion of More Emphasis 4

Students involved with SLICKs gain time-management skills and practice in learning how to learn. Phase II of the course allows students the freedom to design their own learning based on course objectives. Students are not forced to follow the schedule of the teacher; rather, they are strongly encouraged to develop their own. They must also figure out how to overcome difficult problems with resources, since they are not handed a set of directions as a road map to begin. Ironically, many students have initial difficulties with the opened-ended nature of the course, which causes some frustration because most have never been asked to frame an original scientific question or idea for themselves.

The students who are likely to go farther are those who can think and plan for themselves. Those who commonly wait to be told to do something (or memorize something) need the most support in planning an appropriately designed SLICK by the next day. Even when students are not successful in initial attempts at SLICK design, they learn from their failures. A student who classically procrastinates or doesn't look at the objectives knows quickly what he or she must do to be successful. They know the feeling of not planning ahead, and they know the feeling of success when they do plan ahead. Their life in the chemistry classroom becomes the nature of science itself as they begin to ask, "What did I do right that worked?" "What did I do wrong?" "What can I improve upon?" and "What should I do next?"

Unique Features of SLICK Teaching: Specifics of Meeting More Emphasis Criteria with Student Led Investigations for Chemical Knowledge

Figure 2. Teacher-Constructed Views on More Emphasis Tenets

Following are excerpts from an interview with Karl Biedlingmaier, the chemistry teacher, whereby he gives his constructed views about the relevant changing emphasis tenets as they fit his SLICK course structure. Karl views some of the reform-oriented tenets as redundant and envisions many as being woven together and inseparable. That said, it is hoped that the reader begins to gain a good picture into this classroom so that each of the More Emphasis tenets are achieved.

The National Science Education Standards envision change throughout the system. The **teaching standards** encompass the following changes in emphases:

MORE EMPHASIS ON

Understanding and responding to individual student's interests, strengths, experiences, and needs: My goal is to help the kids identify for themselves the best way each one learns best. I try to provide a range of opportunities and tools for the students to decide and pick the way that is most effective for them.

Selecting and adapting curriculum: I begin with a set of what our teaching team has determined to be the minimum amount of the main chemistry concepts that we feel are import for students to comprehend. The concepts are totally interwoven in the way I teach so it really doesn't make sense to follow a rigid order. If a student needs the gas laws, we work on that objective; if osmotic concepts are needed, we work on that area, and so on. It works much better to put the conceptual order in the hands of the learner. In talking to them, I get to know each and I can suggest direction.

Focusing on student understanding and use of scientific knowledge, ideas, and inquiry processes: The SLICK inquiries give students many opportunities to use the processes of science in ways that have meaning for them because the initial idea for the inquiry is theirs to begin with. "Scientific Method" is typically taught as a unified piece of knowledge. We give the various "methods" that scientists use. Students make observations that are real to them and work them into a question for study. I think they carry away the knowledge of the various processes they use more so than the actual findings. They see the many twists and turns they have to go through and when they read about a discovery in the paper or hear it on the news, they will know how much work went into getting that piece of knowledge. They become more scientifically literate.

Guiding students in active and extended scientific inquiry: When students feel they have a need for information, they become interested in learning. For example, with the learning cycle in mind, it makes little sense to say, "This is Charles' Law," or "This is Boyle's Law," before the student has had an opportunity to explore the concept first hand. After they have messed about with a piston, they can go to the text and apply a term to the observation they just made. The notion of extended guided inquiry is the entire nature of the SLICK and the content that is pertinent to each inquiry becomes learned in a meaningful way.

Providing opportunities for scientific discussion and debate among students: There are students who are so listen. They are typically what most would call the "best" students, highly verbal and great at memorizing facts. These students are good at telling back to the teacher what the teacher told them. It is a very easy circle to fall into. It takes no work on the part of the student and they can spit back anything. The majority of students cannot do this. When I begin to listen to students talk to each other I begin to hear the understandings or misunderstandings they have. I can hear and see them using the scientific information in a meaningful way. As we do the SLICK inquiries, we will have three or four running simultaneously. When one student has a problem, we call around to a few students who are nearby to ask them what is happening and how they might help solve the problem. For example, one student was trying to distill Gatorade into its constituent parts. He said, "Well, since materials keep their physical properties within a mixture, why don't I boil off all the water first? Then, I'll deal with separating whatever is left over." Water boils at 100 degrees C and sugar decomposes at 80 degrees C. As soon as the water disappeared, he immediately had charcoal at the bottom of the pan. One student suggested getting the water out by vacuum pump. When I think about that idea I hear application of scientific knowledge and understanding. That student was thinking about vapor pressure and I heard it. That potential solution to the problem didn't work, so he eventually decided to spread the Gatorade over a large area and evaporate the water at room temperature over a long period of time. The concept of surface area had been suggested by yet another student. This wasn't one student struggling by himself, this was a team of students discussing the problem in real time.

Continuously assessing student understanding: While I have end-of-unit assessments that are fairly traditional (multiple choice, short answer, etc.), these pencil-and-paper exams alone would not show me the variety of what they can do. I count a great deal on verbal assessment. Since I spend the majority of my time listening instead of talking, I get a very good picture into the thinking of each of my students. Listening to many is something you simply cannot do if you are lecturing to the class on a daily basis. Some kids do well on tests and others do poorly—despite what they know or what we think they know. The tragedy is when the state requires only the traditional testing system.

Sharing responsibility for learning with students: Since teachers aren't usually given ample time to plan, they have to make decisions that save them time. When I lay out the objectives, I let them choose the direction, the resources that are going to work best for them, and define an appropriate time frame to work through the objectives.

Supporting a classroom community with cooperation, shared responsibility, and respect: The nature of my classroom as I have described in this chapter inherently supports these aspects of a classroom community.

Working with other teachers to enhance the science program: Because of the way my classroom is structured, I seek other teachers out in my building on a regular basis. For example, last week one of the students began a SLICK design around taking pictures. That student was directed to the art teacher who teaches photography in our building. She looked at all the chemicals that were needed to take a picture, how a stopper works, etc. I couldn't have done that, but now the student knows about the process and the chemicals involved because she went to the expert and learned. Other students have worked with the biology teacher, and I have worked with biology students.

The National Science Education Standards envision change throughout the system. **The science content and inquiry standards*** encompass the following changes in emphases:

MORE EMPHASIS ON
(* The nature of the SLICK inquiries was designed with each of these in mind.)

Understanding scientific concepts and developing abilities of inquiry; Learning subject matter disciplines in the context of inquiry, technology, science in personal and social perspectives, and history and nature of science: Since students choose their own questions for each SLICK, they have immediate buy-in. Each SLICK usually has a strong link to the social perspectives of the students. Virtually none of them enjoy doing chemistry for its own sake. I have a student right now who is trying to make connections between athletic performance and the use of Gatorade. As this particular student delves more deeply into the question, more and more variables arise that he has to address. In doing so, he is getting the picture of the convoluted nature of science and how it does not always follow a prescribed method as it is portrayed in most texts.

Integrating all aspects of science content: During SLICK inquires, students often integrate two or more other areas of science. They are guided in various directions and they find the connections themselves. Different branches of science end up in all their projects.

Studying a few fundamental science concepts: Bonding is a major concept. Atomic stability is a big concept. These are a few examples of the topics chosen for each unit. Students focus their attention on these major concepts, as well as related sub-concepts during the course.

Implementing inquiry as instructional strategies, abilities, and ideas to be learned: The SLICK is the implementation of all of these things.

Activities that investigate and analyze science questions: Verification labs with students trying to arrive at a known answer is not an analysis of a scientific question. There is little thinking required of the student. The SLICKs are designed in such a way that the question encourages creative thinking, problem-solving, and use of good scientific technique to discover an unknown answer.

Investigations over extended periods of time: The SLICK's flexibility provides the opportunity for investigations of varying lengths, decided by the student.

Process skills in context: We do have students run through skill-oriented labs so they can have that skill as a tool to understand the processes involved in their SLICK. I have a student now that has done aspirin studies, and she has mastered titration. She can tell you a lot about buffers and antacid solutions. When titration is only taught out of the context of an interesting inquiry understanding is quickly lost.

Using evidence and strategies for developing or revising an explanation: Students ask each other if the evidence they are getting is pointing them in a reasonable direction.

Science as argument and explanation; and communicating science explanations; groups of students often analyzing and synthesizing data after defending conclusions: Students are always talking to each other in supportive ways and questioning the outcomes of various trials that they observe. I make sure that they are able to explain the science concepts that are related to their study. Small group presentations among students who have similar interests elicit meaningful questions and a comfortable exchange of information at the peer level.

Doing more investigations in order to develop understanding, ability, values of inquiry and knowledge of science content: My class is set up so that a student can go to the lab and work on their inquiry every day. The resources are available for them to do all the content work outside of class. No actual classroom time is dedicated to teaching content. Since students are responsible for their own learning in each unit they are free to do all the hands-on they feel they need. Some students move on along with very little teacher attention.

Applying the results of experiments to scientific arguments and explanations: The result of one SLICK leads into the next one. Students are required to do at least six interrelated SLICK inquiries. This is a direct application of results. This helps each student become more aware of chemistry within an everyday context.

Public communication of student ideas and work to classmates: I have found that students presenting ideas and findings to six or fewer of their interested peers seem to be an ideal form of communication. Students who are presenting are into it, and those who are listening are as well.

It is in fact nothing short of a miracle that the modern methods of instruction have not yet entirely strangled the wholly curious nature of inquiry. It is a very grave mistake to think that the enjoyment of seeing and searching can be promoted by means of coercion and a sense of duty.
—Albert Einstein

Experience has shown that most students have a negative psychological association with the term "project." Therefore, the name SLICK was chosen to avoid that negative connotation. A SLICK is a student-designed chemistry inquiry whereby students develop an initial question and design an investigation, including the literature analysis and experiment.

Students' questions often lead to more questions, and their investigations take them down roads they didn't plan to travel. The central notion of the SLICK, then, is to mirror the nature of science in as many ways as possible. The SLICK explicitly demonstrates that knowledge is tentative, that there is no single scientific method, that any results must be able to be argued, defended, and based on evidence, and that observations made must be repeatable and predictable.

SLICK Guidelines are given at the start of the investigation and students are required to keep a lab notebook and write a final report. A scoring rubric is also provided at the start of their SLICK. It is of major import that a significant amount of chemistry and related relevant science disciplines is incorporated into each SLICK design.

The integrated aspect of the SLICK course design limits the amount of time students spend passively learning and maximizes the time they spend actively doing science. National, state, and local science standards are directing teachers to provide students the opportunity for enriching experiences in meaningful scientific inquiry. "Scientific inquiry refers to the diverse ways in which scientists study the natural world and propose explanations based on the evidence derived from their work" (NRC 1996, p. 23). This notion reflects and has its genesis in the Nature Of Science. As stated by Lemke (1993), "Most conventional school and science curricula and the teaching practices that implement them offer students no firsthand working with science." These two themes provide the conceptual framework for this project. That is, to begin the journey of designing meaningful scientific inquiry for students while simultaneously reducing conventional or traditional science education.

While standards are calling for additional inquiry-based teaching and learning, end-of-the-year assessments have not changed to accommodate the standards. End-of-the-year assessments are still highly content- and fact-oriented. In short, they don't match inquiry learning. Therefore, the desire for inquiry-based teaching is often overcome by the requirements for high results on state assessments.

A typical New York State Regents Chemistry class includes several units of information provided to the students through lectures, demonstrations, and verification laboratory experiences. The students generally listen to the teacher a great percentage of the time, try some sample problems, then try to reproduce predetermined results in the lab by following teacher prescribed directions. The science teacher generally dictates the content, timing, and process of student learning for the entire class. Strong students are often bored, and weak students are often left behind. As tradition would hold, this model fits the *Less Emphasis* modes of science teaching.

Due to the open nature of inquiry-based science projects, students require freedom of time and learning style to master the concepts and processes of chemistry simultaneously. The course needs to be designed in a manner that maximizes student laboratory time, teacher flexibility, and student-directed learning, while minimizing lectures, passive student time, and cookbook labs.

To support a positive outcome to this project, a syllabus and support materials were designed that provide students twenty-five weeks of independent laboratory time and self-directed learning. The course contains three distinct phases, described below.

Phase I: Introductory Chemical Concepts and Inquiry Skills

Based on observations during the first few years of teaching this course, Phase I requires about fifteen weeks. Phase I helps students transition from their prior conceptions of a traditional science classroom to a student-led classroom. Students are introduced to Nature of Science (NOS) notions and practice skills they will need to complete their inquiry.

The school year begins with a semi-traditional method in which the class stays together while meeting the learning objectives our science team has deemed essential: the basic and fundamental concepts of chemistry. These objectives were decided upon with the collaboration of four Churchville-Chili chemistry teachers. The students are given these objectives on the first day of class as a relevant road map to follow. It also demystifies learning. The first portion of the course is designed to assist the students with a fairly detailed preliminary understanding of these basic chemistry concepts.

Safety

Safety is the responsibility of all students in the lab. Each day two students are assigned to the special duties of safety guard and clean-up guard. The safety guard watches the lab for safety violations and reports any to the teacher immediately. The clean-up guard announces when ten minutes are left in the period and then again when five minutes are remaining. Students are also reminded by the clean-up guard to clean up their space and put away all equipment before the end of the period. After completing Phase I of the course, students are able to work safely in the lab.

Inquiry

To teach a general yet more real understanding of chemical concepts, traditional skill-based labs are used, as well as a variety of other teaching strategies such as brainstorming, cooperative learning, and meaningful use of technology. During the Phase I of the course the students begin thinking of a question from the world of chemistry that they can investigate in the laboratory. This question is the genesis of their full-inquiry project.

The question development process is not easy for most students. Since they will investigate the question for four months, they are encouraged to pick a topic of genuine interest. Many students select a topic that is too difficult to investigate in a high school chemistry lab, so the role of the teacher in this case is one of monitoring for an achievable question. Other students select a question that is too easy and could be completed in a short time in the lab. The class peer reviews the questions from their classmates and help to refine each question. The teacher, at times, has to help a few students direct their questions to a level that can be investigated in the time and space available.

Phase	Time	Teacher's Roles/Responsibilities	Student's Roles/Responsibilities
I	15 Weeks (Sept.– Nov.)	• Provide objectives • Some lectures • Assist the students in asking a full inquiry investigatable question • Provide open ended laboratory experiences • Direct the flow of the course for the students	• Decide on a researchable question • Peer review other students' questions • Practice designing experiments • Follow the flow of the class
II	20 Weeks (Dec.– May)	• Provide Unit Objectives • Provide support for each Unit • Unit guides • Labs • 1:1 or small group tutoring • Video lessons • Assist students in the laboratory • Teacher does not lecture "live" except to small groups that need assistance • Provide deadlines and exam dates	• Design their own experiments related to SLICK • Review for the New York State Regents Exam • Design their own plan to meet the unit objectives (both in terms of time and method) • Peer review and assist classmates in the lab
III	2–4 Weeks (June)	• Provide a focused, unit by unit, review • Highly structured	

Phase II: Student Directed Course of Study and Student Led Investigations for Chemical Knowledge (SLICK)

Over the twenty-five weeks of Phase II, students perform their own inquiries. Students complete their SLICKs and self-directed studies during this time period. Future curriculum adjustments will likely result in Phase I being condensed even further, and Phase II becoming longer, thereby providing even more time for students to practice science.

During Phase II, students have three major tasks: to meet the chemistry learning objectives, complete the required skill-based labs, and complete a SLICK inquiry project. The SLICK laboratory experiences during Phase II are somewhat open-ended where the students must design procedures to obtain data and then interpret the data in a meaningful way. The students are usually not accustomed to the open-ended nature of this type of laboratory work. Thus the early process is teacher-intensive. These types of labs, best described as guided inquiry, allow the teacher the time to listen to and observe the students, and identify which students will need help during a full-inquiry project.

Students are empowered to take responsibility for their learning during Phase II. The students are given similar learning objectives for each new unit on the first day. The teacher supplies all necessary support materials, such as video-taped lectures, unit notes, textbook readings, worksheets, web references, videotaped demonstrations, and laboratory experiences with videotaped and PowerPoint pre-lab discussions and instructions. The students need an abundance of materials to choose from to meet the objectives of each chemistry unit. The support materials for this course design have been developed over a three-year period and are continuously being updated and improved.

While Phase II of the course requires the students to become self-directing learners, self-direction does not equate to self-teaching. Students select from the support materials and are encouraged to work until they feel comfortable with concepts within the unit. "Enough" is defined by the student and is often set by a period of trial and error where the students assess themselves on teacher provided practice tests to see how well each knows the material. Perhaps most important, they are not all encouraged to work with *all* of the support materials, but rather are encouraged to use the materials most conducive to their learning styles. The changing to *more emphases* here can be considered to be less breadth and much more depth, a focus on different learning styles, and a focus on self and alternative assessments.

Students are required to perform specified and traditional, yet meaningful, skill-based laboratory experiences before a known exam date. They must qualify for each exam by showing evidence of completion of labs and skill-based challenges. There are generally two to four labs per unit and a knowledge/process based exam. For example, titration is a skill which students need to understand and perform only if they need it for their SLICK. The students follow the instructions, practice the skill, and get help if needed. While it may seem far-fetched, students design their own use of class time and quickly learn that they cannot do all of the required work during class. As a result, they must design their own homework and time structure there as well.

While the students are working on the unit objectives in Phase II they are also working on their individualized SLICK inquiry investigation. Students must spend at least five hours in the laboratory during this investigation, although most spend many more. Students decide when they need to do specified laboratory work, provided their schedule is congruent with the school calendar. They can work every class meeting time for several weeks, or they can work one class-meeting period per week for several weeks, or some combination of the two.

In this model of teaching, the teacher is not at all shackled into a lecturer role. However, because lecture is sometimes crucial, all relevant lectures have been recorded on CD-ROM and video-tape and the students can access them when they are needed and as often as they are needed. The videotaped lectures and pre-lab discussions have the same content as in-class lectures; they contain facts and currently accepted scientific understandings of chemistry. The tapes were recorded on nights and weekends when the students were not in the room. They contain straightforward content, solved examples, and a few demonstrations. They are designed for students who feel comfortable listening to the teacher "tell" them what they need to know, while releasing the teacher from the front of the classroom.

Multiple copies of each tape are available and may be signed out overnight. The classroom has at least two VCRs and TVs available for student use. It must be stressed that creation of these tapes required considerable work on the part of the teacher. However, this up-front work pays off substantially during the year. Students may access the teaching tools as much as needed, until they feel prepared. The teacher is free to help in the laboratory, or to work one-on-one, or with small groups of students on the learning objectives.

The Chemistry Textbook

This course uses a textbook as a reference tool, rather than a sole source of information. The relevant sections are listed so that students who prefer the textbook as their primary learning method have a guide to meeting the class objectives. Problems that pertain to the objectives are also listed for practice purposes. The teacher's edition is kept in the classroom and the students can check their answers any time they wish; it is not hidden from view, and the "right answers" are given freely.

Challenge worksheets are provided in a resource folder in the classroom. Students are expected to challenge themselves often with the worksheets (which closely mirror the unit assessments) to see how they are progressing toward meeting the unit objectives. Answer keys are provided for the students. Guided note sheets are also provided as a companion for the videotapes or to be used independently so the students can see what they are looking for in their study.

These departures from traditional teaching come with some drawbacks. For example, students complain that science textbooks are too wordy. They may have a hard time distinguishing important concepts from excess. To reduce this anxiety, a condensed chemistry textbook was compiled with important concepts and examples. The students are given access to print and electronic copies of this book.

Currently, additional support materials are being compiled. These include a unit-by-unit review CD with video, PowerPoint presentations, unit notes, sample questions with answers, and a resource CD that contains all of the lab sheets, worksheets, and pre-lab videos.

Phase III: Preparation for NYS Regents Examination

Phase III is when students review for the current regime of NYS Regents exams. It has been shown that three weeks provides more than enough time for students to review each unit, memorize facts, and take several full-length practice exams. It is, however, beyond the scope of this paper to discuss the negative, unintended consequences such exams have on teaching and learning.

Phase III begins in May and serves as a short-term practice for a high-stakes, state mandated-science exam. Students participate in an intense Regents Exam review session where they are exposed to practice exams that mirror exactly the form and content of the exam. The students also receive topical review along with a checklist of the skills they will need to succeed. This portion of the class utilizes both in-class time and out-of-class time. Review sessions are offered before and after school. Incentives include extra credit for each session attended and for purchasing a review book.

Discussion

"If things go wrong, don't go with them."

—Roger Babson

Observations from First Four Years

Students were able to complete a significant SLICK inquiry while also meeting the objectives of passing the Regents Chemistry Exam. From teacher observations, most students enjoyed the class more when given a greater responsibility for their own learning. Through observation and from student comments, it appears most students had an increase in positive attitude toward chemistry as well. Three groups of students had various responses to the course design. The traditionally low-achieving students, the traditionally high achieving students, and the students who traditionally fall in the middle seem to have fairly cohesive opinions of the course design.

The students who are traditionally considered the bottom of the class seem to excel with this course design. Specifically, they were not forced to sit in rows and "learn" like everyone else—a method they had previously been unsuccessful with. The typically low-achieving students felt empowered to take charge of their own learning. Since the students choose an inquiry of interest, they wanted to do their lab work. This is specifically linked to using student ideas and real-world problems—tenets described in major reform movements in science education. Many students who did not appear interested in chemistry during the first few weeks were stellar students with countless hours of lab time by the end of the course.

The traditionally high-achieving students also respond positively to the course design. These students were not bored and were able to move as far forward as they wished. These students tended to choose SLICK topics that required detailed laboratory work and tended to spend very little time in the classroom learning the objectives. Most of the concepts were learned at home where these students felt most comfortable learning. Again, this is typical of the student who understands written material very easily and does not need hours of lecture to drive it home. In fact, these students had to be reminded that they were not required to complete all of the support material. The only sense of discomfort for these students had to do with being unsure as to when they had done enough work toward the objectives. For this reason, self-assessments will be added to the support materials in the future so that the students will know when "enough is enough."

The students that traditionally fall in the middle of the academic spectrum had the most complaints during Phase II of the course. These students are generally very good at listening to the teacher, taking notes, memorizing what the teacher said (usually the night before the exam), and repeating back what the teacher said on exams. These students generally forget what they had "learned" for the exam shortly later and then re-memorize it for the final exam and then forget it again shortly after the final. These students have mastered this technique and can generally pass a course with very little real effort. These students are not enthusiastic when asked to stretch themselves and take responsibility for their own learning. At the beginning, most of these students protest the very concept of a SLICK inquiry. Many of these students come around and investigate a problem of interest and get excited about the project and process, but not all of them. Some of these students select an inquiry they *think* is easy and it ends up being boring. They lose out on the experience. This point will be addressed in future iterations of course re-design.

Major Evidences of Success

The course design has been implemented for three years at Churchville-Chili Senior High School. Each year there has been no significant difference in Regents exam scores relative to other teachers in the district using traditional teaching methods. During the 2000–01 school year, of the students that completed a SLICK inquiry and participated in self-directed learning for four months (three sections of about 24 students each), 92% passed the exam, and 31% reached mastery (scoring 85–100%). With two other chemistry teachers (6 sections) included, the school had 91% passing and 29% mastery. Students do just as well on standardized tests with this learning structure.

References

American Association for the Advancement of Science (AAAS). 1994. *Benchmarks for science literacy.* New York: Oxford Press.

Bransford, J. D., A. L. Brown, and R. R. Cocking, eds. 2000. *How people learn: Brain, mind, experience, and school.* Washington, DC: National Academy Press.

Burke, P., and S. Garger. 1985. *Marching to different drummers.* Washington, DC: Association for Supervision and Curriculum Development.

International Center for Leadership in Education. (ICLE). 2000. *Instructional strategies: How to teach for rigor and relevance.* Rexford, NY: Leadership Media.

National Research Council (NRC). 1996. *National science education standards.* Washington, DC: National Academy Press.

Tomlinson, C. A. 1996. *The differentiated classroom: Responding to the needs of all learners.* Washington, DC: Association for Supervision and Curriculum Development.

The Sky's the Limit:

A *More Emphasis* Approach to the Study of Meteorology

Eric A. Walters
Marymount School of New York

Setting

The Marymount School of New York is an all-female, independent school in New York City, which features an innovative, engaging, and challenging science curriculum for students from Pre-Kindergarten to grade 12. Upper school students (grades 9–12) engage in a standard high school science curriculum of biology, chemistry, physics, Advanced Placement electives, and meteorology & astronomy. Furthermore, the school has made a significant commitment to the integration of technology into the science curriculum.

The majority of students at The Marymount School of New York are upper-middle and upper class students, who reside on Manhattan's Upper East Side of in the New York City metropolitan area. The school itself is located in four Beaux-Arts mansions on the Upper East Side of Manhattan, in close proximity to the American Museum of Natural History and Central Park. Approximately 95% of all students complete four years of science; all students are required to complete three years of laboratory science.

More Emphasis Review

The curriculum for the senior Meteorology elective was originally structured as a typical course—several topics comprising a unit, followed by a standard assessment. Currently, the curriculum is aligned with the National Science Education Standards (NSES) (NRC 1996) *More Emphasis* criteria, so that students are guided in an active and extended study of weather forecasting. Students are afforded the opportunity to debate and discuss weather forecasts and to work cooperatively to understand the complexities and conceptual basis of weather forecasting.

Assessments are varied, in order to address different learning styles in the class. Students are required to use current weather data for analysis on assessments and to apply their understanding of forecasting to current information as they are tested on their scientific understanding and reasoning. Furthermore, the use of weekly weather forecasts, daily weather briefings, and written justifications allow for ongoing assessment of skill development in forecasting.

The course also addresses content and inquiry standards outlined by NSES. Students are required to understand scientific concepts and develop abilities of inquiry as they study meteorology and weather forecasting. They are engaged in activities that allow them to investigate and analyze scientific questions, and are required to use evidence from weather data and forecasting strategies learned in class for developing and revising an explanation. Furthermore, as they formulate their forecasts, students have the opportunity to argue, explain and debate; working cooperatively, students analyze and synthesize both current weather data and climatological data. This acquisition of weather knowledge is then communicated to both their fellow students (daily weather discussions) and to the Marymount community (weekend weather forecast).

The Classroom

As previously mentioned, the Meteorology course is a senior elective, with an average yearly enrollment of 15 to 20 students (out of 45 seniors). The course was developed as an additional senior elective, geared toward non-Honors students and for students with varied learning styles. As part of their course of study, students use a textbook only as a reference; instead, they use the web as their primary learning tool, accessing real-time weather data. All course information—including the weekly syllabus, online weather resources, student web work, and forecasting guidelines—is found online at the Marymount Meteorology Home Page (MMHP) at: *www.marymount.k12.ny.us/marynet/StudentResources/science/Meteorology/index.htm*. The teacher, Eric A. Walters, serves as the Science Department Chair at the Marymount School of New York, where he teaches physics, AP physics, and meteorology & astronomy. A recipient of the Marymount School Faculty Fellowship, Mr. Walters has developed hybrid e-learning courses in both meteorology and astronomy, and has included digital video and web design into all aspects of the science curriculum. He has also participated in various programs sponsored by NASA and Princeton University, and has presented workshops for NYSAIS, NAIS, and NSTA.

Program Features

Approximately four years ago, the department identified the need for an additional senior elective in science geared toward non-Honors students. A careful review of the Middle School and Upper School curriculum showed that, after grade 7, students were rarely introduced to advanced topics in earth sciences. Thus, the decision was made to introduce an Earth sciences-based, senior, one-semester elective in meteorology.

The course was originally developed with an online presence in mind, where students would be able to access their course syllabus and online links. While it was considered to be an "online course," in its initial iteration, the course was more akin to a standard, textbook-based course.

With the ready access of current weather information on the internet, and the ability to integrate both web-based applications and other multimedia components, the course evolved into a "hybrid e-learning course," which integrates internet applications and real-time data analysis with teacher-facilitated learning.

The course includes an online syllabus, with preparation and review material for students from online sources, as well as links to weather data, weather maps, and forecast information. Students utilize this material as a means of introduction and motivation for each topic. The use of real-time weather data is the basis of classroom activities, and is a means of developing a conceptual understanding of meteorology and skill development in data analysis and weather forecasting. Homework assignments are usually long-term, open-ended, and require the application of forecasting skills and conceptual ideas to weather data.

As an example, consider a recent class in meteorology on atmospheric stability. Prior to this class, a student's only understanding of stability would have come from physics, where concepts of static equilibrium are discussed, or in chemistry, where they would have learned about chemical equilibrium. Now they were going to take this knowledge and apply it to the atmosphere.

Before arriving in class, a student would be required to check the online syllabus and review the material found online at the University Corporation for Atmospheric Research (UCAR) site on atmospheric stability. Students would take notes on the reading, outlining specific questions about the material. Class time would involve a brief review of the material and a discussion of the appropriate maps and charts, such as the Stuve diagram and skew-T log-p diagrams. Questions may include: What information do these charts offer us in terms of atmospheric stability? How we can use these charts as forecasting tools?

Students then access current skew-T log-p thermodynamic diagrams online (at *http://ametsoc.org/dstreme*) and relate the information presented on these diagrams to current weather conditions. For homework, the students complete a similar analysis, either using current weather data from later that day or archived data from earlier in the week. Students do not receive this homework assignment on paper; they are required to find the necessary information online to complete the assignment.

More often than not, classroom activities follow this organizational pattern. Other times, activities are inquiry-based (for example, units on satellite imagery and radar analysis) where students are required to analyze images and make conclusions about the validity and value of various image types. Student discussion of these conclusions follows, and students then use their understanding, developed from both these discussions and their independent work, to apply this understanding to similar analyses.

Each class begins with a student discussion of weather. Students are assigned a specific day to present a weather briefing to the rest of the class. Prior to arriving in class, the student needs to review current surface maps, radar and satellite images, and numerical forecast products, and then share their conclusions with the rest of the class. Students in class also have an opportunity to debate or to challenge the presenter about their conclusions. This year, student forecast discussions will be posted on the Marymount Meteorology Home Page (MMHP) on a daily basis for the school community to access.

On a weekly basis, each student is required to complete a Friday forecast for Central Park in New York City. The forecast requires a prediction of the maximum and minimum temperatures at Central Park as well as a "Yes" or "No" prediction for 0.01 inches of precipitation in Central Park. Students are also required to justify their forecasts by including a discussion of the current weather conditions and numerical forecast models that support their forecast. Forecasts are submitted through an online form on the course website.

Verifications are posted on the MMHP on Saturdays, with the actual maximum and minimum temperatures, as well as precipitation total for Central Park. Student forecasts are scored as follows: one point for each degree away from the actual maximum or minimum temperature; five points for an incorrect precipitation prediction. Student scores are weighted by the number of forecasts. At the end of the semester, the student with the lowest weighted score is declared the winner.

Students present a weather briefing to the class.

The forecast justifications are assessed for completeness and for correctness. Inconsistencies between justifications and forecasts are identified early in the semester as students develop their forecast skills. As these skills develop during the course of the semester, peer analyses are used as students critique and evaluate individual forecasts.

Students also participate in a national online forecast contest sponsored by the University of Wisconsin at Milwaukee. In this online activity, students are required to forecast and justify the maximum and minimum temperatures, together with wind direction and speed for a specific city for one day during the week.

Sponsored by Bravenet.com, students in meteorology are also involved in an online discussion forum called the Marymount Meteorology Forum. Each Monday, a "question of the week" is posted on the forum. The question is related to weather and climate, either locally or globally. Sample questions include "Do you believe the media is truthful in the presentation of weather information?" and "What do you think is the biggest challenge to using numerical models in forecasting?" Students are required to provide an initial response to the question by Thursday; two comments on other student postings are due by Sunday. The teacher facilitates the discussion by offering additional comments and insights, and maintains the site for content and appropriateness.

During significant weather events such as snowstorms, students are required to post observations on an hourly basis, if possible. This includes local temperature, sky cover, precipitation and precipitation type. The following day in class, students use these postings to understand the impact of significant weather events on the New York City metropolitan area as well as variations in weather conditions during these events. Furthermore, this understanding deepens the students' knowledge and comprehension of the challenge of forecasting weather in New York City.

Such forums are also beneficial as they allow students to interact beyond the walls of the classroom and to have this discussion extend to their entire class, as opposed to individual emails. The forum also allows students to have a medium to express their opinions and ideas, to share data and to become even more fully involved in the course curriculum.

A side benefit to the online forum has been the increase in class participation. Often student responses are significantly more numerous than required as discussions become more involved and more intense. As Young suggests, "some students who rarely participate in classroom discussions are more likely to participate online, where they get time to think before they type and aren't put on the spot" (Young 2002). This has been evident with the Marymount Meteorology Forum. The more vocal participants online, those who post the most, are those who are the least vocal in class.

On a weekly basis, one student writes, produces, films, and edits her own weekend weather forecast. This requires the students to utilize their forecasting and analytical skills in developing the three-day forecast. The video, completed using a digital video camera, is often taped on the school grounds or in the neighborhood. During the course of the year, guest forecasters have included the Headmistress and the Director of Technology.

After filming is complete, the video is edited using either Apple's iMovie or Adobe Premier, and then compiled as either a Quicktime or RealPlayer movie. The video forecast is then posted on the MMHP.

On the following Monday, the forecaster reviews and verifies her forecast. As part of her assessment,

Every student in the class has the opportunity to lead classroom discussions on weather forecasts.

she is required to identify sources of error in her forecast or validate her precision. Forecasts are also produced for significant weather events, such as snowstorms and severe weather, as well as for significant school events, such as retreats and field trips.

More importantly, the forecaster quickly learns how difficult it is to be a "meteorologist." The student becomes responsible for informing the softball coach that rain is in the forecast for the big game, or telling the maintenance men to prepare for six inches of snow. The student also quickly learns to bear the brunt of criticism when her forecast of sun turns into a rainy Saturday.

Students are also involved in several data sharing and data analysis projects. In the fall and spring semesters, students exchange weather data with schools in Australia through Project

Atmosphere Australia (PAA) online (*www.schools.ash.org.au/paa1/paa.htm*). Students at Marymount take daily readings of maximum and minimum temperature, as well as precipitation, and, through e-mail, post these observations to PAA. Marymount also receives postings from across the globe; these postings and observations are used as springboards for discussion of variations in weather conditions and climate across the globe, as well as understanding the difficulties of forecasting for different regions.

Clearly, it would have been possible for the course curriculum to focus on covering every topic in the textbook. Instead, in developing the goals and objectives, we decided to frame the curriculum around the art of weather forecasting. Thus, the topics selected were those that helped the students develop not only their forecasting skills but also the physical and conceptual background for those skills.

Evidence of Success

It is also difficult to assess whether this *More Emphasis* approach to the study of meteorology has been successful. First, because of the uniqueness of the course, it is almost impossible to compare results with other schools or other districts. Most New York City independent schools only offer Advanced Placement courses or senior electives such as astronomy or marine biology. The New York state regents' guidelines offer only a minimal weather & climate component.

Trends in forecast scores over the past two years suggest success in this approach to the study of meteorology. Because the weekly forecast requires students to apply their knowledge and understanding of forecasting and meteorology, based on classroom activities, the weekly forecast scores are probably the best evidence that the teaching, assessment practices, and content are involved in achieving the *More Emphasis* conditions. The forecast results for the past two years are presented in Figure 1 and Figure 2.

In general, as the trend suggests, student-forecasting scores generally improve during the course of the year. As Occam's razor would suggest, this improvement can be directly tied to the acquisition and development of weather forecasting skills during the semester. However, the average score increased between 2001–2002 (6.56) and 2002–2003 (6.70). First and foremost, this can be attributed to the fact that weather forecasting is not an exact science. There are several variables, including sudden shifts in expected weather patterns as well as tricky and complex forecasting scenarios, which may introduce errors into a forecast. Moreover, the winter season of 2002–2003 featured numerous snowstorms, some of which exceeded expectations, while others did not. A case in point is forecast 15—with an average score of 11.3. On this date, it remained considerably warm until immediately after midnight, a point most forecasters missed.

Prior to the focus on *More Emphasis* conditions, student forecast scores were considerably more varied. While this data is not included, average forecasting scores for 2000–01 and 1999–00 averaged approximately 10.0. This is primarily due to the fact that the development of forecast skills was not related to concepts learned in class.

By focusing the course content on the development of weather forecasting skills, as well as a physical and conceptual understanding of these skills, coordinated with assessments that seek to evaluate these skills, the *more emphasis* conditions have been achieved.

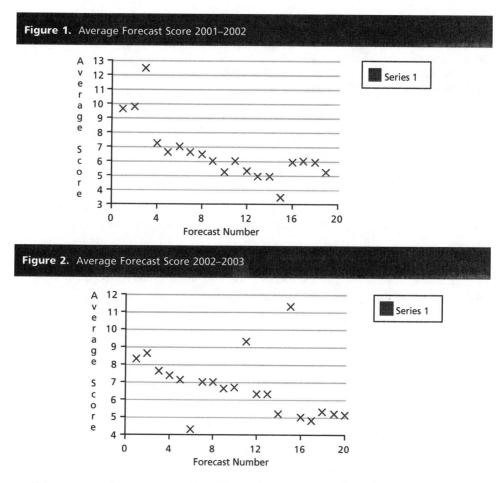

Figure 1. Average Forecast Score 2001–2002

Figure 2. Average Forecast Score 2002–2003

Moreover, student comments from the course assessment show that they find the *More Emphasis*, "real-world" applications engaging. Their comments are summarized in Figure 3 below.

Figure 3. Summary of student comments

When asked in the end-of-course assessment about the pros and cons of e-learning, the students responded:
- This has made meteorology an every day topic.
- Gives us variety in how we learn.
- Allows for access to global information.
- Allows me to interpret current weather data, and then look out the window to see if I'm right.
- Current information makes class more interesting and less textbook-based.
- I don't feel like we are rushing through material to finish the textbook; instead, we get time to develop our understanding.
- Our tests allow us to apply what we know; it's not just multiple choice and fill ins.
- We get to share our knowledge with the Marymount community.

- This is much more "hands-on" learning.
- We have a teacher to guide us and we get good training in technology.
- Using the web is not a hindrance at all.
- I need the web in front of me to complete assignments.
- Long loading times; failing server.

Summary

In conclusion, the development and implementation of a hybrid e-learning course in Meteorology as a method of meeting the NSES conditions for *more emphasis* has been most successful. Student enrollment has been consistently high; the variety of learning activities and opportunities in different media has promoted better student performance, better student learning, and better student understanding of weather forecasting. Students feel that they have ownership over their learning through the use of more participatory, inquiry-based, and student-centered learning activities, as well as through a variety of activities that require them to apply what they have learned in class. More importantly though, students now feel that they "understand the weather" and can accurately criticize and evaluate meteorological information and forecasts presented in the media.

References

Kahl, J. 2001. Meteorology online. *The Science Teacher* (Feb): 22–25.

Lago, M. E. 2003. The hybrid experience: How sweet it is. *Converge* (1 April). Available online at *http://www.convergemag.com/Publications/CNVGNov00/hybrid/index.shtm.*

Learning Technology Center.2003. *Student issues.* Available online at *http://www.uwm.edu/Dept/StudentIssues/why-teach.hybrid.html.*

Learning Technology Center. 2003. *What is required of faculty?* Available online at *http://www.uwm.edu/Dept/StudentIssues/why-teach.hybrid.html.*

Learning Technology Center. 2003. *Why teach a hybrid?* Available online at *http://www.uwm.edu/Dept/StudentIssues/why-teach.hybrid.html.*

Young, J. R. 2002. "Hybrid" teaching seeks to end the divide between traditional and online instruction. *The Chronicle of Higher Education: Information Technology.* (22 March): 17–22.

Bust That Castle Wall!

Vicki Wilson
Rockwall High School

Setting

Rockwall, Texas is a suburb of Dallas. The city is located 25 miles east of downtown and is known for having a small town way of life, with the convenience of being located near the big city. There is one high school, where 2,000 students attend grades ten through twelve. All socioeconomic levels are present, but the community is predominantly middle class.

More Emphasis Conditions Implemented in the Classroom

The National Science Education Standards have been used to guide the evolution of my teaching style for the physics course. The specific standards covered in this chapter include selecting and adapting curriculum, as well as guiding students in active and extended scientific inquiry. The course is intended to make students aware that physics is all around them. Most of the fall semester is spent studying mechanics. The payoff is the final project of the semester—building a trebuchet! Another teacher at Rockwall (Scott Townsend) had pursued this project with his students at the end of the previous school year, before I began teaching there. After looking at Scott's work, I decided it would be an excellent way to structure my first semester mechanics lessons.

The students are excited about building a trebuchet after hearing about it from previous students. The project works well as a way to connect the various concepts they will be learning, and also serves to bring real-world uses for book learning to the students' attention. Too often, students view school as isolated bits of stuff, memorized in order to pass a test and then forgotten. By presenting students with a problem to be solved, and making sure that the solution requires a thorough understanding of the laws of motion, a deeper understanding of physics is obtained.

Description of Teacher, Student Body, and Classroom

The classes are taught by Vicki Wilson. She is a veteran educator with experience teaching chemistry and physics. She has spent a good deal of time in workshops learning new ways of teaching science, as well as spending time reading journals such as *The Science Teacher* and *The Physics Teacher* in search of new ideas. The classes are regular and pre-AP physics. The classroom contains a seating area with 25 desks and six lab tables in the back. The school is on an alternating block schedule. The students are in the lab for part of the period on most days.

The teaching style is often inquiry-based, with open-ended questions being asked of the students. This requires them to learn good lab technique and procedures for gathering information. The students then work together in groups to make sense of their results. They are required to demonstrate their lab skills in assessments, and are tested using problems that call for critical thinking and an extension of the concepts learned in class. The course requires students to learn in-depth about a few concepts, and to tie those concepts together instead of doing the book a chapter at a time.

Features of Program and Alignment with *More Emphasis* Standards

The unit covered during fall semester is mechanics. Instead of rigorously following the textbook author's idea of when and how material should be taught, the unit is divided into conceptual segments. The students are introduced to one-dimensional motion, velocity, and acceleration. After obtaining a good understanding of those concepts, vectors are studied. Falling bodies and projectile motion are analyzed. A little torque, a lot of forces, and some centripetal motion set the stage for the project everyone has been looking forward to—trebuchets!

The first lab of the year is to promote the standard of having students understand scientific concepts and develop abilities in inquiry. Many of the students have not been previously exposed to inquiry-type investigations. They are used to cookbook labs where they simply follow directions and are not required to initiate the procedure themselves. To guide the students in active scientific inquiry, a good lab to begin the year with asks them to calculate how long they could breathe if the room were sealed off. The only tools they are given are a meter stick and a plastic trash bag. There is a clock in the room they can use to measure time. No instructions are provided. The students are divided into teams of four to five students and told to begin. The students go down a lot of wrong trails. This provides an opportunity to stress that mistakes are simply learning experiences. They come up with some inventive methods for measuring the volume of a trash bag. They look to see what other groups are doing. Eventually, they calculate a time for using up all of the air. The class then compares their answers and discusses which are most reasonable. The teacher can use this activity to get a better understanding of students' ability to problem solve and reason, and can also discuss the importance of precise measurements whenever possible.

Another standard focuses on students' understanding and use of scientific knowledge, ideas, and inquiry processes. As the class moves on to reviewing basic math and graphing skills, they are learning to take a skill and apply it in order to make sense of the data they will gather in the lab. Since many of the concepts in *motion* are deduced from graphs produced in the lab, it is vital that all of the students have good graphing skills. Measurement units are stressed in these beginning labs since they are an integral part of interpreting slope and area under the curve. As a way of teaching process skills in the context of the material being covered, the students learn these graphing skills by doing a lab. They are required to measure the circumference and diameter of different cylinders and then graph circumference versus diameter. They are given several measuring tools, such as a yardstick, a ruler, and a piece of string, and told to measure the cylinders in two different ways. This is easy for the teacher to check, since all of the slopes should equal pi (but don't tell the kids that). The students then compare the slope of their graph to the ratio they got for each individual cylinder. The class then discusses the problems with measurement and data collection, together with the value of scatter plots in averaging out mistakes.

The next topic covered is *constant velocity*. After a brief discussion of what velocity is, the students are sent into the lab to graph distance versus time for constant velocity. This is in keeping with the standard of using process skills in context. Unfortunately, no constant velocity cars were available, so the students used almost frictionless cars. They went into the hallway and one student gave the car a good push. Another student called out every second according to a stopwatch. A third student ran in front of the car and made a mark on the floor with a highlighter when the seconds were called. This procedure was highly entertaining. When the students felt they had a good run, they measured the distance between their marks and made a graph. They then calculated the slope of the line to find velocity. Using units to make sure that the slope represents what you are looking for is stressed. Some of the students graphed the distance between individual marks and some students graphed the cumulative distance. This led to interesting discussions on the different ways to graph results in order to get the best interpretation.

To look at a position versus time graph for an accelerating object, the students made ramps out of meter sticks and books and rolled a marble down them. This activity follows the standard of using multiple process skills—manipulative, cognitive, and procedural. They marked the position of the marble at four seconds, then at three seconds, then at two seconds, and finally one second. Only one or two books were used to hold the end of the ramp so that the marble would not pick up speed too quickly. After graphing position versus time, the students could easily see that this line did not have a constant slope, so there was not a constant velocity. The concept of instantaneous velocity was introduced, along with average velocity. Since they had constructed a graph of accelerating velocity, showing average velocity on a graph was a simple step forward. The equation was derived from the graph using concepts they had learned in math class.

After working with several more of the position versus time graphs, the students took their data and calculated the velocity at each point. They then graphed velocity versus time. This gave them a visual picture of the changes in velocity, otherwise known as *acceleration*. The students did several more activities, including going into the parking lot to measure the various lines and displacements for walking, jogging, sprinting, and skateboarding. They took their data and graphed position versus time. The slopes were calculated for each line. The velocity was calculated for each data point. These numbers were averaged and compared to the slope of the position-time graph. The velocities were then graphed against time. The slopes were calculated in order to figure acceleration. The area under the curve was calculated in order to compare the distances traveled. After this, they seemed comfortable with what the graphs could tell them.

A goal of the class is to select and adapt curriculum, as recommended by the NSES. During this period of learning, various sections of the textbook were assigned which dealt with the particular skill the students would be working with the next class period. Parts of several different chapters were combined in order to back up what they were doing in class. This made quite a few of the students uncomfortable, especially when they wanted to know which chapter the test would be covering. The answer was no particular chapter, the test would cover everything we had learned in class, including sample lab data, which they then had to manipulate and explain.

When it came time to learn about acceleration due to gravity, the students found places in the building where they could drop a tennis ball from one floor to another. Using a measuring tape, the distance was measured and converted into metric units. After obtaining a good average time, the students calculated average velocity. Initial and final velocities were extrapolated. This led to the derivation of the formula for acceleration. This is an example of the standard for using evidence and strategies for developing or revising an explanation. Velocity seems to be an easy concept for the students to grasp, but changes in velocity are difficult for them. In order to make the kinematic equations more real to the students, they went outside to see how high they could throw a ball into the air. They were allowed to take a stopwatch and had to use their calculated gravitational acceleration to calculate the maximum height the ball reached. The boys thought this was a really cool lab.

Vectors were the next topic of discussion. After a review of basic trigonometry, the students were sent outside with approximately 20 meters of string and directions for laying out the string. After making a series of 90-degree turns, they were delighted to find that they had formed the outlines of letters. They then had to draw a vector map from their house to the school. From this map, they had to figure distance, displacement, and the resultant vector. Using this type of assessment to learn what students understand meets another of the standards.

Before starting *two-dimensional motion,* the students needed to understand that the vectors do not affect each other. Since the NSES recommends using activities that investigate and analyze science questions, this concept was taught using a boat and a river. The boat was a marble rolled down a stationary ramp onto a large piece of bulletin board paper. Since the ramp was stationary, the boat hit the paper with the same velocity each time. The students timed the boat going across the river while it was still. Then they timed the boat going across the river when it was moving perpendicular to the direction of the ramp. This was a real eye-opener for them, since they expected the boat to take longer to cross the river when it was moving. This led into great discussions about frame of reference and relative velocity. The concepts seemed to make more sense to the students since they had discovered them on their own instead of being told by the teacher.

As a way of extending this vector situation to gravitational acceleration (addressing the standard of active and extended student inquiry), the students used a ruler to launch several pennies off a lab table. If one end of the ruler is held, and the other end is pivoted, the pennies will have different horizontal velocities, so will hit the floor at different places. But they all hit at the same time. After making sure students were comfortable with this idea, they went to the football field and threw various balls. They varied the angle of the throw and the mass of the ball thrown. The landing spot of the ball and the time spent in the air were recorded. They calculated the initial horizontal velocity, the maximum height achieved, and the velocity in the *x* direction. Using their velocities as vectors, they were able to calculate the angle of release. The effects of the angle of throw on the time in the air and horizontal distance achieved were to be referred to later when it was time to build the trebuchet. In this way, the students would develop a greater understanding of scientific concepts and the ability to conduct experiments using the inquiry method during their building and testing phase.

Force was the next topic. Several activities were performed and discussed by the students in order to get them thinking about forces and acceleration. One of the activities was a space race. The students used graph paper and Newton's laws of motion to send a rocket ship through an asteroid field without crashing. This was approximately the time when they started understanding that while Star Trek was a great television series, there were some serious errors of science in the show. They were able to apply the results of experiments to scientific arguments and explanations (another standard).

Following a lab on torque and learning about centripetal acceleration, the students were ready to put it all together. It was time to build the trebuchet! The discussion was begun by talking about seesaws, and moved from there to throwing objects. A video from NOVA on trebuchets was shown which helped the students picture what a finished trebuchet should look like and how it should work. This is an example of the standard of selecting and adapting the curriculum.

The standard of supporting a classroom community with cooperation, shared responsibility, and respect was implemented by dividing the students into groups to work on their projects. The teams were encouraged to share ideas, since the assessment was not going to be competitive. The students had six weeks to work on their project. They could work in groups of two to four people. They could use the internet or other sources to research trebuchets, but they were required to build an original (not buy one ready-made). The requirements were that the projectile go 40 yards and hit a castle wall. They could use a projectile of their choice as long as they cleaned up any mess made. The accelerating force had to be from a source other than human power—e.g., falling weights, springs, or having a person stand on one end of the throwing arm and letting gravity work on them. The trebuchet needed to have a fulcrum. Other than that they could use their imagination. The standard of assessing rich, well-structured knowledge was the basis of this project.

Building the trebuchet required the use of mathematical skills such as measuring and calculating angles and forces. Understanding the concepts underlying parabolic motion allowed the students to know where to tinker with their machines in order to achieve the maximum results. Many of the students found engineers in their families or among neighbors to help them with their projects. This was an extension of the classroom learning to allow the students to apply multiple concepts in solving real-world problems.

Setting up the trebuchet.

The successful groups began by researching the trebuchet and drawing up designs for what they thought theirs might look like. The construction phase took the most time, and those groups that didn't start on time really paid for their procrastination. After construction came testing, testing, and more testing. Nobody's trebuchet launched anywhere near 40 yards when first tested. Through trial and error, most groups came up with a satisfactory load and a good length for the throwing arm. A recurring problem was the attachment of the throwing arm to the trebuchet. The stresses from accelerating the projectile wreaked havoc on most of the bars used for the fulcrum.

Those groups who had started on the project early were able to overcome their problems and had some very successful throws. Those groups who waited until the last minute were usually not successful. The choice of partners also proved to be crucial to the success of the group.

This project was a definite hit among the students. In talking with them at the end of the year, it was mentioned most often as the best part of the physics class. Parents were mostly supportive of the endeavor, and some even came to watch the launches. The students seemed to learn more about force and motion with this project than if they had simply worked problems out of a textbook. The textbook is a valuable reference tool, but should not be the main focus of the course, as the standard of selecting and adapting curriculum recommends.

Evidence of Learning Using the *More Emphasis* Conditions

The inquiry-based teaching style and adaptation of the curriculum seems to support student learning. The students are not given a bunch of random facts to memorize, but are expected to learn through trial and error what happens in a given situation. They are then asked to apply these concepts to a different situation in order to assess their depth of understanding of the concept. Ties are made to their perceptions of the world and to activities they are rou-

Students learn about force and torque in trebuchet distance trials.

tinely involved in. As the different concepts are introduced, the history of the discovery and the people involved are discussed. Ongoing issues that involve the concepts are brought up and researched, then discussed in class. These discussions do not have a set agenda or a preferred viewpoint, but instead are discussed as problems with different possible solutions. This follows the standard of focusing on student understanding and use of scientific knowledge, ideas, and inquiry processes.

As an educator, teaching conceptually rather than by the book is much more enjoyable. The lessons can be paced to the students' ability to grasp the material rather than lurching along on a schedule set by the publisher of the textbook. A concern at the beginning was the extra amount of time this method of teaching would take, but at the end of the year, my classes were actually a little ahead of the classes who had gone straight through the textbook and learned most of the material through the lecture method.

At first, the students are fearful of trying something new. Not having one exact right answer or one best way of gathering data is very frustrating for some of the children. However, it eventually allows them to try new things and not worry about what happens if they fail. They are still learning, and have the freedom to try new things just to see if they work. This spills over into their problem-solving skills when doing homework. They are inventive when solving problems and come up with some unique ways of working out answers. Thinking outside of the box is encouraged and applauded, while being wrong is not necessarily bad, but instead presents an opportunity to discuss the underlying concepts in order to understand what is really going on. Since much of physics is counterintuitive, the first guess about a physical process is oftentimes wrong, and students must dig deeper for an answer. Overall, the students seem to enjoy the inquiry method of laboratory investigation and the projects assigned to them over the course of the year.

Over the last several years, during my shift to the inquiry-based, conceptual method of teaching science, overwhelming positive feedback has been received from the students and their parents. Not all students like this method, but the ones who do not are generally more prone to learn an accepted truth instead of seeking out the truth for themselves. The state-mandated graduation test in Texas is moving toward conceptual questions instead of the rote memorization of the past, and my students did very well this year. On the *force and motion* portion of the test, students enrolled in physics scored an average of 67% correct. Students in the inquiry-based classes had an average score of 81% correct on the *force and motion* portion.

The tests in the classroom have become more problem-based, and by the middle of the year, the students are doing well on these types of ques-

Students make adjustments to the trebuchet to increase distance trials.

tions. Each teacher writes their own tests during the year, but all physics students take the same semester exam. The students in the inquiry-based classes scored an average of 8.5 points higher on the mid-term semester exam than the students in the lecture-taught classes.

Through the use of portfolio and performance tasks, the students are given a chance to apply what they have learned in the classroom to events in their lives, thus addressing the standard of assessing scientific understanding and reasoning. In this way, the students can be assessed on what they have learned, instead of what they don't know, which bears on the standard of assessing to learn what students do understand. As the class moves through the year, the students will often bring up previous projects they have done and apply the newly learned principles to those projects. Research is done on current issues as they relate to our course of study, and possible solutions and outcomes are discussed by the class.

The failure rate has gone down since shifting to this method of teaching. This is due to the fact that the students are more in charge of their learning, and so feel a sense of ownership, thus meeting the standard of sharing responsibility for learning with students. While employing the lecture method of teaching, failure rates were often 20% for the course. In this past year, only 4% of the students in the inquiry-based classes failed the course. The standards are higher now than in the past, and when the inquiry students transfer mid-term to a lecture-based teacher, they usually will stop by later to visit and complain of being bored. The transfer students do not lack any of the underlying conceptual understanding, and have no problem picking up where the new class currently is.

Another clue that program is working consists in the increased enrollment in Pre-AP classes. All of the Pre-AP physics classes are inquiry-based and the enrollment has increased from 78 students this past year to 124 students for next year. The overall physics enrollment has remained constant, so this suggests that more students are willing to do the extra work involved in Pre-AP in order to enjoy the inquiry-based, conceptual method of teaching.

Summary

Knowing that they are going to build a trebuchet kept the students interested during the difficult process of covering mechanics. It gave the class a central idea to relate all of the concepts they were learning, and provided a practical application for the math. Learning by inquiry encouraged the students to question and try new things instead of waiting for someone else to feed them the answers. Seeing real-world applications of textbook ideas helped them to feel ownership of the material. Working on a big project like this helped to build the students' confidence in tackling problems they knew little about. On the first day of class next year, the first thing asked will be, "When are we building trebuchets?"

References

Herreid, C. F. 2001. Case method teaching. *Journal of College Science Teaching* 31: 87–88.

Iri, D. A. 1998. How long can we breathe? *The Physics Teacher* 36: 36.

Vinson, M. 1998. Space race: A game of physics adventure. *The Physics Teacher* 36: 20.

Successes and Continuing Challenges:

Meeting the NSES Visions for Improving Science in High Schools

Robert E. Yager
Science Education Center
University of Iowa

The authors and co-authors of the 15 chapters in this monograph represent an intriguing set in respect of their types of school, program foci, and attention to the National Standards. Evidence for the success of the programs in regard to their impact on students, schools, and communities proved the most difficult feature for many. It was generally easier to describe a program than to establish its impact on students and their scores on a variety of assessment efforts.

Noteworthy is the fact that many of the 15 exemplars did not arise in typical schools, especially in view of the 16,000 public schools operating in the United States. Certainly it is easier to change and to implement the Standards in special schools with an atypical teaching force than in communities without nearby colleges, special facilities, or funded projects to draw from. Nonetheless, these examples provide impressive information as to how the NSES can be (and are being) used to achieve the goals summarized at the end of each chapter.

The exemplars comprising this monograph have not made significant progress with respect to *all* the standards listed in the *More Emphasis* recommendations, which include 9 suggestions for needed changes in teaching, 14 features recommended for programs designed to prepare and/or provide continuing education projects for in-service teachers, 7 new directions for assessment efforts, and 17 new guidelines for general content and those associated directly with inquiry. A full listing of all *Less/More Emphasis* recommendations can be found in Appendix 1, page 172.

More Emphasis in the Teaching Standards

The high school programs discussed in this monograph all provided evidence of changes in teaching. Five of the nine *More Emphasis* teaching standards were judged as having been met in an exemplary manner. The remaining four standards were found to have been demonstrated by over half of the 15 exemplars.

By far the greatest need (at least as evidenced by the exemplars described in this monograph) was in the ninth teaching standard (NRC 1996, p. 52), namely, "working with other teachers to enhance the total science program." Perhaps too often exemplary program teachers are individuals who do not affect the total school program as much as they should.

Other aspects of recommended changes in teaching where more progress is warranted focus on: (1) *Understanding and responding to individual student's interests, strengths, experiences, and needs.* Too often even the exciting programs come from unique situations, teacher planning and leadership, whole class activities, and content foci. (2) *Selecting and adapting curriculum.* Too often the materials were used without flexibility and without a real shift of focus. (3) *Continually assessing student understanding.* Too often standard measures from other instructors were used; too infrequently students were asked to demonstrate their understanding by using the information and/or skills taught in new situations and contexts. Again, progress was reported—but these were the weakest areas noted after analyzing the analyses and conclusions of the 15 preceding chapters.

Most would still maintain that changes in teaching are the most critical needs if the reforms of the NSES are to be realized generally in classrooms around the world. The 15 programs described in this monograph have succeeded in showing how teaching can change, while also identifying some areas where continued attention is needed.

More Emphasis in the Professional Development Standards

An evaluation of the high school programs in this monograph yields more information that progress is being made in implementing the Professional Development Standards. Nearly all reported that the following *More Emphasis* conditions recommended for the education of teachers were being met and working in an exemplary manner:

1. Learning science through investigation and inquiry;
2. Integration of science and teaching knowledge;
3. Integration of theory and practice in school settings;
4. Collegial and collaborative learning; and
5. Teacher as intellectual, reflective practitioner.

Four additional areas where significantly more attention is needed are:

1. Staff developers as facilitators, consultants, and planners;
2. Teacher as source and facilitator of change;
3. A variety of professional development activities; and
4. Teacher as producer of knowledge about teaching.

Five other areas were in evidence in some chapters, but missing in others:

1. Inquiry into teaching and learning;

2. Long-term coherent plans;
3. Mix of internal and external expertise;
4. Teacher as leader; and
5. Teacher as a member of a collegial professional community.

More Emphasis in the Assessment Standards

The seven *More Emphasis* standards envisioned to improve assessment practices were also used by the 15 exemplars for the high school level. Most progress was reported in the following areas:
1. Assessing what is most highly valued;
2. Assessing to learn what students do understand; and
3. Assessing achievement and opportunity to learn.

One area of the assessment standards was rarely considered or described as significant in any of the exemplars: the recommendation that teachers be involved in the development of external assessments. Perhaps external examination groups should seek out more teachers who are preparing such exams, and who are knowledgeable and skilled in meeting the NSES visions.

More Emphasis in the Content and Inquiry Standards

As might be expected, all of the exemplars reported significant progress concerning the NSES recommended content standards; 12 of the 17 *More Emphasis* conditions were mentioned and illustrated in all 15 reports:
1. Understanding scientific concepts and developing abilities of inquiry;
2. Learning subject matter disciplines in the context of inquiry, technology, science in personal and social perspectives, and history and nature of science;
3. Integrating all aspects of science content;
4. Studying a few fundamental science concepts;
5. Activities that investigate and analyze science questions;
6. Process skills in context;
7. Science as argument and explanation;
8. Communicating science explanations;
9. Groups of students often analyzing and synthesizing data after defending conclusions;
10. Applying the results of experiments to scientific arguments and explanations;
11. Management of ideas and information; and
12. Public communication of student ideas and work to classmates.

The only areas where the 15 programs in this monograph indicated room for improvement were in the following *More Emphasis* conditions pertaining to content (and even so, the scores were impressive):
1. Implementing inquiry as instructional strategies, abilities, and ideas to be learned;
2. Investigations over extended periods;

3. Using multiple process skills—manipulation, cognitive, procedural;
4. Using evidence and strategies for developing or revising an explanation; and
5. Doing more investigations in order to develop understanding, ability, values of inquiry, and knowledge of science content.

Conclusion

Attention to the Standards among all authors indicates to what degree we have succeeded in finding real exemplars in teaching, professional development, assessment, and content consistent with the NSES recommendations. We now have data regarding a great variety of content, continuing growth and professional development programs, grade levels, discipline samples and geographical regions. The diversity of teachers, schools, and plans is extraordinary. Perhaps we should have anticipated that the most remarkable and successful teachers, classes, and schools world vary greatly from the norm.

All told, the 15 programs described herein illustrate where we are with respect to realizing the vision of the 1996 National Standards—eight years after their publication and acceptance as needed new directions. Our exemplars have scored in terms of what the content of the 15 chapters indicate. The range is a high of 96% of the *More Emphasis* conditions met by one program to a low of 74% by another. When all are considered, the 15 exemplars meet the NSES *More Emphasis* conditions with an average score of 87%.

We hope and expect that the stories told will inspire teachers. There are still areas to explore and to stress more diligently. However, if all teachers and all schools were to develop similar models with similar evidence of their success, we would have achieved much of what those involved with the development of the NSES envisioned over four years of debate. At that point we would need to consider new Standards as suggested ways that we could be even more successful at creating scientifically literate high school graduates, such as our society sorely needs.

There are two years remaining in the decade that the NSES leaders predicted would be needed to make major advances. We hope there will be many more exemplars in the years to come and that NSTA and the profession will continue to support searches for them so that they, too, can continue to light a path to a better tomorrow.

Appendix

The *National Science Education Standards* envision change throughout the system. The **teaching standards** encompass the following changes in emphases:

LESS EMPHASIS ON	MORE EMPHASIS ON
Treating all students alike and responding to the group as a whole	Understanding and responding to individual student's interests, strengths, experiences, and needs
Rigidly following curriculum	Selecting and adapting curriculum
Focusing on student acquisition of information	Focusing on student understanding and use of scientific knowledge, ideas, and inquiry processes
Presenting scientific knowledge through lecture, text, and demonstration	Guiding students in active and extended scientific inquiry
Asking for recitation of acquired knowledge	Providing opportunities for scientific discussion and debate among students
Testing students for factual information at the end of the unit or chapter	Continuously assessing student understanding
Maintaining responsibility and authority	Sharing responsibility for learning with students
Supporting competition	Supporting a classroom community with cooperation, shared responsibility, and respect
Working alone	Working with other teachers to enhance the science program

Reprinted with permission from National Science Education Standards. 1996. National Academy of Sciences, courtesy of the National Academies Press, Washington, DC.

National Science Teachers Association

The *National Science Education Standards* envision change throughout the system. The **professional development** standards encompass the following changes in emphases:

LESS EMPHASIS ON	MORE EMPHASIS ON
Transmission of teaching knowledge and skills by lectures	Inquiry into teaching and learning
Learning science by lecture and reading	Learning science through investigation and inquiry
Separation of science and teaching knowledge	Integration of science and teaching knowledge
Separation of theory and practice	Integration of theory and practice in school settings
Individual learning	Collegial and collaborative learning
Fragmented, one-shot sessions	Long-term coherent plans
Courses and workshops	A variety of professional development activities
Reliance on external expertise	Mix of internal and external expertise
Staff developers as educators	Staff developers as facilitators, consultants, and planners
Teacher as technician	Teacher as intellectual, reflective practitioner
Teacher as consumer of knowledge about teaching	Teacher as producer of knowledge about teaching
Teacher as follower	Teacher as leader
Teacher as an individual based in a classroom	Teacher as a member of a collegial professional community
Teacher as target of change	Teacher as source and facilitator of change

The *National Science Education Standards* envision change throughout the system. The **assessment standards** encompass the following changes in emphases:

LESS EMPHASIS ON	MORE EMPHASIS ON
Assessing what is easily measured	Assessing what is most highly valued
Assessing discrete knowledge	Assessing rich, well-structured knowledge
Assessing scientific knowledge	Assessing scientific understanding and reasoning
Assessing to learn what students do not know	Assessing to learn what students do understand
Assessing only achievement	Assessing achievement and opportunity to learn
End of term assessments by teachers	Students engaged in ongoing assessment of their work and that of others
Development of external assessments by measurement experts alone	Teachers involved in the development of external assessments

The *National Science Education Standards* envision change throughout the system. The science **content and inquiry standards** encompass the following changes in emphases:

LESS EMPHASIS ON	MORE EMPHASIS ON
Knowing scientific facts and information	Understanding scientific concepts and developing abilities of inquiry
Studying subject matter disciplines (physical, life, earth sciences) for their own sake	Learning subject matter disciplines in the context of inquiry, technology, science in personal and social perspectives, and history and nature of science
Separating science knowledge and science process	Integrating all aspects of science content
Covering many science topics	Studying a few fundamental science concepts
Implementing inquiry as a set of processes	Implementing inquiry as instructional strategies, abilities, and ideas to be learned

CHANGING EMPHASES TO PROMOTE INQUIRY

LESS EMPHASIS ON	MORE EMPHASIS ON
Activities that demonstrate and verify science content	Activities that investigate and analyze science questions
Investigations confined to one class period	Investigations over extended periods of time
Process skills out of context	Process skills in context
Emphasis on individual process skills such as observation or inference	Using multiple process skills—manipulation, cognitive, procedural
Getting an answer	Using evidence and strategies for developing or revising an explanation
Science as exploration and experiment	Science as argument and explanation
Providing answers to questions about science content	Communicating science explanations
Individuals and groups of students analyzing and synthesizing data without defending a conclusion	Groups of students often analyzing and synthesizing data after defending conclusions
Doing few investigations in order to leave time to cover large amounts of content	Doing more investigations in order to develop understanding, ability, values of inquiry and knowledge of science content

Concluding inquiries with the result of the experiment

Applying the results of experiments to scientific arguments and explanations

Management of materials and equipment

Management of ideas and information

Private communication of student ideas and conclusions to teacher

Public communication of student ideas and work to classmates

The *National Science Education Standards* envision change throughout the system. The **program standards** encompass the following changes in emphases:

LESS EMPHASIS ON	MORE EMPHASIS ON
Developing science programs at different grade levels independently of one another	Coordinating the development of the K–12 science program across grade levels
Using assessments unrelated to curriculum and teaching	Aligning curriculum, teaching, and assessment
Maintaining current resource allocations for books	Allocating resources necessary for hands-on inquiry teaching aligned with the *Standards*
Textbook- and lecture-driven curriculum	Curriculum that supports the *Standards*, and includes a variety of components, such as laboratories emphasizing inquiry and field trips
Broad coverage of unconnected factual information	Curriculum that includes natural phenomena and science-related social issues that students encounter in everyday life
Treating science as a subject isolated from other school subjects	Connecting science to other school subjects, such as mathematics and social studies
Science learning opportunities that favor one group of students	Providing challenging opportunities for all students to learn science
Limiting hiring decisions to the administration	Involving successful teachers of science in the hiring process
Maintaining the isolation of teachers	Treating teachers as professionals whose work requires opportunities for continual learning and networking
Supporting competition	Promoting collegiality among teachers as a team to improve the school
Teachers as followers	Teachers as decision makers

The emphasis charts for **system standards** are organized around shifting the emphases at three levels of organization within the education system—district, state, and federal. The three levels of the system selected for these charts are only representative of the many components of the science education system that need to change to promote the vision of science education described in the *National Science Education Standards.*

FEDERAL SYSTEM

LESS EMPHASIS ON	MORE EMPHASIS ON
Financial support for developing new curriculum materials not aligned with the *Standards*	Financial support for developing new curriculum materials aligned with the *Standards*
Support by federal agencies for professional development activities that affect only a few teachers	Support for professional development activities that are aligned with the *Standards* and promote systemwide changes
Agencies working independently on various components of science education	Coordination among agencies responsible for science education
Support for activities and programs that are unrelated to *Standards*-based reform	Support for activities and programs that successfully implement the *Standards* at state and district levels
Federal efforts that are independent of state and local levels	Coordination of reform efforts at federal, state, and local levels
Short-term projects	Long-term commitment of resources to improving science education

STATE SYSTEM

LESS EMPHASIS ON	MORE EMPHASIS ON
Independent initiatives to reform components of science education	Partnerships and coordination of reform efforts
Funds for workshops and programs having little connection to the *Standards*	Funds to improve curriculum and instruction based on the *Standards*
Frameworks, textbooks, and materials based on activities only marginally related to the *Standards*	Frameworks, textbooks, and materials adoption criteria aligned with national and state standards
Assessments aligned with the traditional content of science	Assessments aligned with the *Standards* and the expanded education view of science content

| Current approaches to teacher education | University/college reform of teacher education to include science-specific pedagogy aligned with the *Standards* |
| Teacher certification based on formal, historically based requirements | Teacher certification that is based on understanding and abilities in science and science teaching |

DISTRICT SYSTEM

LESS EMPHASIS ON	**MORE EMPHASIS ON**
Technical, short-term, in-service workshops	Ongoing professional development to support teachers
Policies unrelated to *Standards*-based reform	Policies designed to support changes called for in the *Standards*
Purchase of textbooks based on traditional topics	Purchase or adoption of curriculum aligned with the *Standards* and on a conceptual approach to science teaching, including support for hands-on science materials
Standardized tests and assessments unrelated to *Standards*-based program and practices	Assessments aligned with the *Standards*
Administration determining what will be involved in improving science education	Teacher leadership in improvement of science science education
Authority at upper levels of educational system	Authority for decisions at level of implementation
School board ignorance of science education program	School board support of improvements aligned with the *Standards*
Local union contracts that ignore changes in curriculum, instruction, and assessment	Local union contracts that support improvements indicated by the *Standards*

Contributors List

Karl Biedlingmaier, coauthor of *Stop Talking, Start Listening: Turning Didactic Science Teaching On Its Head,* is a chemistry teacher at Churchville-Chili High School in Churchville, New York.

David L. Brock, author of *It's the "Little Things" that Can Change the Way You Teach,* is a high school biology teacher at Roland Park Country School in Baltimore, Maryland.

Brenda Capobianco, coauthor of *Teacher Action Research on Interactive Lectures: Engaging All Students in Verbal Give-and-Take,* is assistant professor in science education at Purdue University in West Lafayette, Indiana.

Donald Dosch, coauthor of *Student Inquiry at the Illinois Mathematics and Science Academy,* is a biology teacher (NBPTS certified) at Illinois Mathematics and Science Academy in Aurora, Illinois.

Steve Fletcher, coauthor of *Guided by the Standards: Inquiry and Assessment in Two Rural and Urban Schools,* is a science teacher at Sunnyside High School in Tucson, Arizona.

Therese Forsythe is coauthor of *Technology and Cooperative Learning: The ITT Model for Teaching Authentic Chemistry Curriculum.* She is a teacher at Northeast Kings Educational Centre in Canning, Nova Scotia.

Carolyn A. Hayes is the author of *Inquiring Minds Want to Know All about Detergent Enzymes.* She is a biology teacher at Center Grove High School in Greenwood, Indiana.

Harry Hitchcock, coauthor of *Teaching Ecology by Evolving and Revolving,* is chair of the science department at Clinton High School in Clinton, Tennessee.

Stacy S. Klein, coauthor of *Biomedical Engineering and Your High School Science Classroom: Challenge-Based Curriculum that Meets the NSES Standards,* is a research assistant professor at Vanderbilt University in Nashville, Tennessee.

Robert E. Landsman, author of *RIP-ing Away Barriers To Science Education: Inquiry Through The Research Investigation Process,* is research scientist, science education specialist, and president of ANOVA Science Education Corporation in Honolulu, Hawaii.

Earl Legleiter is author of *Modeling: Changes in Traditional Physics Instruction.* He is a senior science consultant at Mid-content Research in Education and Learning (McREL) in Aurora, Colorado.

Julie A. Luft, coauthor of *Guided by the Standards: Inquiry and Assessment in Two Rural and Urban Schools,* is associate professor of science education at University of Texas, Austin in Austin, Texas.

Gregory R. MacKinnon, coauthor of *Technology and Cooperative Learning: The ITT Model for Teaching Authentic Chemistry Curriculum,* is associate professor of science and technology education at Acadia University in Wolfville, Nova Scotia.

Claudia Melear, coauthor of *Teaching Ecology by Evolving and Revolving*, is associate professor at University of Tennessee in Knoxville, Tennessee.

Carmela Rivera Minaya, author of *A View from One Classroom,* is a science teacher at Hanalani Schools in Mililani, Hawaii.

Cindy Moss, author of *Sing and Dance Your Way to Science Success,* is a K–12 science curriculum specialist for the Charlotte Mecklenburg School System in Charlotte, North Carolina.

Teresa Potter, coauthor of *Guided by the Standards: Inquiry and Assessment in Two Rural and Urban Schools,* is a science teacher at Rio Rico High School in Rio Rico, Arizona.

Steven Rogg, coauthor of *Student Inquiry at the Illinois Mathematics and Science Academy,* is associate professor of science education at DePaul University School of Education in Chicago, Illinois.

Judith A. Scheppler, coauthor of *Student Inquiry at the Illinois Mathematics and Science Academy,* is coordinator of student inquiry and director of the Grainger Center for Imagination and Inquiry at Illinois Mathematics and Science Academy in Aurora, Illinois.

Robert D. Sherwood, coauthor of *Biomedical Engineering and Your High School Science Classroom: Challenge-Based Curriculum that Meets the NSES Standards,* is program director, elementary, secondary, and informal education at the National Science Foundation in Arlington, Virginia.

Susan Styer, coauthor of *Student Inquiry at the Illinois Mathematics and Science Academy,* is a biology teacher (NBPTS certified) at Illinois Mathematics and Science Academy in Aurora, Illinois.

Ruth Trimarchi, coauthor of *Teacher Action Research on Interactive Lectures: Engaging All Students in Verbal Give-and-Take,* is a science teacher at Amherst Regional High School in Amherst, Massachusetts.

Peter Veronesi, coauthor of *Stop Talking, Start Listening: Turning Didactic Science Teaching On Its Head,* is associate professor of science education at State University of New York, College at Brockport in Brockport, New York.

Eric A. Walters is author of *The Sky's The Limit: A More Emphasis Approach to the Study of Meteorology.* He is science department chair at The Marymount School of New York in New York City.

Vicki Wilson is author of *Bust That Castle Wall.* She is a physics teacher at Rockwall High School in Rockwall, Texas.

Index

Page numbers printed in **boldface** type indicate tables or figures.